ARCHITECTURE IN A REVOLUTIONARY ERA

ARCHITECTURE IN A REVOLUTIONARY ERA

Julian Eugene Kulski

AURORA PUBLISHERS, INC.

Nashville, Tennessee • London

Copyright (c) 1971 by AURORA PUBLISHERS, INC., NASHVILLE, TENNESSEE

LIBRARY OF CONGRESS CATALOGUE CARD NUMBER: 70-114779

STANDARD BOOK NUMBER: 87695-016-0

DESIGNED BY KURT WIENER
PRINTED IN THE UNITED STATES OF AMERICA

NA
680
K78

TO ISABEL

CONTENTS

PART ONE

SPACE AND MAN'S ENVIRONMENT.................................... 15

    1. Freedom, Poverty and Architectometrics......................... 17
    2. Movement, Space and Architecture.............................. 21
        Space and Movement.. 21
        Pre-Moon Movement.. 22
        Post-Moon Movement... 24
    3. Stimuli, Response and Psychoenvironment....................... 27
        Interaction of Man and Environment............................ 27
        Psychoarchitecture and Perspective............................ 28
        Psychophysics of Design Elements.............................. 31
    4. Urbanism, Pollution and Social Progress........................ 40
        American Urbanism.. 40
        Pollution and Architecture................................... 45
        New Social Demands... 47
    5. American Architecture in the Post-Moon Movement Era............. 51
        Development Corporation...................................... 53

PART TWO

ENVIRONMENTAL DESIGN OF THE LATE TWENTIETH CENTURY.......... 63

    1. The Macroenvironment: Towns and Cities......................... 64
    2. The Dwelling Group..142
    3. Transportation Complexes......................................162
    4. Places of Work..197
    5. Places of Learning..220
    6. The Arts, Recreation, and Religion............................259
    7. The Evolving Microshelter.....................................286

SOURCE OF ILLUSTRATIONS...302
INDEX...304

Acknowledgments

Preparation of this analysis of the contemporary movement in architecture began in 1965, and although the author alone is responsible for the findings and conclusions reached in this work, the book would not have been possible without the assistance of many individuals who supplied suggestions, criticisms, and information. Although it is impossible to give due credit to all, particularly helpful assistance was provided by a few individuals who cannot go unmentioned.

I owe a particular debt to William Pullin, who first brought to my attention the need for explaining the contemporary movement in architecture; to my friends and colleagues at Notre Dame, The George Washington, and Howard Universities for their intellectual stimulation; to Dominic de Lorenzo for his assistance and friendly encouragement; to Daniel Urban Kiley, who inspired me with ideas and concepts; and to my graduate students, whose perceptive questioning about the true nature of the future of architecture and city planning forced me into this research.

For the section on city planning, Edmund Bacon, past director of the Philadelphia City Planning Commission, was the source of many valuable and inspiring ideas. The same is true of the planners of Brasilia, Chandigarh, and Islamabad. The airport section was greatly strengthened by the cooperation of my classmate at Yale, Roy Harrover, and that on schools by Eliot Noyes and John Johansen.

To Robert E. Koehler and William Dudley Hunt of the Journal of the American Institute of Architects go my thanks for their helpful conversations and discussions. Special gratitude is due to the Embassies of India, Pakistan, Brazil, Mexico, Australia, and New Zealand, which gave me valuable assistance.

I owe special thanks to Kurt Wiener, who, besides being the designer of these pages, was my best and severest critic during the final stages of the preparation of the book.

J.E.K.

McLean, Virginia
January 1971

Introduction

The architecture of all previous eras reflects the society in which it was created. What, then, is the effect of the social revolution taking place today in America, and indeed in the world, on contemporary architecture? What effect do the environmental deficiencies in our polluted and decaying cities have on the architecture produced today in this country? What effect do the great advances in technology, systems building, management and production have on the quality of design in architecture produced today in America? What effects have citizen involvement, the voice of the common people, and the citizen input in community development had on the character, quality, and direction which urban design is taking in this country and throughout the western world? Is architecture in this revolutionary era being created to satisfy the ego of the affluent; to enhance the income of the building investor; to further polarize economically the rich and the poor; to aggravate racial differences by providing separate and inferior facilities for minorities; to perpetuate, by monumental but useless structures, the memory of a great hero or statesman; to build magnificent edifices for religious worship one day per week? Or is architecture today being produced on such a humanized scale that it creates a man-made and continuous-use environment where good housing, transportation, employment, education, recreation, and a meaningful life are experienced by all?

These and other timely, relevant, and thought-provoking questions are inspired by *Architecture in a Revolutionary Era.* Dr. Julian E. Kulski, a sensitive critic of the deficiencies of present-day architecture, has in this book made an in-depth analysis of the trends in contemporary architecture and urban planning both in this country and abroad. Every architect, urban designer, and city planner will find this book stimulating, informative, evocative, and exciting reading, one which concerns itself with the day-to-day challenges of our society and with ways in which we can solve many of our problems of ecology, housing, transportation, employment, education, recreation, open space, noise, and water and air pollution.

Dr. Kulski's outstanding ability as an organizer and leader in the fields of architecture and city planning education has been demonstrated at Notre Dame University, where he taught architecture and planning and laid the foundations for a Graduate Program in Urban

Planning; at The George Washington University, where he established the Graduate Program in Urban and Regional Planning; and at Howard University, where he now serves as Director of the Department of City and Regional Planning. A frequent contributor to professional journals, he is also the author of the widely read book *Land of Urban Promise* (Notre Dame, 1967). As an authority on architecture and planning education, he serves on committees relating to education of the American Institute of Architects, the Association of Collegiate Schools of Architecture, the American Institute of Planners, the Association of Collegiate Schools of Planning, and the American Society of Planning Officials.

Dr. Kulski's response to the challenge of planning the rebuilding of cities in New England, of planning new resort towns in Europe and South America, and designing educational campuses in Africa and the Far East over the past decade and a half have given him the unique background of a professional, deeply involved participant in the process of architecture in our fast-changing times. This intimate knowledge of the changing form and nature of architecture is also one of Dr. Kulski's prime qualifications as an author. His exposition in this book provides a fresh and completely new insight into the role of architecture as a catalytic force in human development.

Howard H. Mackey, FAIA

Washington, D.C.
January 1971

PART I

SPACE
AND
MAN'S ENVIRONMENT

Chapter I

Freedom, Poverty and Architectometrics

Freedom is impossible without space. Space exists only in the presence of light. In darkness, space is not visible and motion is impossible. The emotional content of space disappears and with it, man as a free individual.

Yet tens of millions of families on this planet are deprived of space, of environment conducive to public mental and physical health and human development. In many cities throughout the world today families live in rooms so small that there is barely space for the individual to lie down. Rooms are devoid of light during the day as well as at night and the individual members of the family grope around in almost total darkness and cannot see each other without the help of a fire. Fresh air is missing. Man and animals live in proximity. Often in those inhuman hovels rooms are constructed back to back allowing ventilation for susbsistence only.

In countless villages which are inhabited by the two-thirds of the population of this globe, man still lives without a protected and assured water supply and in an environment in which both soil and water are polluted, in which mosquitoes and flies are the chief inhabitants of the space, and cattle his bedfellows.

It is, therefore, not surprising that we have found ourselves in the 1970s in the center of a revolution of rapidly increasing expectations and demands to end the inhuman living conditions in which two-thirds of our fellowmen hopelessly find themselves. The pressures to put an end to hunger and to the lack of decent environmental conditions are mounting as we move towards a five milliard global population in the year 2000.

Technical Ecstasy

The implications and inherent dangers of this social and economic situation are appreciated by too few environmental planners, who live today in a world of technical ecstacy, enamored with space travel and forgetful of the shrinking scale of this planet.

The revolutionary nature of recent changes made reorientation from individual, fragmented approaches to a synoptic view of the environment seemingly very difficult. For many centuries the role of the environmental designer was relatively simple—he enclosed a small space with materials at his disposal and occupied the space himself. Today the requirements of our global environment are so complex and so differentiated and fragmented that we have trouble even conceiving of problems and expressing them in words, let alone attempting to solve them. Recent jaw-breaking and style-jarring euphemisms and hyphenated semantics are simply an expression of this chaotic state. Overlapping professional responsibilities and fast disintegrating disciplinary boundaries are disturbing to our mid-twentieth-century minds. We spend great effort redefining concepts and creating new words instead of welcoming the opportunity to approach the development of our spatial environment in a comprehensive unity of effort. Unity is multiplicity.

Architecture Is Space   Instinctively we know that architecture is space, and space, environment. The slightest problem in the balance of the universe has an immediate impact upon architecture.

Man's movement through space, which has been responsible for his knowledge and discovery of the universe, has at the same time created serious environmental problems. Recent movements of population of megaproportions, greedy and absolute use of land, air, and water resources have quickened the tempo of biological, social, and behavioral imbalance. Our architecture reflects this, too.

Furthermore, behavioral science research has in recent years discovered the extent of the effect of environment upon man. It is known that during a man's first formative years the environmental factors are crucial in increasing the child's chances of enlarging his mental and physical capacity as a creative individual. The effects of noise, air and water pollution and of space upon man's mental and physical health, well-being and cultural development are constantly being brought to the attention of the architects.

Measured awareness of the great effect of man-made environment upon the individual has brought the importance of biological, behavioral, technical, social and economic factors into the architect's central focus. His traditional preoccupation with molding man's living space, coupled with revolutionary new scientific discoveries, has broadened his concern into one of synoptic environment and synoptic architecture.

Synoptic Environment   Evolution of synoptic environmental design from the prime concern for man's immediate shelter, a place to live, work and worship—architecture—to that of building cities and urbanized areas—urban design—is of vital interest today. Since the creation of a decent and inspiring urban environment lies in the hands of those who plan the priorities and policies which guide our future development, this book is addressed to the urbanologist—the economic development expert, be he an economist, political scientist, lawmaker, educator, administrator or elected official. It is also addressed to the concerned and sophisticated student of today who is interested in overcoming the traditional academic barriers and who searches in an interdisciplinary way for knowledge which will enable him to contribute towards the solution of explosive social problems facing him in the fateful days ahead.

Sociophysical Design

The revolutionary changes which have occurred in architecture, city planning and urban design have left us all in a quandary, not only about the nature and status of these arts but about their role in assisting man in shaping a prodigious urban environment. This book is intended to be a reintroduction of basic elements and principles of design—of space, light, sound and structure, and of man's interaction with space. This book also contains a study of some of the most recent significant achievements of architecture, showing the ever-increasing scope of sociophysical design. In addition, it attempts the use of architectometrics to study selected problem areas which require immediate attention to allow more extensive and more successful creation of man's environment and solution of the pressing socioeconomic problems.

Architectometrics is a method of numerical particularization of environmental laws established by architecture and based upon specifically described environmental processes through statistics as yet to be developed. There is little doubt that architectometrics would serve as an important tool for particularizing to the highest possible degree the laws and theories formulated by environics and architecture and thus serve as a means for their verification. Architectometrics would, of course, assure only an approximate identification of environmental processes, but it would serve as a bridge between the science of architecture and environics and the science of statistics. Planning, programing and budgeting, systems theory and cybernetics are paving the way to eventual development of architectometrics. In this work, architectometrics is used in the sense of an analysis of the interaction of man and environment.

Psychology of Space

The goal of architecture and of synoptic environmental design is to maximize opportunities for all men and to create spaces which respond optimally to the needs of people. Our failure to develop a more responsive urban environment has, in large part, been due to the fact that although the psychology of man's interaction with man is well understood by contemporary society, the psychology of man's interaction with urban space and architecture remains a largely unexplored horizon. Furthermore, there has been a lack of appreciation of the fact that the content and context of urban architectural space is social and economic. The indissolubility of socioeconomic and aesthetic objectives in urban design and architecture becomes at once apparent when we try to visualize urban space without man or man outside his physical environment. Much of this dichotomy between social psychology and urban design is the outcome of viewing architecture as a purely physical creation—mass rather than space—and the tendency in psychology to look at the interaction of people without relevance to the world of physical space.

The impact of architectural space on man is extremely powerful and all-inclusive. The monotony, repetition, hopelessness and boredom native to urban slum areas is neither merely "physical," "social," "economic" nor "psychological," but the result of the lack of opportunity, of choice, and of an unresponsive environment.

Ghetto environment is a critical example of the unresponsiveness of much of urban space to basic human needs. The results of this kind of nonarchitectural space are dramatically expressed in the riots which have shaken America in the 1960s; deprived Black society can well be expected to prefer destruction to chaos. Conditions of housing and schools in the Black ghetto intensively contribute to personal despair, failure and revolt of the individual. When basic human requirements are denied, when the individual is refused access to such basic urban functions as employment and recreation, when he is denied architectural space, he has little left in life to lose.

Environmental design is an integral function of economic development. Man needs architecture at all levels and scales of his existence. The quality of environment of the future city will rest upon the ability of the future citizen and policy planner to comprehend, appreciate, and demand a greater role for architecture and environmental design in synoptic development, and upon the creative and intellectual vigor of the design professions to translate these demands into significant and responsive environment.

Chapter II

Movement, Space and Architecture

SPACE AND MOVEMENT

Man's movement through space is the way to understanding the nature of his environment, to discovery and to learning how to shape space, to architecture. The last two decades have seen unprecedented movements of man in space on land, in air and in outer space. The automobile and the airplane have each become an American way of life, constant and rapid travel desirable since man is almost instantly learning about the nature of his environment through intimate discovery of the universe.

The significant effects of this new perception of space upon the concepts and ideas concerning man-made environment and postwar American architecture are clearly discernible.

The previously clear distinctions between the city and the country are in the process of disappearing; the city, only a few years ago the center of economic and cultural life, has become mainly a service facility and home to large numbers of the poor and the disadvantaged. The vast land and air transportation network has opened distant space for development; technology of communication has made decentralization economically feasible and culturally desirable. The next two decades will witness the disappearance of the time-established contrast between what is urban and what is rural.

Man is fast adapting to change and, in spite of professional hue and cry about the disappearance of a more static way of life and values, is benefiting and developing by the great movement through space.

Increased Tempo

The use of land, water and air has undergone drastic revisions as the result of man's movement through space. As always, he developed new machines and new tools to help him adapt his way of life and his environment to this increased tempo of life and motion; but again, as always, the development of political systems, administrative organizations and building concepts follows rather than leads the speed with which man moves through the environment.

Architecture has been known to reflect a way of life as well as to shape man's environment, but the extent to which these two goals have been and are being achieved today varies with interpretation. Unless it first reflects the changing morality, ethics, economic values and new concepts of religion, education and personal values, architecture loses touch with those for whom it is creating an environment; it stops communicating and loses the opportunity to educate, to be relevant, significant and meaningful to man.

Inevitably, American architecture of recent times expresses all the changes which are occurring in this revolutionary era. What we find wrong with today's architecture mirrors only the difficulty man finds in adjusting his concepts of life and building to the dynamic changes in his perception of space, travel and new knowledge. That which we admire and are satisfied with relates directly to the new discoveries and their inherent excitement.

Sense of Flight

The massive, monumental, static structure exuding a feeling of permanence and timelessness feels most uncomfortable since it relates little to our new sense of flight, motion and freedom. As our civilization is emerging from the cave, we no longer need to fear environment and can now seek an ever greater communion with space.

Light and continuity of space and spatial experiences become fused as the predominant objective of environmental architecture, and spaces which serve to move man with greater ease, comfort and perception through space become the "great" architecture of the latter part of the twentieth and the first part of the twenty-first centuries. The well-designed highway, the airport space, such as the Dulles International Terminal in Washington, D.C., or any building which expresses the newly found freedom are of this age and are architecture.

PRE-MOON MOVEMENT

The contrast is enormous between the views of the environment in the latter part of the twentieth century and the views of it in the pre-moon landing era. The effect of man's recent great movement through space upon his approach to the design of his own environment can be immediately noticed when compared with views of space held by past civilizations.

The attitude of the ancients toward space originated with their philosophy that all things should be easily comprehensible, well defined and finite. The size of the ideal city, for example, was conceived by the Greeks to be between ten and twenty thousand population. They located their cities in a clearly defined environment against steep hills or along the shores of rivers or the sea, often on irregular terrain. When a town reached its ultimate capacity, satellite new towns were built.

Non-mechanical Movement

These towns expressed in their scale and organization of urban space a predominant order and continuity, all within the walls which totally and absolutely contained them. Within this clearly defined city-space there was a rich variety of spatial experience based upon a nonmechanical movement: the center with agoras and temples self-contained and defined by building elements; the freely located but adamantly geometrical stadiums and theaters; and the many narrow residential streets and inner courts designed predominantly for the pedestrian. The city-space expressed the needs of a community living to a rhythm and movement basically different from our own. Little importance was attached to private houses, which were considered the building blocks or elements used to define public space, and movement on land and water was expressed in accordance with the scale of its speed, which to us appears almost static by comparison.

The Middle Ages, spiritually preoccupied with the afterlife, feudalism, and monasticism, considered nature as the all-powerful element. Its glorification, rather than its control, was sought after. Buildings and cities were constructed to enhance nature rather than to subjugate it.

Primordial Space

This respect for and enthrallment with the discoveries of the nature of primordial space gave rise to new forms of molding man-made environment. The development of transcontinental communication routes, the movement of great armies, and the rise and expansion of monarchies all led to a great new town-construction era. The building of new communities, new outposts and new roads preoccupied man in the Middle Ages as he searched the mysteries of earth space while forging civilizations out of the wilderness.

In the Renaissance, spatial investigations and research into natural forms and phenomena gave way to a rather academic revival of structural and decorative elements of Roman architecture, while important discoveries regarding mechanical means of propelling man through space took place. The Romans creatively developed new forms and spaces; Renaissance architecture, based as it was upon the imitation of ancient Roman forms, was best in developing an almost all man-made environment based upon revolutionary space-movement perception, which was to form the foundation of our own twentieth-century philosophy. Instead of the concept of a building in nature and space, the Renaissance concept was one of the maximum

Man in Motion control and enclosure of space and nature for man in motion.

Up through the eighteenth century, man's development of cities, public spaces and buildings was based upon nonmechanical means of transportation. Housing, more than any other building type, was almost always expressive of the rapid changes in man's mode of living and of his migratory underlying nature. Mass housing was built in the cheapest and fastest way possible, and this is one of the reasons none of it has survived, while the cities, with their public buildings of more static nature, stand to this day.

The advent of the mechanized movement-through-space era, with its concomitant industrialization and urbanization during the nineteenth and twentieth centuries, permitted, in the more technologically advanced countries, a major effort towards the improvement of the family's immediate living space, yet without making it any more "permanent" than in the past. While man concentrated in the twentieth century on newer and faster means of mechanized motion, there followed a general slowdown in the building of new towns and cities throughout most of the world.

Scales of Movement

The creation of a spatial composition in the city depends primarily upon the manipulation of various scales of movement. In order to create points of emphasis, there has to be a certain middle level of spaces and buildings which may be considered "normal" or background architecture in which movement is relatively slow. The role of these buildings in the urban hierarchy is based upon man's generally accepted norms of motion and the treatment of these buildings undramatized. Within such an established framework it is then possible to dramatize the significant nodes, or places where major modes of movement converge, thus creating spaces where great concentrations of people move and interact.

The individual space in the city has no inherent scale quality of its own. The effectiveness of a space depends entirely upon the relationship between its movement scale and the scale of the macro-environment in which it is located. There is no experience of an individual space apart from the larger space and no architecture of an individual building divorced from the architecture of the city.

Civilizations are judged by the way they express their basic values of life and motion in organized and synoptic design of the environment— in architecture as a form coherence of movement systems. Responsive space for the individual is possible only in the context of contemporary movement responsive environment.

POST-MOON MOVEMENT

Space is visible and apprehensible only in the presence of light and motion. The innate emotional meaning and significance of space is absent in the totally static state and disappears in total darkness. Man perceives space through all his senses and this is why optimization of spatial experience is possible only under conditions in which man's total sensory perception can function, interact and develop.

Spatial Disorientation

The kinetic sequence of man's spatial experience is a never ending process throughout his life, and the sensations he encounters during his travels through the complex hierarchy of spatial routes, departure, transfer, and destination nodes form the total of his personal, immediate environment. Spatial disorientation, to which contemporary man is so often subjected, is the combined result of man's inability to adapt to his continuously changing environment; to his frequently occurring breakdown in the process of past experiences and iron-curtaining of his future; and to the man-made environment's chaotic and often formless space which reflects little the dynamic balance of today's existing movement systems.

As we enter the post-moon movement era of space exploration, we have suddenly come to realize that our concepts of space and of the universe are extremely outdated and reflect little if any of the realities of today. Just as we begin to learn how to perceive and comprehend space while moving at fifty to eighty miles per hour on land and five hundred miles per hour in the air, we are facing travel at as yet undetermined speeds. Mechanized travel at these miraculous speeds revolutionizes the very foundation of perceiving, understanding and controlling the environment.

Environmental Variables

Man's ability to master the complexity and enormity of newly discovered environmental variables and the degree to which he will be able to continue to relate to his immediate living space on earth, and that space in turn to the environmental megastructure of the cosmos, causes the greatest challenge to our civilization in the years ahead. Fortunately, since understanding and perception is largely a component of memory retrieval system based upon prior experience, and the speed of perception is also dependent upon past experiences, the more we move through space the better are our chances of perceiving and comprehending the environment.

Psychoarchitecture

At the same time, man's time-space perception itself is undergoing revolutionary changes. The relationship and relevance of various spaces and places of psychoarchitecture measurable in distance are being drastically changed. No longer is the domestic place, the home, related to the place of work in terms of distance but rather in terms of time. Even the abstract objective element of time is undergoing revolutionary changes as the rate of movement increases in speed, variety and complexity. When it becomes increasingly possible to live in New York and to work in Los Angeles or Paris, a new syntax of environmental perceptions of comprehending and measuring movement through space and time evolves.

Environment becomes a system of movement patterns with the points at nodes of major and minor transition areas slowly taking the place of previous topographic and building landmarks. No longer is the physical or geographic center necessarily the center of activity patterns, or the inner, center city the hub of the metropolis, as in the past when the majority of people worked there. Rather, the environmental patterns have a multitude of centers where the individual lives and works, each center with widely different variables in terms of space, time and distance. The architecture of the post-moon movement era thus becomes psychoarchitecture—the art and science of organizing and understanding spatial movement systems at all scales and speeds. The degree of its application to man's ways of viewing his immediate environment will vary greatly from his concepts of the outer space, but the interaction and interrelationship between these two various worlds will remain and become even more powerful in the decades ahead. Further, the acceptance of the process of constant change, the dynamic way of viewing and shaping man's environment will replace the more static principles which have characterized architecture of the previous eras.

Chapter III

Stimuli, Response and Pyschoenvironment

INTERACTION OF MAN AND ENVIRONMENT

Much of the existing dichotomy between social psychology and environmental design is due to the tendency of architects to look at the molding of space, at best, as a simple two-way process: man defines space to his needs and the defined space in turn affects him. There is no doubt that this is so, but the process is far more complicated, at least as complicated as man himself. The individual and the group have a significant impact upon the man-made environment. Their individual and group personalities, their motivations, their ways of movement and life have a dynamic effect upon a given space. It is important to remember while we make decisions for forming and structuring our environment that the personality of each individual who will experience it will in turn affect and influence the given environment.

Process of Development Therefore, the process of development and education of the individual must proceed side by side with architectural research in individual and group psychology if the delicate balance between the mutual effect of structured environment and man is to be approached. Since man-shaped space has a tremendous influence upon the emotional state of the individual, affecting his mental health, and is in turn equally affected by the people who occupy it, it requires a balanced integration of emotional stimuli. Because of the pervasive and significant relevance of man-sculptured space to group psychology as well, affecting directly the extent and the form of communication between men, in creating our environment we should aim at also achieving an equilibrium of architectural-psychological sensitivity.

The individual is now in ever increasing daily contact with a greater and greater number of individuals and experiencing constantly newer and varied contact with groups of individuals. Our apartment complexes are increasing at a tremendous rate and the child of today goes to a megaschool which prepares him for an ever greater social contact in his future life. Yet, communication between individuals seems to be proportionally decreasing and a man often finds himself without any actual interaction or contact with the members of the larger group in which he finds himself. As a result, the following

Paradoxical State paradoxical state exists: Man in a crowded urban environment cannot often find the privacy and solitude he requires, while at the same time he is unable to establish a true human dialogue with others with whom he is sharing this space. The business of architecture is to provide for man a genuine, communal contact which, at the same time, assures him a degree of privacy needed for his physical and emotional well-being.

Such communal contact may be found in the complex system of multivariable environmental elements which can be referred to as man's psychoenvironment—those environmental variables to which man responds in a generally satisfactory and adequate way. Man's reactions and responses to these variables vary widely with the individual and the particular set of environmental elements he encounters in a specific time, place and space. The native constraint, constants and uncertainties found in the structure of psychoenvironment all assist man in recognizing and disseminating certain specific units of perceptive variables, thus enabling him to satisfactorily perform social interaction and the retrieval of the complex mass of information and impulses.

Social Interaction

In architecture the search for structure in the primal and man-made environment is a search for space-man related constraints, similarities and variations. Recognition of certain groupings of spaces in the city, the suburb or the country; perception of specific types of building or movement corridor spaces based on past experiences is the method through which we disseminate and comprehend the nature of the psychoenvironment. This comprehension through classification is necessary for logical and creative shaping of man's total environment.

Man's comprehension of the psychoenvironment dates from the time he began to explore the primal space through movement. This process which has been gaining momentum through the centuries of man's cultural and technical development is the history of psychoarchitecture.

PSYCHOARCHITECTURE AND PERSPECTIVE

The elements of psychoarchitecture are elusive. Man and space are so naturally unified that the question of where man stops and his environment begins has been continuously raised by philosophers, scientists and artists. The inherent difficulty lies in the fact that both man and environment are dynamic, moving, open systems in constant interaction and interchange with each other. It is therefore quite logical to find that the system of psychoarchitectural space is perceived and discovered by man's movements through it. Moving through space, man encounters constantly changing elements and variables. He participates in spatial experience through all his senses,

Moving Open Systems

perceiving space change as he moves through it. The same space is differently perceived by each individual. The specific evoked responses depend to a large degree on the speed with which man moves through it and his position while in motion. Elements which evoke certain definite motions in the intimate contact of walking become lost when man is mechanically propelled through the same space.

Since the basic quality of perceiving space is movement, which implies constant and continuous change of viewpoint and dimension, it is not surprising that viewing architecture from a single, stationary and limited point of perspective is unsatisfactory. However, this is exactly how architecture has been viewed for the last few hundred years, and the habit has become so ingrained in our whole attitude towards viewing space that it is extremely difficult to view architecture as it really is—experiencing space while in motion.

Perspective as a device for the representation of space design on paper before implementing it in real life was an invention of the Italian Renaissance. The ancient and medieval architects were able to visualize space in its full dimensions and employed only measured drawings to assist them in shaping space and in constructing buildings. Until the Renaissance, both a building in space and space itself were viewed from various vantage points. Buildings and spaces were well integrated. When it became possible to create illusions of space by temporarily arresting it on the canvas by means of linear perspective, a dichotomy between space and buildings began. The discovery of perspective, which proved to be a great milestone in the development of the two-dimensional art—painting—has been partially responsible for retarding spatial perception in architecture.

Retarding Perception

The development of scientific perspective made possible simple representation of a spatial concept before construction, but at the same time substituted a rather rigid discipline of its own for viewing and apprehending space. Thus, it became possible to represent and view space through the use of lines converging on a vanishing point on an artificially established horizon and picture plane. An excellent tool in itself, perspective superimposed its own discipline on the designer's ability to sculpt space. This discipline was limited by the size of the drawing, choice of the eye level, and the number of vanishing points. By making it possible to observe a stationary set of objects at one specific moment in time, it assisted in turning attention away from spatial exploration and toward the design of individual buildings.

Exploration of Space

The late Renaissance, however, began to discover that the one-point perspective could be used not only to delineate and study the mass of the building, but also for the exploration and sculpting of space. The one-point perspective became the dominant discipline of painting, architecture and city design. The street was viewed as a tunnel of space along a strong single axis of movement. Opening of transverse spaces, squares, and setbacks of buildings and variety in building heights started a significant movement in urban design.

The seventeenth-century architects began to apply to the city as a whole the principle of space-time experience of movement along a single axis. Main avenues were selected as the predominant axes of design, and the juncture points which they crossed became the central spaces of the city—places where simply by turning one's head, it was possible to view various architectural spaces simultaneously. The city, instead of being simply an assortment of streets, began to take a defined form and order, with various spaces and spatial progression organized into a multidirectional structure. High buildings, obelisks, church steeples, and other dominant landmarks were used to accentuate this structure and make the spatial organization clearly perceptible to the man moving in urban space.

Nineteenth-century preoccupation with buildings rather than with space misused perspective. In the twentieth century the three dimensions of perspective—height, width, and depth—became too limiting for a person to perceive space during increasing mechanical mobility. The architect found that it was no longer possible to represent expressions of architecture by a view from any single, stationary point in space.

Continuity of Space

The movie camera and the increasing speed and frequency of man's movements led to a new concept of space. This concept was based upon perceiving objects in space from many points and many levels. It broke with the absolute and relatively static Renaissance concept of perspective based primarily on visual perception. It viewed architectural space dynamically, from inside and outside, from below and from above. It acknowledged the continuity of space. Space of a building, a group of buildings, of a city or of a megalopolis was expressed by receiving thousands of different impressions and gaining from them an appreciation of the continuity of space. This new dimension, or rather infinite number of variable dimensions, became the element of perceptual psychology and information theory of psycho-architecture.

Hierarchy of Variables

Man's dynamic patterns of perception in the latter part of the twentieth century are the very skills he needs for manipulating his environment. The more clearly defined the behavioral patterns are, the more skillful is man's control of his environment. The selection of these magnitudes and energy patterns also forms man's hierarchy of sociophysical variables, assists him in setting certain priorities and helps him in emphasizing selected value systems.

Classification of social patterns and physical forms in accordance with specific responses, stimuli and emotions further assists in developing architectometrics, the science of measuring the process and performance of psychophysical elements of architecture.

PSYCHOPHYSICS OF DESIGN ELEMENTS

All objects and all spaces generate a certain degree of stimuli. The individual who is in constant and immediate communion with his environment responds directly to this continuous flow of energy which stimulates his total system of sense. Those variable objects, spaces, shapes and forms which can be considered as being at the level of ecology rather than micrology or cosmology have more direct and immediate impact on man. The stimulation of the gamut of these arrays of perceptual elements forms the basis of psycho-architecture.

Emotion-evoking Space

Multidimensional objects, ground forms, buildings, roads, trees, contain these more elementary perceptual variables and constitute the basic elements of our environmental composition. They are used directly to define and create space through an arrangement of specific units of perceptual stimuli. While in the graphic arts, drawing and painting, emotion-evoking elements of mass and space can be produced by using lower order variables of frequency and intensity and by comparatively more illusory measures, in architecture and environmental design perceptual variables of a higher order are employed and thus they appear much more real.

Isolating Variables

Geometry and textured patterns of optics assist in studying and isolating the psychophysical design variables of higher order. By reducing design elements into textured optical and geometrical patterns, it is possible to view mass and space in relative terms and to discover under what environmental conditions mass may be viewed as the form, the mold which space fills and surrounds—the sculpting of space.

Every architectural object, mass or space, has a generally distinguishing boundary and can be reduced to a series of planes or shapes by ignoring other dimensions and by isolating the variables by ingredients. Thus, the shape of a building or a city can, for more immediate apprehension, be expressed in two-dimensional shapes. The unique surface shapes and recessions are produced by employing the density variation ratio method. The edges which define these elemental variables are the places where sudden and rapid changes in densities occur. When the rate of change of an edge is uneven, discontinuities occur; when the edge is uniform and closed, it becomes a shape. Shapes have a specific character and personality according to certain sets of impulses and stimuli connected with their form as viewed in specific environmental conditions, and in accordance with the way they are manipulated. They may evoke a wide range of energy reactions and thus may be considered as single and comprehensible, calm or active, static or dynamic, certain or imprecise.

Shapes may also be categorized according to their implied or defined direction. Point is static and has no direction. Line is the path of a

Inherent Directions

point in motion and an edge of shape. Each shape has a number of inherent directions. A straight line connecting two points is an axis. A rectangle has two implied axes—a major or longitudinal one and a minor or transverse one. The dominant direction of a rectangle is determined by its major axis.

A circle does not have a major and minor axis; instead, it has a number of equivalent axes, and for this reason it is often referred to as being multidirectional. The equilateral triangle also has equivalent axes but these are limited to three. The elongated triangle has a major and a minor axis like a rectangle, but instead of being symmetrical along the minor axis and predominantly two-directional, it possesses a certain degree of asymmetry, and its dominant direction is determined by the apex.

The square is the simplest of shapes, yet possesses the greatest potential for variety in a composition. A simple arrangement with great spatial possibilities is a composition consisting entirely of squares. It is the only shape that possesses two equivalent axes and the only one that may be assembled into a cube. The circle and the square are complementary, and it is not surprising that we see these shapes in unison in the architecture of buildings and cities throughout history.

Matrix of Confusions

In order to minimize the matrix of confusions and to achieve optimization of stimuli and responses, it is necessary to organize shapes as visual variables into systems. Groupings of elements into systems can be achieved by using the laws of proximity, similarity, or continuity. These constraints help to reduce the level of uncertainty in the environment and to structure space.

Law of Proximity

The law of proximity tends to group elements of approximately the same number of stimuli and to locate them near each other into forms. The proximity of elements to each other creates distinct groups in a spatial composition, establishing meaningful sequence of magnitudes.

The law of similarity is employed in organizing relationships across space of elements which are identical in shape, location, texture, color, direction, and which contain an equivalent number of stimuli. In urban composition this dynamic principle is employed in relating similar masses and spaces across distances, thus assisting in establishing a relevant structure and in achieving visual legibility of urban form.

Law of Continuity

The law of continuity, the use of equally probable stimuli, is used to achieve unity—linear as well as spatial. The inherent constraint in the application of the law of continuity is that it assists in obtaining economical, nonredundant systems by eliminating unrelated uncertainties and superfluous forms.

The modern city contains shapes and masses which interpenetrate each other, change form and direction, break up, provide contrast and variety, and characteristically express the multidirectional nature and form of the city—shapes which interweave in a highly ordered activity—incorporating all psychophysical laws and variable design elements.

Balance and Order

Balance is the rudimentary law of universal order. Balance of stimuli and emotion-evoking variables is necessary to prevent total environmental chaos and to assure mental health. Symmetrical balance is the equal distribution of mass and space of identical stimuli. The obvious symmetrical arrangement of groupings which have similar or identical elements placed on either side of the central axis is a recurring phenomenon in the history of man-made environment.

Symmetrical designs in architecture, as in other arts, are usually impressive, possessing qualities of dignity and serenity, which come as a result of clarity and simplicity. These buildings are easy to perceive and to comprehend and are therefore familiar.

However, there is a real danger in axial balance of complete repose, of too much repetition, too much inertia, not enough dynamic opposition of elements and insufficient variety in stimuli producing variables. Dynamic opposition of elements can be found in the occult, asymmetrical composition, with similar elements balanced in equilibrium. When such balance is achieved by the interplay of unequal forces at varying distances, the possibilities of arrangement of spaces become infinite and the psychologically necessary relevant uncertainties are optimized.

The preference of balanced symmetry over dynamic asymmetry varies with cultures. The Greek, Roman and medieval architects generally employed balanced symmetry in their buildings, but in manipulating their urban space they often employed dynamic asymmetry. The Romanticists generally abhorred the monotony and limitations inherent in the static concept of balanced symmetry. Contemporary art and architecture representative of the dynamics of modern life tend to be based upon a concept of unequally distributed, counterbalanced forces.

Human Systems

Perceptual proportion is the relationship between the relevant parts of a psychophysical system. This relationship is not too difficult to apprehend but is extremely difficult to structure. Perceptual proportion of man's environment is not only the relationship of space to space, of mass to mass, and of mass to space but of the various human systems to the systems of environmental variables. In spite of man's never-ending search for perfection in apprehending and directing perceptual proportion and the many generally futile attempts to reduce the problem to purely mathematical formulas, the law of perceptual proportion stubbornly remains, to a large degree, man's unresolved mystery. However, the significance and value of perceptual proportion as a prerequisite to an environmental balance and order has always been recognized.

The ancient Greek temple was evolved through centuries of development of a highly stylized system based on the radius of the column as the module of its rather fixed perceptual proportions. The Roman and the Renaissance architects continued their search through complex mathematical means. This century, Le Corbusier, in his search for a system in architecture, developed his "Modulor," a skillfully designed mathematical system of selected proportions related to the human body—a modern adaptation of the "golden section" based on optical geometry developed by the ancients.

Sequences of Magnitudes

The perceptual proportions of a traditional Japanese house are based upon a strict mathematical discipline related to man. The basic shape or module is a sleeping mat six feet long and three feet wide. Planning of the entire sensory space is based upon this standard. A great latitude of establishing hierarchies of significant sequences of magnitudes is possible within this system. The use of this unit throughout the house establishes a very strong organization. The composition is carried further into the structure of the house, with columns, ceilings, movable partitions and furniture consistently in accord with the total system. The result is one of perceptual balance, proportion, order, extremely deceptive simplicity and an almost total elimination of uneconomical and unrelated uncertainties.

The principle of perceptual proportion of the Japanese house may be found in some contemporary architecture. Instead of the sleeping mat, the basic unit of perceptual proportion may be a precast concrete floor slab, or a prefabricated structural element, as in the geodesic dome. The lack of a strong unifying element of perceptual proportion in the average house of today is largely responsible for the lack of relatedness, order, and spatial organization, resulting in too many unrelated uncertainties in the contemporary suburban house.

Stimuli and Impact

Perceptual proportion, in addition to being the relative relationship of physical variables in a system, is an aggregate of scale, function, structure and time. Satisfactory perceptual proportions of a larger system, if reduced unchanged to a more intimate scale, lose stimuli, meaning and impact. The reverse can also be true.

Function also significantly affects perceptual proportion. The principles of the characteristics of vision, touch and audition which apply to the design of an educational facility, an office building, or a zoo are each different. It is also largely by means of the specific characteristics of perceptual proportion that we distinguish the innate function of the specific space.

The inherent properties of materials also affect the principles of perceptual proportion. The concept of perceptual proportion itself changes with and in time. The difficulty with which man accepts new forms and new uncertainties is the reflection of certain established norms of psychophysical behavior at a given time. The skyscraper form, when first introduced, contained new uncertainties and thus had a very disturbing effect upon man, who was used to stimuli of predominantly horizontal forms. Today, emotions created by the vertical forms are familiar and offer a dynamic range of perceptual parameters.

The difficulty of adjusting to new perceptual proportions, to new dimensions, to new stimuli, and to new types of movement systems in the twentieth-century city has been one reason for the flight from the city to the suburb. This trend today is showing some signs of reversal as people accustomed to or born in the new kinetic world of spatial perception are returning in search of the voluminous, interlocking, juxtaposed environmental variables found in the modern city.

Repetition and Variety

Unwanted sound—noise in the auditory system of perception—is analogous to chaos and clutter in the visual system, where dissimilar and irrelevant objects occur. Repetition of similar or identical physical variables is a rudimentary law of order of man's environmental system. Psychologically, man needs in his environment spaces and masses which are familiar to him, which evoke certain expected responses and which, through manipulation and repetition, create balance and order. Certain repetition of identical elements and of similar stimuli in structure and space may create a psychologically and physically moving environment. Stonehenge is one of man's earliest attempts to create order through repetitive use of stone slabs, each a constant, to create a highly mystical, self-contained and concise space which even today retains a certain degree of kinetic energy and form coherence.

Constants and Uncertainties

Repetition is also elementary for creating movement in space. The staccato placement of columns in ancient temples established movement as basic to architecture as the base note is to music and alliteration to poetry. A continuous and uninterrupted flow of impressions in an architectural composition is important to achieving harmony in design. However, repetition without variety and constants without related uncertainties mean monotony. As in ecology, architecture must possess variety and repetition combined.

Variation in both micro and macroenvironment can be achieved through rhythm, contrast, or by gradual step-by-step procession leading to a certain degree of climax. A process distinguished by rhythmically spaced constants and uncertainties can provide a stirring processional route of emotional stimuli, of highly rewarding and satisfying experiences. The climax, or a system of highly concentrating kinetic energy, inherently provides needed variation and gradation.

Variety through contrasts is used in environmental design to clarify, dramatize, or modify mass and space, to suggest movement or activity, and to focus attention on the basic environmental structure.

Contrast of spatial direction in an environmental composition evokes vibrant energy and resultant psychological impact.

In the late Renaissance architects became so frantic in their search for variety by the use of often unrelated uncertainties—mannerism—that the practice sometimes led to the destruction of the structure itself. Mannerism in architecture is not limited to this period in history, however; many of the designers of our spaces today are so hamstrung by regulations and customs that all that remains to them is this meaningless search for unrelated uncertainties.

Stimulus of Rhythm

Repetition of similar impulses, or rhythm, is one of the strongest elements of environmental design for evoking emotion and response. It is as basic to architecture as to the life process in general. Man breathes in rhythm, his heart beats in rhythm, within overall rhythms of the setting of the sun and the changing of the seasons. It is not surprising, then, that in manipulating space, as in ecology, the stimulus of rhythm plays an enormously important part.

Rhythmic patterns are selected in accordance with the desired emotions to be evoked. A slow, even, repetitive rhythm tends to create slow movement and a sense of monumentality. Single, strongly articulated and accented spacing of environmental constants found in some spatial compositions is reminiscent of the great temples of the past.

To achieve a less formidable environmental composition, the regularity of the beat of the primal rhythm can be broken by inserting a minor secondary rhythm. Sometimes the structure of a given environmental system itself contains an innate variation of perceptual proportion within the cellular repetitive unit. In spaces with large numbers of environmental constants, monotony is avoided through simple variation within the basic unit while at the same time maintaining the repetitive modular rhythm.

Full perceptual orchestration is also possible and sometimes desirable. In certain psychophysical systems the use of repetition and variety of design elements and variables can be extremely intriguing and intricate, with various systems of perceptual proportion, such as vision, touch and audition, exquisitely composed into a strongly expressive harmony.

The element of time has an important place in environmental rhythm. The character of a culture is significantly expressed through the type of rhythm, the inner excitement of the architecture of the period.

A balanced integration of the emotional stimuli—between monotonous repetition and endless variety, between oppressive control and complete lack of definition—is as much a part of space design as of ecology, music, poetry, art and drama.

Every decision while sculpting and manipulating space must derive

Light, Color and Texture

from the awareness of the effect light, sound, color, and texture will have on the completed artifact. Without light or sound there is no space, and environmental space is experienced to a large degree by texture and color of the surfaces that define it. These surfaces are revealed to us through the medium of light. Contrasts in light value in the luminous environment are used to articulate mass and space. The sun as the critical source of radiant energy provides man with a wide spectrum of interaction with the luminous environment, ranging in brightness from ten thousand foot candles in direct sunlight to a wide range of intensities to completely overcast atmosphere when the level of illumination reaches as low as one hundred foot candles.

Value Relations

Tropical sun provides maximum value contrasts in architecture, but value relations exist in all climatic zones. Moods of spaces change with changing light conditions. A flood-lighted space seen against an ink-dark sky appears completely different from the same space in strong daylight, with its recesses and openings etched with natural shades and shadows. In nighttime the artificially illuminated mass is the dominant element of architecture—in the daylight, the sunlit space.

Our experiences in space and evoked emotions are directly affected by the light condition. A city skyline at sunrise is far different from the same space at evening, when the contours of the mass of the city are painted with the full range of colors of the setting sun. In the one case, mass reflects the light; in the other, the city is seen against the background of light. A different mood effect is yet created by the midday haze, when the same mass appears much farther away from us than on a clear day. This atmospheric mood is created by the fusion of colors, giving an illusion of farther distance.

Constantly changing shadows cast by buildings on ground bring life and movement to the open spaces within a city. Flying over an urbanized region under clear atmospheric conditions, it is possible for us to perceive at noontime the three-dimensional sculpture of the mass below and detect the organization of its spaces mainly by the articulation of the forms within the luminous environment.

Kinetic Elements

Skyscrapers, domes, and steeples—the kinetic elements of urban space—are dominant only when in light. Interior spaces are similarly perceptually dramatized by the degree of light intensity allowed to penetrate the enclosing envelope. In Notre Dame du Haut, Le Corbusier uses light to paint the interior and to create a constantly moving, psychophysical space. Light values and intensities are also used to create balance and order, repetition and variety in environmental space.

Color is the quality of light intensity reflected from a particular surface. The actual color sensation of any surface depends upon its relationship to the light source.

Color in space is either the natural color of materials and of the primal environment, or of applied, man-made chemical color, or a combination of both. Color is one of the space designer's means of creating space and of achieving variety, repetition, emphasis and unity.

The basic, predominant color of a spatial composition is often, as in paintings, the local color. A specific space appears to have a certain basic color by absorbing elements of light energy and reflecting others.

Space-ground Relationship

The use of local materials to unite the man-made with the primal environment is characteristic of the Romanesque and medieval periods. The ancients, the architects of the Renaissance, the Mayans and the Thais used color to underline a conscious distinction between what is man-made and the color of the undisturbed natural environment. The site as an integral part of the mass of the building versus the site as a podium on which the building is placed are still two diametrically opposed movements of space-ground relationship in architecture. Color is extensively used to dramatize each design philosophy.

With architecture rapidly approaching an almost all-synthetic environment, the matter of choice of colors becomes of utmost importance.

Texture is a visual quality—dark or light, advancing or receding. Texture is also a tactile quality—soft or hard, firm or coarse. Textural variation is used to accentuate space. Since texture is both a visual and tactile quality, it is perceived by symbolic associations. Thus, a person seeing the smooth surface of glass or a rough stone wall can perceive the quality of these materials without having to touch them. The more indentations and various projections or recesses a surface possesses which produce a variety of shadows under light, the more textured the surface becomes.

The element of time and movement is also important in perceiving texture. At a certain distance or speed or under certain other environmental conditions, texture disappears. The study of texture in the environment is a study of environmental variables, their nature and arrangement.

Organic Unison

Architects of the Italian Renaissance exploited contrasting textures of rough and smooth stone work to achieve spatial variety. To achieve a feeling of stability and organic unison with the ground, effects of the mass of a building were dramatized by employing large scale, bold texture on the first floor, gradually diminishing its scale on each successive floor, as in the Palazzo Riccardi in Florence. Among some of the greatest articulations of spaces through sculptural texturing are the Gothic cathedrals, Seljuk mosques, the Thai, Mayan and Aztec temples.

Texture can also be used to accentuate or diminish the emotional impact of environmental design. It must, however, be used with care and always be subjugated to the overall composition; otherwise it comes into conflict and obscures the clarity and coherence of the basic forms of the created space. In the psychoenvironment a texture is perceived as a grouping of determinable environmental variables, in themselves insignificant, but when combined into units creating a magnitude of visually discernible elements. Densities of texture establish surfaces which, in turn, define space. When textures are destroyed both the surface and the space lose some or all of their psychological meaning and being.

Chapter IV

Urbanism, Pollution and Social Progress

AMERICAN URBANISM

The hectic American urbanization has upset almost all of the established prewar land values, made the old taxation on land obsolete, and revolutionized land use. As such, it has created the need for new architecture, new uses and developments of land.

The majestic individual skyscraper as the symbol of the first half of the twentieth-century in America, representative of the conquest of space and of gravity and of the centralization of corporate power on central urban land, is gone. It has been replaced by commercial megastructures which, in turn, are being integrated with the movement corridors. The future will see the end of greedy, single-purpose, massive and static structures. Central urban spaces will, in the future, contain multiple-function megastructures, capable of constant and rapid adaptation to increasingly new needs.

Multiple Megastructures

In the shift from central to suburban developments, the old nineteenth-century concepts of urban land economics disintegrated the economic base of the center city. In a desperate attempt to continue the development of central urban land under obsolete national tax structure and lack of national or any other urban land development policy, it became impossible to mold space within any kind of behavioral, social or artistic logic. Our central urban commercial areas are devoid of architecture or space and, allowing little, if any, spatial experiences, are but glass enclosed, dead boxes.

In addition, movement in and out of these structures is made twisted and awkward. In their failure, these inept spaces portray man's inability to maintain a reasonable distance between his increased speed and technology and his political-legal systems. Architecture has no place in these urban hubs and can be blamed little for the handcuffs rigidly installed by past politicians, planners and lawyers.

Environmental Policies

It is not too much to say that architects are only too aware of this situation, but only by their immediate involvement and action in bringing about the long overdue changes in national tax policies, local codes and ordinances, and in the development of environmental policies will the shaping of meaningful central areas again become possible. The use of total resources of our central urban environment, above ground as well as subterranean spaces, will then constitute the new total architecture.

With almost complete mobilization of our people being an established fact, the long maligned suburban phenomena are much more illustrative of the postwar migratory era and of the spirit of the times. True, for basically the same reasons as the center city, the development of the suburban environment has been haphazard, uneconomic and unconducive to social and behavioral development. In the almost blind faith that any type of use of land, any type of frantic building and constant action is preferable to more analytical and less frenetic activities, huge expanses of suburban space were thoughtlessly cut up, creating massive social, economic and human problems.

Yet, it is in the builder's box on an individual lot, untouched by the hand of the architect, that we can detect the new desire of man to live in an intimate way with the newly discovered environment. The exodus from the city to the suburb is only partially due to economics and obsolete national and local tax policies, only partly due to new roads, and the new and better facilities available outside the urban core. And it is certainly not due to any historical or romantic "back to the land" movement, with its roots in early American developments, as some urban historians would have us believe.

Rediscovered Space

Man in his automobile and freedom of movement and new leisure time has rediscovered space as his environment, space as his being. He has discovered his need to live in places which enable him subconsciously to feel the continuity of space. To be able once more to place his feet on soil, to look at the sky, to study the structure of the tree and to look at the moon walked upon by his fellowman seem so important that these desires overshadow the grave problems created by unnecessarily long travel and, in many ways, a cumbersome style of life.

Glass (badly or well used) as the material for constantly remaining in touch with the total environment is a prized possession of modern man. Television and other means of spatial communication have given him wings.

Architecture as a conscious shaping of environment shows its rebirth in the suburbs in the planned new communities. The courthouses, row-houses and dwelling towers in the new "towns" are evidence of this rebirth. With a new national movement of community building, we will see environmental architecture on a completely new scale.

Cultural Ecology

Self-criticism is the way to self-improvement and to improvement of the environment, unless this criticism stifles or replaces creativity. Cultural ecology, on the other hand, recognizes man's relationship to and basic dependence upon his cultural environment—the man-shaped spaces of his natural surroundings.

A basic difference in the structure of city architecture of the past and of today and tomorrow is the movement of man through space by mechanical means. As long as man moved within a city primarily on foot, the distances which he could cover determined to a large degree the formal structure of a town or city. Application of the automobile as the basic mode of movement in the city, a unit much larger, faster and more impersonal than the human body, had more impact upon the structures of urban areas than any other previous development.

The norms of size, space and scale in the city up to the nineteenth century expressed only a gradual evolution from Greek city-states. The spatial organization of these cities is easily comprehensible. They provide experiences expressing an extremely high quality of order of city life within a hierarchy of building masses and stimulating spaces. The industrial and technological revolution drastically altered the structure of the city.

Element of Time

The unprecedented rate of urbanization, combined with population explosion, new sociopolitical systems, expanding technologies and the unprecedented growth of cities, added a new basic dimension to the urban structure—the element of time. Up to this point the physical structure of the city was measured mainly in terms of distance, its length, width and height. Mechanical means of movement and communication made time the basic measure, completely altering the traditional concept of city structure.

The structure of an individual building is gradually changing under the impact of these new forces, but not nearly as fast as the function of the building in the overall urban composition. In the city of the past, each building type had a clear and defined role which it had to perform within a given system. The location and character of each component structure was determined on the basis of where people worked, lived and played, and their interrelationship was based on convenience of movement and the existing social and cultural hierarchy of values. Thus, the center of the city was symbolically, as well as in reality, the place where the dominant structures of the community were located—the cathedral, city hall and marketplace defining the central space of communal activities. Until the advent of time-space perception, this central place was reachable from any part of the city in about the same time, regardless of whether in a horse-drawn carriage, on horseback, or on foot. The designer of the historical city had to deal only with a simple system of perception and basically a one-movement system.

Revolutionary City

Inevitably, modern city life has grown around the twentieth-century mechanical mobility and communication, demanding revolutionary new city structure to meet the new living patterns. The old cities have shown a fairly constant and concentric pattern of housing based on a regular distribution of income-level groups from the lowest at the periphery to the highest near the center. This centralization principle has now radically changed, with low income families often occupying areas previously inhabited by the highest income groups, who vacated them as the result of commercial expansion and socioeconomic changes.

The rapid growth of the modern city has been and still is basically unplanned and uncontrolled. The history of city planning offers no examples of urban development directed by man on this unprecedented scale. Application of architectural theories and techniques of the past are generally futile, and yet many of the solutions offered today for rebuilding cities, as well as new town planning concepts, are still predicated on man's being predominantly a pedestrian. Environmental changes have happened so fast that the traditional structure of the city changed with no guidance from man.

In city planning and design, which is basically anticipatory in nature, lack of foresight in the past was not so disastrous as it is today, when technology has almost completely overtaken humanity. The enormous increase in the size of the metropolis requires new images, new techniques, and new approaches if the structure of the environment is to retain any semblance of order.

Sinews of Population

The environmental structure of human settlements is global. The circulation system, air, water and ground, spans and connects continents. The sinews of relatively dense population create continental structures, megalopolises, whose form interconnects centers of population generally along main lines of transportation. The megalopolis is a region containing many cities and a multitude of subcenters, yet organized into an easily distinguishable and cohesive form. These conurbations have central urban spaces arranged into highly individual, dynamic and organic relationships.

These regions, lately referred to as megalopolises, vary widely in the size of their populations, densities of their centers, and in their functions, forms and geophysical characteristics. There are eight such large urbanized complexes around major cities which fall into this classification at the present time in the United States: Los Angeles-San Francisco, Seattle-Portland, Houston-New Orleans, Daytona-Miami, Atlanta-Raleigh, Columbus-Cincinnati-Louisville, Chicago-Detroit-Pittsburgh, and Boston-New York-Washington.

These large urban structures are expected to grow rapidly in density in the future under an increasing pressure for urban land, and their structures are expected to become constantly more elaborate. With the increase in urban population and the advent of new means of transportation and communication, these great conurbations will face unprecedented pressures on their urban centers, which will increase in importance, dimension, and structure.

Metropolitan Scale

The major structural unit of the megalopolitan system is the metropolis. The metropolitan scale is a relatively new unit of architecture. Just as the city block has replaced the individual building as the basic unit of city structure, the metropolis, a highly complex urban organism, has replaced the city. During the last decade there have been many attempts to mold space on this scale.

The Satellite City

The challenge inherent in the search for viable forms of a structure of the modern metropolis is illustrated by certain basic evolving forms: the planned metropolitan sprawl, ring of satellite cities, and a radial corridor plan.

The structure of the planned metropolitan sprawl accepts the existing low-density suburban sprawl based on automobility and attempts to bring some degree of order to the growth of the modern metropolis by limiting planned controls to new, small urban subcenters and high-density development to the old metropolitan center.

The ring of satellite cities concept directs the growth of the old hub along the lines of mid-Manhattan and prevents furtherance of sprawl by separating the old city from a ring of new communities with a green belt, the only connection between the satellites and the old city being radiating transportation routes.

The radial corridor plan is an attempt to find a compromise between the acceptance of the inevitability of continuing present unplanned horizontal developments and the rigid and utopian concepts unworkable in a democratic society. The Year 2000 Plan for Washington, D.C., is an example of a metropolitan radial corridor plan. This plan is based on an urban configuration resembling the form of a six-pointed star with its centroid the old centrum of the city. The rapid transit and freeway radials focusing on the metropolitan center would carry mass transit as well as automobiles and connect the new and old subcenters into a comprehensible composition defined by green wedges.

Simultaneous Control

Shaping man's environment on a metropolitan and megalopolitan scale requires not only the understanding and guidance of extremely complex systems of transportation, communication, social and economic organization, political and administrative structure, and technological functions of man (housing, education, work, recreation), but requires most of all their simultaneous control and development if the continued unplanned and chaotic growth of cities is to be terminated.

The systems approach to urban design offers the potential of comprehensive development of man-made environment. The tool for a systems design—the modern computer—can now be utilized for analysis of complex controllable environmental variables such as the density of population. The synoptic interdisciplinary design team, by manipulating the multivariable complexes of the environment, while working within a common design policy, is capable of creating meaningful spatial experiences and significant forms on a scale entirely new to mankind.

POLLUTION AND ARCHITECTURE

Air Pollution

The great American architect visionary, Frank Lloyd Wright, predicted in the first half of this century that the city as we know it is doomed to die. Unchecked environmental pollution, together with the unresolved national problems discussed earlier, is at the base of the agony in which our metropolitan centers find themselves at the dawn of the twenty-first century.

Air Pollution Almost ten thousand communities in the United States have air pollution problems and, according to the United States Public Health Service, almost every community with a population of 25,000 or more is contaminating its air beyond the minimum safety standards. The automobile is but one culprit, pumping tons of carbon monoxide into central urban spaces. At levels found in rush-hour traffic, carbon monoxide is known to produce mental and physical imbalance expressed in headaches, dullness of vision and reduction in muscular reactions. In addition, hydrocarbons produced by man's favorite means of movement through space, the automobile, play a major part in creating smog and are seriously suspected of causing cancer. Although many air pollution sources have been reduced or eliminated, the almost one hundred million motor vehicles remain the most numerous and widespread contributors to pollution of the American environment.

The significance of these findings upon architecture is all too obvious. Human contentment is an object of architecture. Contentment is also recognized as an important factor in good health, and therefore, poorly shaped space and any disturbance to man's senses, such as smells, dirt and noise, seriously impair his health. Health is defined by the World Health Organization as "a state of complete physical, mental and social well-being." Public health concerns of environmental architecture are unfortunately only now being recognized.

Noise Pollution

Environmental noise may be defined as unwanted sound. With the increase of mechanical mobility in the last part of the twentieth

Noise Pollution

century, there has been a drastic increase in the level of noise, particularly in and around our metropolitan areas. Since all sounds or vibrations travel through solids as well as through space, the architect is concerned with controlling unwanted sound through manipulation of space.

In recent years there have been investigations into the possibilities of using air rights over urban highways for housing, particularly for low-cost housing for the urban poor. Subterranean urban highways will create new and unique problems for the architect in having to reduce the high level of reverberating highway traffic, and to control highly concentrated escaping noise at points of openings.

However necessary and partially successful may be the reduction of noise level through screening and other spatial manipulations, architects are becoming increasingly aware that the reduction of unwanted sound must be first controlled at points where it originates. Thus, the reduction of motor traffic in cities and the location of airports serving supersonic and other aircraft become of great concern to the environmental planner.

In connection with the advent of the supersonic plane, it is estimated that approximately one-third of the population of the United States will be subjected to unexpected, sudden noises as often as fifteen to twenty times a day. Man is expected to adjust to some of this forthcoming phenomenon of increasing speed and frequency of his treks through space, but it is clear that the air corridors of the future will affect development of land and environment as much as the highways have done in the twentieth and the railroads in the nineteenth centuries.

New modes of travel revolutionize life and create entirely new living patterns. The street and the urban square, traditionally the centers of contact between men, have lost their civilizing influence through noise. As it is impossible to carry on a conversation on the sidewalks of a busy city street, social intercourse has had to find new spaces.

Since noise level is proportionate to the speed with which a vehicle travels, the greater the speed, the greater the noise; one of the prices for man's desire and ability to explore his environment faster and faster has been pollution of the environment by noise. As history shows no indication of man's willingness to give up space explorations, architects and planners must use all their ingenuity and knowledge to localize and control noise in man's environment. Any architecture that ignores environmental noise pollution is anachronistic. The future findings of science on the more specific effects of noise upon man's auditory and other systems and his psychological well-being will have a significant impact upon the future of architecture and city planning.

Water Pollution

Space, life and architecture would not exist without water. On the earth's surface alone there are some 336 million cubic miles of water of which ninety-eight percent is contained in the oceans and most of the remaining two percent is ice. What remains for man's consumption is a miniscule .027 percent in fresh water, which is replenished by an even smaller .000053 percent in the atmosphere. It is this balance that makes man's life on this globe a reality.

The rate of water consumption through industrialization, urbanization and population growth in the United States has long since overtaken the rate at which the atmosphere can provide purification of this relatively small body of water for human use through nature's cycle of precipitation and evaporation. Thus, the problem of pollution of this life-giving environmental element is basic to man's future life and development. With an average supply of approximately 500 billion gallons of water daily available in the United States, Americans are using almost 400 billion, or ten times the amount of water they consumed at the turn of this century. With such a rapid growth of consumption of clear water, the provision of adequate supplies is crucial.

Although misuse of clean water is partially responsible for diminishing our available supply, pollution of our streams, rivers and lakes is by far the most important culprit. Countless quantities of water are being spoiled by pollution and, as our population grows and creates more and more waste, these quantities will further increase.

The realization of the importance of clean water to the economy, health and development of man and his environment has brought water, and water pollution concern, before the American architect. Throughout this country, planners and architects in regions which are affected by haphazard urban development around fresh water sources are organizing and helping to champion the cause for preservation of our natural water resources.

This concern with the total environment is a radical and welcome change from the irresponsible attitude towards our environment which previously prevailed in America. Unitl recently we stood by, unconcerned, as we let our land, our forests, our air and our water become defiled and polluted.

NEW SOCIAL DEMANDS

The recent widespread and increasingly intensive public demand for much faster change in our institutions and for more relevancy in our

New Social Demands

social, economic and physical planning, development and implementation is the result of the new and revolutionary era of movement, communication, fast and efficient means of disseminating and absorbing information, of education and of the fruits of technological progress available to the billions who inhabit this planet. These demands and mandates are particularly strong in the more developed countries and nowhere so powerful as in the country which enjoys the highest per capita level of income—the United States of America.

This apparent dichotomy in the nation consisting of over 200 million individuals represents the continuously rising waves of expectations based, not on political slogans and promises, but upon the growing public awareness of the feasibility of their demands, of the great needs for reform in all of the sectors of our economy and in our social environment. It is the epic achievements of American twentieth-century industry, agriculture, education, and space movement and exploration that have convinced the people of the possibility of solving their mounting environmental problems and of the righteousness and feasibility of their goals for social progress.

The Kinetic Process

The goals and demands, the advantages and disadvantages of urban growth, technological progress and strides in mobility and the way they affect the shaping of environment pose grave questions before the environmentalist. The consequences of the urbanization of large parts of the environment and of the kinetic process of megapolitanization are social, economic and environmental. The inherent advantages of this epic growth are reflected in the economies of increased freedom of movement, of educational and occupational choice, of increased consumer choice through boosted competition and of increased communication and institutionalization of knowledge and discovery. These positive consequences of growth have to be balanced against the socioenvironmental diseconomies of urbanization which are staggering. They are: huge inner city slum areas, residential social separation and segregation by race and income groups, inequity of educational and neighborhood facilities, shortage of locally available job opportunities, poor transportation, higher living costs particularly for housing, pollution of environment, loss of the psychologically needed sense of constancy of the community, political and administrative fragmentation, large and difficult-to-manipulate sprawl areas, less space, much higher cost of public services, estrangement of the tax base for public service needs, estrangement of the individual from the environment and the resultant increases in crime.

To attempt to resolve the seeming imbalance of economies and diseconomies of urbanization, the new social objectives may be summed up as those of environmental equity in the distribution and redistribution of income, opportunity and relevant space, economic affluence through increased productivity, higher income and wages, and national economic stability through more advanced fixed monetary and land development policies.

The effect of these new social goals and demands upon architecture in this revolutionary era is extremely pressing and direct. The optimization of the environmental opportunities and maximization of the economic and psychological environmental stimuli as the basic responsibility of environmental architecture must be met at all levels of the environmental scale. Architecture as a tool of social and economic development has a crucial responsibility for participating in the heavy investments required during an era of epic technological, institutional and environmental change.

Era of Epic Change

At the international level the environmental architect can play a major role in studying the problems of environmental pollution and development which recognize no national or continental barriers. On the national scene, architects' involvement in social, economic and political planning will assist in increasing the optimization of social progress and in meeting the environmental goals. By assisting in the development of systems which allow greater citizen-participation in the decision-making process necessary for creating a more meaningful and relevant environment, the architect will be in a position to know the people's way of life, their needs and to help improve their economic and social well-being. By assuming a more active and leading role in the political decision-making process and in assisting to initiate and develop the political design decisions themselves—which today are made mostly by nonprofessionals—the architect would again be in a position of becoming the shaper of the immediate and relevant space.

Political Decisions

By recognizing the modern movement systems as the basis of contemporary environmental planning and development theory, the architect may take a much more intimate and enthusiastic interest in the development and construction of balanced transportation systems and their influence upon shaping the architectural environment of the future.

The imbalances, disparities and diseconomies of the social environment must become the environmental architect's prime concern if the goal of architecture—the process of optimization of environmental opportunities for all—is to ever be even partially achieved.

Optimization of Resources

Environmental architecture has a leading role to play in meeting the new social demands. The far greater degree of man's freedom of movement necessary to accommodate the future population of the twenty-first century is today being planned, based on 1970 projections and envisioning the population of the future as basically living a 1970 pattern of life—traveling in today's vehicles, living in today's homes, and participating in today's leisure activities. The study of alternate futures, particularly in the field of movement systems theory, must be further developed to enable the environmental planner to make realistic long range plans. Without such planning, architecture will continue to meet past needs rather than to provide an environment reflective of current requirements and philosophies and to assist in shaping the future.

Without a more economic use of resources, the gulf which exists today between technical ingenuity and social wisdom will doubtless continue to grow. The architectural profession, by focusing greater attention on its responsibilities for the social environment, would assist in eradicating this dichotomy which exists between capability and responsibility. The architect in the first part of the 1970s faces the challenge and the opportunity of helping to meet the new social demands. These demands include optimization of leisure time activity; more economic use of resources; redistribution of income and amenities; the increase of the citizen's role in environmental development; maximization of the freedom of movement, and choice of educational and job opportunities; improved uses of technology for mass consumption, particularly in the case of industrial techniques as applied to meeting housing needs; and elimination of poverty and racial and economic inequities.

The great challenge of the post-moon movement era—an age of change, of exploration, and of flight—has made it abundantly clear that the architect's actual client is the public and his primary responsibility is social and environmental.

Chapter V

American Architecture in the Post-Moon Movement Era

CONCLUSION

The spirit of American architecture in the post-moon movement era is as unique as the American way of life at the threshold of the twenty-first century. The great mistakes and the fabulous achievements live side by side. On this continent, long known for contrasts and dramatic inequities, for unequaled exploration of its natural resources and a long history of spatial blindness, the man-made environment clearly evinces this epic dichotomy.

The early American had already begun to suspect the universality of space as his exploration of space and search for new lands led him to increased mobility. His treks through America's primal environment indicated that beyond the prairies lay the mountains and in the mountains lay secreted valleys and beyond was water, and land and more space.

The more he carved the natural environment, the more skilled he became at adapting it to his needs. In the period of three decades he built more towns and cities than were constructed in Europe over a period of centuries. Today these great spatial explorations continue unabated on a new and fantastic scale.

While older, more mature and more patient civilizations painstakingly develop and improve the mass of building structures, the American explores space.

It is not surprising, thus, to find that it is in the nature of American architectural space that we find the basic differences which distinguish it from those of other lands.

Environmental Visionaries

From spatial manipulations of Thomas Jefferson and William Penn, through the work of environmental visionaries of the nineteenth and twentieth centuries, to the great spatial orchestrations of Frank Lloyd Wright, Paul Rudolph, Louis Kahn and a multitude of others, the form of American environmental space evolved. It is distinguished by its spatial continuity and communion between the environmental elements untouched by man and those strongly shaped to his needs and in his image.

The selected buildings in this book do not purport by any means to be the best of the architecture of the postwar period in America and were chosen simply because they illustrate the actual ferment, change and reconceptualization of the American way of life. It is for this reason, among others, that some of the work of America's best known architects has been consciously omitted. Yet, the great majority of spaces included are in concert with the evolution of American style of living in recent years. They also portray the problem of shaping environment without clearly defined goals and objectives.

Development Policy

The United States of America entered the 1970s in a singularly unique position among the world's community of developed nations—without a comprehensive land and environmental development policy. At the same time, the domestic and global responsibilities of the world's richest and most powerful nation are without comparison. The architects of this economically most developed and technically most advanced continent are among the national leaders who recognize the expanding challenges and problems of environmental architecture and are rapidly readying themselves to face the task of controlling and molding the future environment.

This task requires, first of all, the development of a comprehensive environment development policy at the federal and regional levels, as well as the development of new administrative, economic and legal tools for an effective implementation of this policy according to a new set of national priorities, resource distribution techniques and a twenty-first century approach to the use of environmental resources: air, water, land and, predominantly, space.

The past efforts of the 1950s and 1960s at building a new environment in the United States have failed for a multitude of reasons, among the major ones being what can be characterized as a purely pioneering, experimental, disjointed, and filled-with-gimmicks-and-individual-programs attempt to renew our nineteenth-century cities basically within the nineteenth-century framework and with no attempt at creating a new environment, which is absolutely necessary for the future social and economic development. Without a new community land development policy and without channeling adequate resources for urban development, the release of highly volatile and powerful forces into the streams of existing urban complexes have proved terribly wasteful, grossly inadequate, and have given rise to social urban problems never before encountered in urbanized nations.

Architectural Education

Many American architects recognize that the creation of a decent and inspiring environment under these conditions is, in fact, impossible; that they are presently entering an era of vital improvement in environmental policy formulations at all levels of government, while at the same time expanding the concept of architecture and of architectural education into all environmental sciences.

Man's search into the nature and mystery of his environment can be seen in the production of books and articles which, in the area of science alone, amounted to 500,000 books, 20,000,000 patents and countless original contributions in articles, products and designs during the last decade alone. This sea of documented, though unclassified, undisseminated, and often unrecorded knowledge poses great problems to the future of planetary development and to the practice of environmental architecture.

Through modern environmental information retrieval centers, this sea of knowledge can be made available quickly and precisely at the time that it is required to all concerned with the improvement of man's environment. Furthermore, this information could thus be made available in the exact form in which it is needed independent of time and place. The development of regional, national and international environmental data processing centers is without doubt a number one priority of environmental science and architecture.

Without architectometrics and with the dearth of information which is available to the architect concerning the impact of environment upon the activities of man in space, upon his work efficiency, his cultural and emotional development, and upon the learning process, the efforts of contemporary architects to create an environment based on more scientifically grounded knowledge are retarded.

DEVELOPMENT CORPORATION

At this time of socio-economic history of the United States, it becomes abundantly clear that in order to meet the critical needs of society, there is a pressing need for capital to finance the reconstruction of the cities destroyed by decades of neglect and to increase the education, productivity and living standards in the underdeveloped areas of the United States, rural as well as urban. The task is so great and involves financial risks of such magnitude that private capital alone is obviously unable to undertake them.

The development of urban areas and implementation of sociophysical designs requires an entirely new approach to planning design and development. This undertaking must of necessity go far in excess of presently employed methods and available Federal, state, municipal and private resources. Two decades of urban redevelopment and renewal efforts stand witness to the gross inadequacies of the Department of Housing and Urban Development, and of its predecessor the Housing and Home Finance Agency, in coping with the mammoth problems of renewing urban America and solving its sociophysical problems. The history of private, municipal or county sponsored urban development is even more insignificant and less magnanimous than the national effort. Since the end of World War II, we have attempted to meet the demands of housing for our burgeoning urban population by simply producing more of the same.

Hardly utilizing the space age mass production know-how, and misusing urban land, we have created suburban wastelands and enormous problems in the center city. Since 1945, the United States has built almost 40 million housing units but only several hundred thousand of these have been within the low-cost range, built for low-income people who account for about one quarter of our urban population. Public apathy has kept down government housing programs and increased congressional appropriations required to meet these demands.

Loans and Credits

The creation of a national investment institution capable of authorizing, granting or guaranteeing loans and credits for productive reconstruction of blighted areas and for economic development projects through mobilization of private capital resources, and provided with a structure under which the risk of investment in the inner city and rural areas of poverty would be shared by Federal, state, and local governments, is embodied in the concept of a United States Environmental Development Corporation. The Urban Development Corporation in New York State is a first, though minute and grossly inadequate, step in this proposed general direction. However, no single political entity or state-wide organization alone, even of as rich a state as New York, is capable of providing the required financial assistance.

The proposed Environmental Development Corporation, an interstate governmental institution, with all of its capital stock owned by the United States member states and territories, could begin operation with as little as one-tenth of the subscribed authorized capital. Thus, with about a $30 billion operating capital, the Environmental Development Corporation would have $300 billion of authorized capital which could be called in, if the Corporation needed it to meet obligations as a result of its borrowing or guaranteeing loans.

High Risk Areas

Such a basic capital structure would enable the institution to borrow much more sizable financial resources by selling its obligations to private investors. Through the sale of bonds and notes to investors, the Environmental Development Corporation would draw upon the tremendous resources of the private sector. It must be emphasized that no single resource, however large, is capable of meeting the environmental crisis. Therefore, the Corporation's paid in capital would simply be a feasible means by which the private capital of the United States could be enhanced to move into the underdeveloped, high-risk areas. Thus, although the Environmental Development

Corporation is envisioned as an inter-governmental, inter-state institution, it would rely mainly upon private investors for its financial base. The degree of the risk guaranteed would be limited only by the requirement that the total amount of outstanding loans and credits made or guaranteed by the Corporation would not exceed the total of subscribed capital plus reserves and surplus.

To avoid defaults, it would be incumbent upon the Corporation to insure that loans are not made without careful attention to the borrower's ability to repay. The borrower might be a state government or a political subdivision like a county or municipal government or even a private business enterprise located in the territory of a member state. However, should the borrower be a private enterprise or a community group, duly incorporated in the member state's territory, the state government would have to act as the guarantor. Furthermore, the Environmental Development Corporation would have to ensure that the proceeds of each loan are used only and exclusively for the purposes for which the loan was initially made and would have to insist that the borrower pay utmost attention to economy.

Economic Considerations

In order to obtain maximum success, in its primary role as an economic development institution, the Corporation would also have to make sure that it does not grant loans in cases where the borrower could obtain funds from other reasonable sources. Only economic considerations would be relevant to the Corporation's decision in making a loan or granting a credit, and political considerations would have to be minimized, if the basic objectives of the proposed Corporation were to be implemented.

Technical Assistance

In order to optimize the economic and technical assistance objectives of the Environmental Development Corporation and to minimize adverse political pressures, the legal statutes, membership and organization of the institution would have to be carefully structured. Membership would be open to all states, with subscription to the capital stock based upon each state's comparative economic standing, with voting power relative to shareholdings. The powers of the Corporation would be vested in a Board consisting of the state governors, who would delegate the authority to Executive Directors. The latter would in actuality be responsible for the general operations of the Corporation—loans, financing, budgets, policies and technical assistance operations.

The technical assistance operations of the proposed Corporation would be handled by Technical Assistance Departments, which would be responsible for conducting continuing economic studies of all regional and metropolitan areas of the United States. They would also conduct studies of sectors like Housing, Transportation, Education, and Industry as well as pollution control, in an interdisciplinary and intersectorial manner. They would be responsible for identifying projects, for determining priorities within sectors, for appraising projects, for financing and for supervision. Basically, the objective of the institution would be to provide a unified data bank for economic development of urban and rural areas, for provision of funds, technical assistance and for formulation of policies and procedures for the administration of such assistance. The Corporation would cooperate with all agencies of the Federal Government, including especially the Department of Housing and Urban Development, Department of Transportation, Department of Health, Education and Welfare, Department of Commerce, Department of Interior, and other departments of the U.S. Government in order to provide the important link for a truly effective approach to economic development, to coordinate the private and public effort, and to provide funds in quantities and in a manner which are presently not available. The present efforts are disjointed, inadequate and to a large degree wasteful. Instead of supporting economic development projects, which would provide maximum economic returns, urban development projects to date have been to a large measure based upon political and hand-to-mouth decisions. The proposed Environmental Development Corporation would assist in the establishment of economic development priorities, provide much needed low-interest loans for environmental development, and no-interest credits for economic development of underdeveloped urban and rural areas in the United States. It would further provide the country with a new power structure whose basic and immediate task would be to assist in attaining a significant environment for the millions who so far have been denied this basic human right.

Maximum Returns

Education is one of the major industries in the world. The growth of education into a major source of employment in the twentieth century has to date been largely unaffected by the technological revolution and little by the rapid changes which are occurring in commerce and industry. The growth and development of educational spaces from the one-room schoolhouse to the mega-high school and university city has been impressive in terms of variety, complexity and number of teaching spaces. However, not only have teaching methods, productivity of teachers, and use of modern means of communication lagged behind this rapid increase in the teaching plant, but this unilateral growth has tended to increase the barriers which separate academic life from the rest of the world.

Educational Spaces

At the same time, automation and changes in required skills and employment patterns have been responsible for incorporating education as an integral part of the employment process. So far these demands have been largely met on an *ad hoc* basis—evening courses, educational leaves of absence for workers and managers to pursue further studies away from their place of employment, and consultation and short-term employment in industry and government for teachers and professors. While the demands for greater cross-pollination of employment and education have been growing, the actual spaces which have been built for both have been largely single-purpose in nature, e.g., the industrial research and development park in an entirely different urban location from the university campus.

Urban Activity Systems

It is important to emphasize that the simultaneous nature of all urban activity systems in the modern city tends to develop in a very opposite direction, one towards greater amalgamation of functions and activities and in particular to demand closer integration of educational and employment spaces. We know that education as well as employment is relevant to the development of the retarded urban areas, and that integration of the two makes a more effective worker, more creative manager, better administrator, and in general permits further human development. Starting with the urban ghetto, we are going to see in the years ahead a greater amalgamation between industry and the technical school, between places of research and teaching spaces, between the administration of urban areas and the administration of high schools and universities. This development will evince itself in the building of spaces which will serve this multiple role.

Developments of composite, synthetic materials have so far been used primarily in experimental ways in the building industry and have until now made little impact on our ability to create significant new spaces within the greater economy. Metals, plastics and the composite materials have been ingeniously applied to building spacecraft, jets, autos and household implements but generally not to enclosing man's living space.

The shortage, skyrocketing costs of processing traditional "natural" building materials, prohibitive on-site labor costs, together with revolutionary demands for social investments and accompanying economy, offer the greatest promise for completely new ways of building, for enclosing a maximum of space with a minimum of mass, for entirely new architecture which will make "modern" architecture of the last fifty years look obsolete by moving it entirely out of the present handicraft stage.

These new synthetic materials in prefabricated buildings, allowing a greater economy in capital and operating costs, are occupying the ever-increasing attention of the architect-engineer-scientist not only in actual construction but also in the search to find better ways to transport these structures from the plant to the site. Present experimentation with folding structures capable of being stored in the nose cone of the spacecraft, to be later unfolded and assembled on the moon, paved the way to the type of architectural research which requires application of mathematical formulae heretofore considered entirely inapplicable to the building industry. Besides the require-

Architectural Research

ments for minimum weight and maximum strength, keeping the number of folds of such a structure at a minimum becomes of paramount importance.

Economic studies show that the drag of excessive population growth, excessive preoccupation with military development, is quite independent of population density. More economic use of materials will help to finance the needed social investments and in turn spur economic development of other sectors.

The history of contemporary movements in urban planning and architecture points towards an increasing awareness and preoccupation with the problems of macroenvironment. Yet the present-day distribution of natural and human resources makes it apparent that our efforts are directed more at increasing the size and scale of spaces along functional lines of a bygone era than in a concentrated attack on primary sociophysical problems. The limitants to the creation of urban spaces conducive to economic and cultural development of deprived and disadvantaged peoples are multitudinous: national planning continues to fail to recognize economic development of urban ghettos and building new communities as top national priority; development of urban space is retarded by the meagre source of loans and the almost complete lack of economic development banks; political boundaries and administrative systems are generally obsolete and do not coincide with the realities of the problem areas; and industry, government and the design professions are attacking design of space in a compartmentalized and highly individualistic fashion, preferring short-term stop-gap remedies to socioeconomic reform.

Urban Ghettos

The token interest recently evinced in the underdeveloped areas is only a reaction to the riots which have taken place in the heart of the American city. As such, these half-hearted efforts cannot be expected to produce anything more than a continuation of sporadic and highly experimental urban renewal, which to date has been largely responsible for attempts to destroy the indigenous quality of urban neighborhoods, for Black removal and for accentuating already enormous social and economic problems of the inner city.

The Black Neighborhood

The doleful socioeconomic conditions of the Black inner city neighborhood are but a demonstration of the underdeveloped pockets of poverty throughout the world. Lacking in decent housing, employment and the educational opportunities and amenities of life that are so plentiful in the areas which surround it, the space of the ghetto is in every sense cut off from the space of the universe. In order to reestablish these places as significant urban spaces, as spaces conducive to further urban development and as integral parts of the space of the urbanized world, they must first be assisted to redevelop, to renew, and to reform from the inside. No amount of token assistance from government or private outside sources can be expected to accomplish this task. The inner city is fully capable of accomplishing its own renaissance, given the powers to govern itself and given adequate financial and technical assistance. A national Environmental Development Corporation, which would channel needed financial and technical resources required to strengthen the various economic sectors of these areas, would provide this much-needed assistance.

The inner city neighborhood as an established urban entity must have its own representative government responsible for charting and planning its own development and with accompanying powers to borrow long-term, low-interest, or interest-free loans. Such a largely independent and largely self-governing urban entity would be capable of redeveloping the area to the point where integration, spatial and human, would become a reality. Partnership between unequals is politically and spatially impossible.

Social Responsibility

The established professional and educational institutions of the American architectural profession can at best only partially meet the environmental, interdisciplinary challenges and the demands for new social responsibilities of the environmental profession of our epoch. The Task Force on Social Responsibility and the Professional Development Program of the American Institute of Architects have been engaged in individual efforts to meet this challenge. It would indeed be unfortunate and futile for the American architect to abandon his basic social responsibility for shaping man's environment through environmental systems architecture and to replace it with disjointed and non-professional social action programs. To optimize the chances of being able to meet most of the new social responsibilities which face the architectural and other environmental design professions would be to improve the competence and to broaden the social responsibility of the professions. In addition, the professions should assist in the education of the greatest possible number of well-qualified architects from predominantly Black and disadvantaged sectors of our society, all through the systematic, highly concentrated injection of excellence into the top (but missing) level of the educational system itself.

Mid-career Opportunities

The problem which faces the profession, the dichotomy which still exists between the world, practice and education and the needs of the society is but a reflection of the dichotomies which exist in the world of today in which social progress has been far outstripped by the technological genius. To bridge this gap there is a need for more than mere random attempts to initiate new schools of architecture and of environmental studies, for more than mere reorganization of the existing schools' philosophies and curricula which is, of course, needed, and much more than the Professional Development Program's valiant and to a large degree successful effort to provide the profession with coordinated and systematic mid-career educational opportunities. But there is little hope of being able to achieve the much needed coordinated improvements and of setting the desired levels of excellence in architectural education and practice through these individual efforts alone. The distinguished and interested practitioner and professor of architecture and environmental studies must be assured an opportunity of high level interdisciplinary study and of research opportunities in the environmental sciences and environmental systems architecture in his mid-career.

The distinguished military officer has the Staff College for his professional development, and so does the Foreign Service Officer. The socially and environmentally motivated architect or architectural educator has no such facility and no opportunity of professional and educational support for his continuing professional development. It is, therefore, not surprising that the existing dichotomy, instead of disappearing, seems to be widening with disastrous effects on both the society and the environmental professions.

If the American Institute of Architects is really serious about its responsibility to meet the social challenges of the 1970s and the 1980s, if it is vitally interested in assisting communities in solving these social, racial and economic problems, and if it is actually committed to the idea of faculty and practitioner improvement in an effort to resolve its goals for excellence in architectural practice and education, then it may well be worth considering the establishment of a top level national academy for a systematic, intensive, interdisciplinary and synoptic professional development of the American architects and environmentalists.

Environmental Academy

Such an Academy of Environmental Sciences would provide the professions with an opportunity of being able to offer to the members research, scholar-in-residence, and practitioner-in-residence facilities in an interdisciplinary setting. The inherent goals of the advancement of the science of architecture and environics and at the same time the advancement of the well-being of the society through greater environmental knowledge and application would then have an opportunity of being met by the environmental professions.

The establishment of the Academy of Environmental Sciences by the American Institute of Architects, with the joint cooperation of the American Institute of Planners and the other major professional environmental societies, would meet the urgent need for a center for synoptic and environmental studies. It would help meet the social responsibilities of improving professional competence; it would broaden the responsibilities of the professions, and would improve and strengthen the role of the environmental design schools in directing the entire spectrum of professional development programs and activities on a national and regional level.

Professional Competence

Instead of wasting the limited professional resources on various random and, at least partially if not wholly, diseconomic schemes and projects, the Institute's major effort in the early 1970s might be to jointly charge the Professional Development Program, the Task Force on Social Responsibilities and the Urban Design Center with the responsibility for developing an Academy of Environmental Sciences by a target date of 1976.

Man at the threshold of the twenty-first century is faced with the brutal truth of either finding a better, faster and more economical way of enclosing space, or of perishing at the hands of his fellowman. Never in the history of mankind has the architect-environmentalist had a clearer and more demanding mandate.

PART II

ENVIRONMENTAL DESIGN
OF THE
LATE TWENTIETH CENTURY

Chapter I

The Macroenvironment: Towns and Cities

A. THE HORIZONTAL CITY

1. *The Garden City*

The problems of the twentieth-century city have their roots deep in the nineteenth-century era of industrialization. The end of the last century saw the industrialized urban space becoming overcrowded with rural newcomers, with traffic, commerce, and unbounded land speculation. The living conditions of the tenement-house population were appalling, and the architecture of the towns and cities was no longer a viable force.

Among the leading social reformers of the urban scene of this period was an Englishman, Ebenezer Howard. After observing the disintegration of city space in Chicago and London, he developed a fresh, new concept of groups of cities in the country as a solution for stemming the uncontrolled growth of the industrial city. His concept was published in London in 1892 in *Tomorrow: A Peaceful Path to Real Reform*.

Deeply concerned about the seeming impossibility of providing decent living conditions in existing cities under the system of private land ownership, Howard proposed new cities whose land would remain in the ownership of the community. In the belief that land located away from existing urban centers can be purchased economically, avoiding undue land speculation and costs associated with urban renewal, he offered his planning concept as a means of providing decent, low-income housing.

Howard's constellation of new communities consisted of a central city of 58,000 people ringed by garden cities of 30,000 each. These satellite cities were to be separated from the center city by a permanent green belt and connected by highways and rapid transit.

Pages 65, 66, 67

Each satellite city was envisioned not as a bedroom, suburban-type community, but as a self-sufficient urban entity with places of employment located on the outskirts. There would be six residential neighbor-

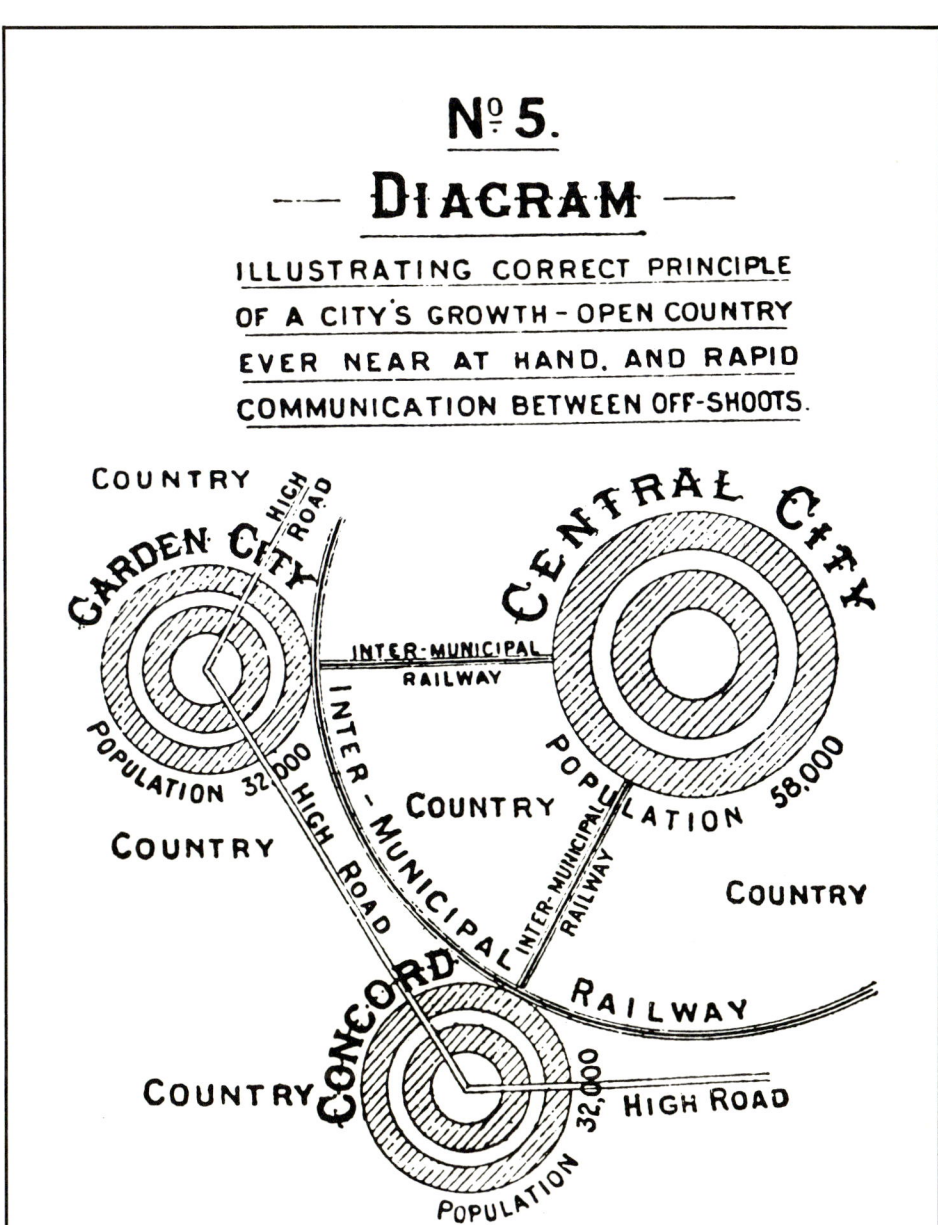

Ebenezer Howard's ring of satellite towns around the central city. A highly theoretical nineteenth century vision of a solution to the center city ghetto through decentralization and an alternative to uncontrolled suburban sprawl. The concept of the Garden City is as controversial today as when it was published in 1898. The problems of the inner city have in the meantime only magnified.

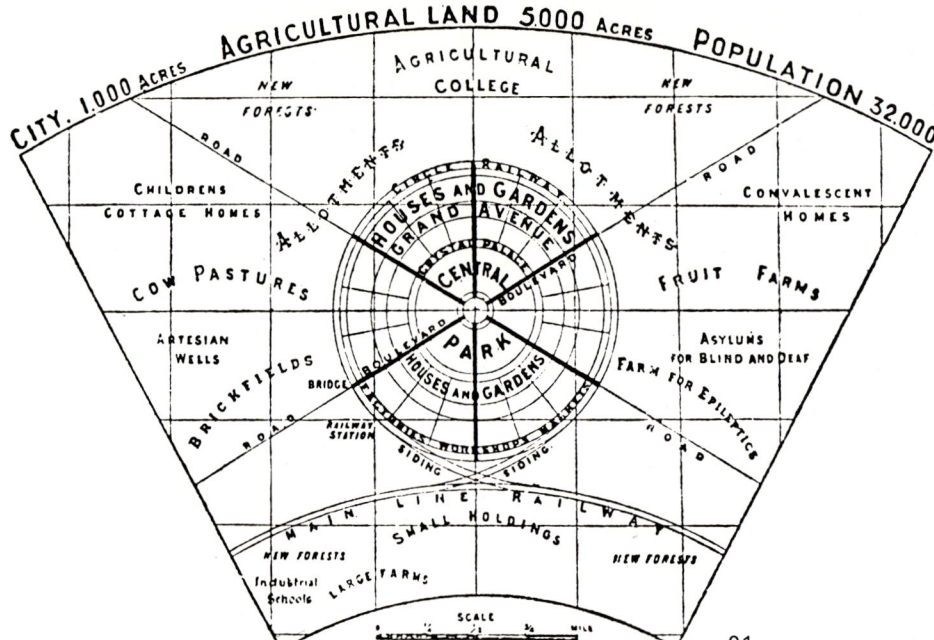

The satellite Garden City concept was envisioned as a densely built town with its own covered shopping mall and centers of employment, surrounded on all sides by suburbia.

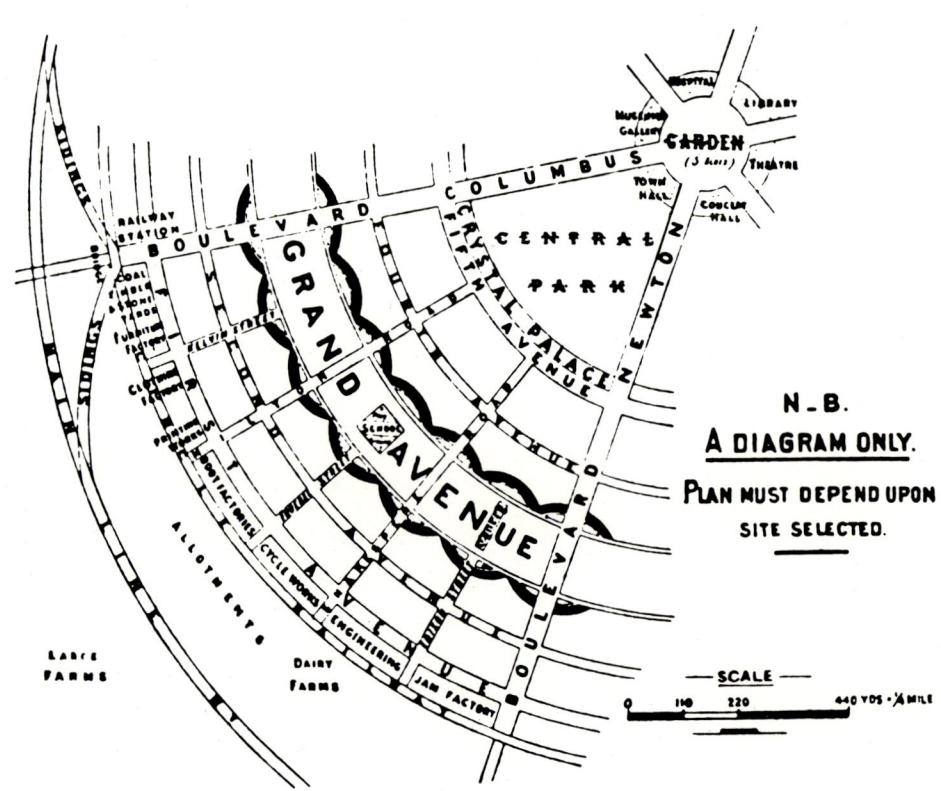

This abstract scheme was drawn to illustrate Howard's socio-economic concepts rather than a proposed physical city form.

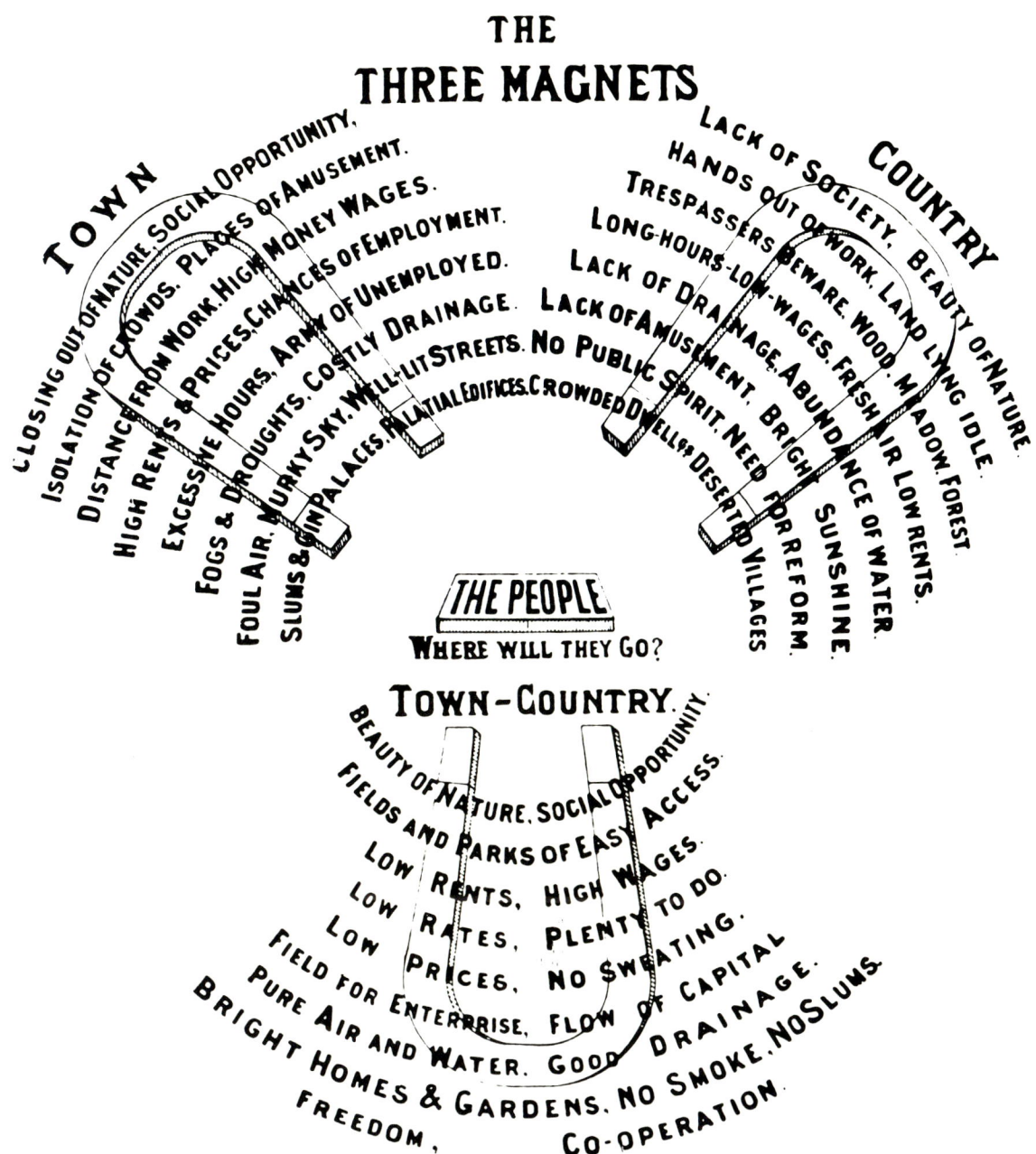

The Garden City was based upon an oversimplified idea of the perfect mix of the town and the country. The revolutionary developments of the twentieth century have overtaken man's ability to control his environment and have resulted in the emergence of mostly negative qualities of Howard's town-country "magnet." Today on a megalopolitan and national scale there is a need for a comprehensive and systematic land-use policy.

hoods, each facing the town's interior (420 foot wide) green belt, and each containing schools, churches and other community functions. The center of each new town would contain public buildings and a small park.

Howard's garden city was to have a significant impact upon twentieth-century concepts of new towns. His idea met with widespread interest, not only from those who foresaw public ownership of land as a means of breaking an architectural stalemate, but also from traditional private enterprise groups who saw a great opportunity in participating in a large-scale building of mass housing. As early as 1902 the garden city idea was applied to building a new community, Letchworth, designed by Barry Parker and Raymond Unwin, and located thirty-five miles from London.

The new dimensions of twentieth-century architecture and their application to creating a new urban environment were further reinforced by the prophetic English planner, Patrick Geddes, in his *Cities in Evolution* published in 1915. The author, himself a designer of approximately fifty new towns in India and Pakistan, analyzed the spatial and socioeconomic causes of "conurbation" in the creation of ghetto slums. Disturbed by the obvious inadequacies of architecture as practiced in the nineteenth century, he proposed an interdisciplinary system approach to the design of urban space.

Today's uncoordinated urban space of the megalopolis is largely the combined result of the great real estate activity and the automobile boom of the 1920s. The automobile permitted unbound horizontal growth of cities, and uncontrolled urban land speculation is still "designing" urban space.

2. *Radburn* The new town of Radburn designed in 1928 by Clarence Stein and Henry Wright, located in New Jersey less than an hour's drive from Manhattan, was the first town conceived and built in the motor age. The design objective was a town with primarily an automobile circulation system, yet preserving the human scale in its environment. Complete separation of people and vehicles was achieved by interlocking autonomous systems of walks and roads.

The walks were located in greenways which were separated from the roads by bridges and crossovers. These paths interconnected the cul-de-sac clusters of houses with schools, churches, shopping and recreation centers. Houses themselves were designed to take full advantage of the green areas, with only their service areas facing onto the streets. The town as conceived was to house a population of

25,000. The Great Depression prevented its completion. The places of employment were never built, and today the completed residential neighborhoods are encased in suburban sprawl.

This important experiment started a significant new town movement: the "New Deal" towns of Greenbelt, Maryland; Greendale, Wisconsin; Greenhills, Ohio; and today's Reston, Virginia, and Columbia, Maryland.

3. *Broadacre City*

The case for an all-horizontal city in the twentieth century was unequivocally presented by Frank Lloyd Wright in his 1935 Broadacres project. Never built, it represents a strong plea for the retention of human scale, space, and contact with nature in the architecture of the contemporary city. Wright goes beyond the proposals of Howard, Geddes, and other sociophysical reformers in advocating regional decentralization—a major effort directed at building new communities rather than rebuilding the old urban structure.

Instead of viewing the automobile as a foreign element in urban space, Wright saw it as the means for escaping the shackles of the rigid, overcentralized, and obsolete form of the city of the past. Aided further by the new media of communications, Broadacre City was envisioned as a self-contained "agrarian urbanism"—a city in communion rather than at war with nature.

The area of the proposed community was to cover a square, two miles on each side. The individually owned house on an individual lot was to form its basic unit. The city's network of roads was to connect all employment, recreation, and commercial centers. Significantly, the central government unit was not to be the city hall but the county courthouse, further underscoring the new organizational structure of the community.

Pages 70, 71

The entire proposal met with almost universal criticism from the day it was unveiled. It was considered an embodiment of the anti-city movement, retrogressive and useless in solving contemporary urban problems. In the forefront were those who still believe that the megalopolis has the capacity of absorbing unlimited population and of being restructured to meet the demands of the new society and new technology. In the meantime, the uncontrolled process of suburbanization continued, gaining impetus until today it has reached a form resembling a mediocre caricature of Wright's artistic concept —unplanned sprawl in place of the balanced planned community.

As mature judgment for a comprehensive economic development of regions replaces either city or country theories, the Broadacre City proposal may seem far less of a utopian dream than it did when Wright unveiled it.

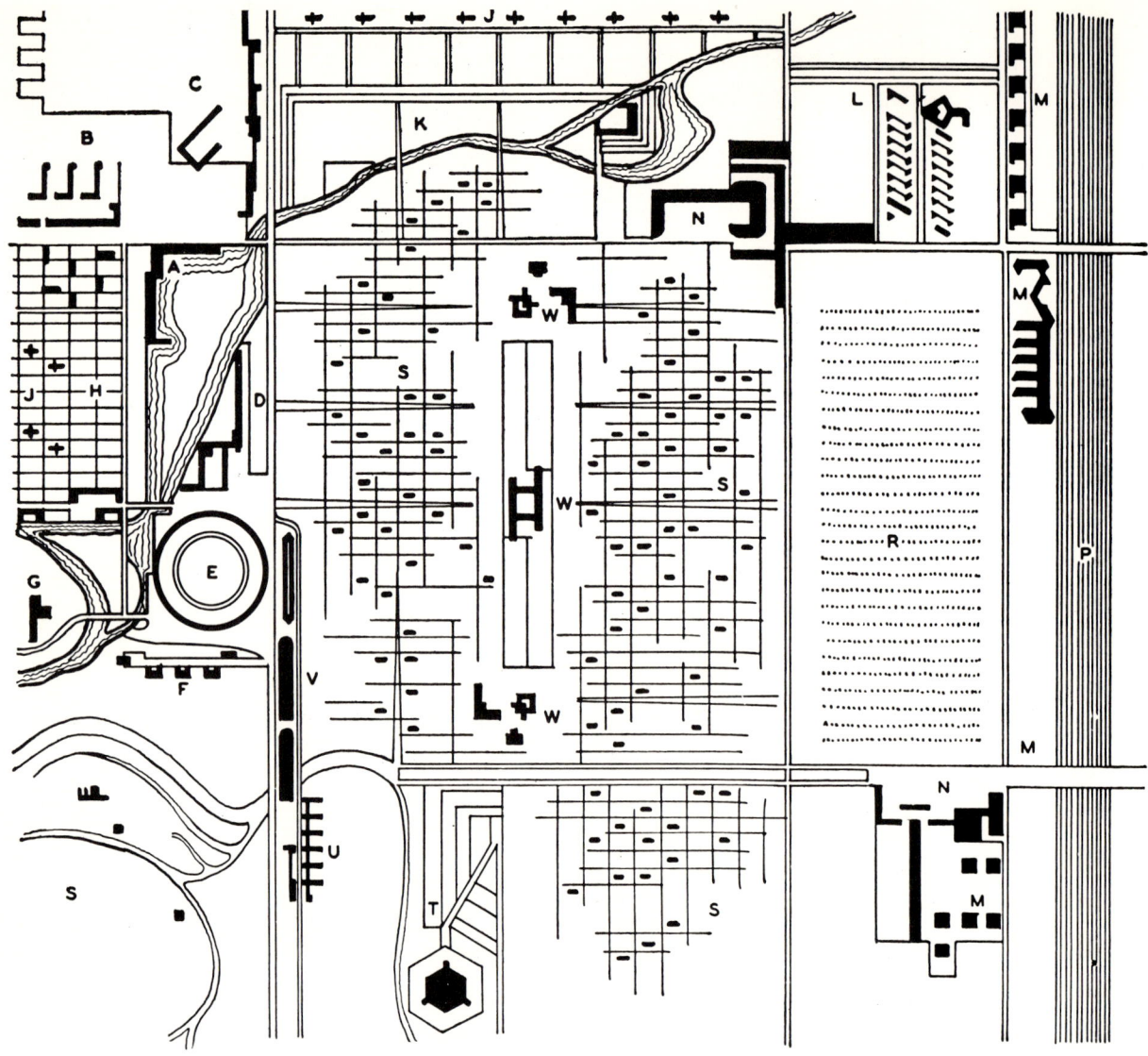

Frank Lloyd Wright's 1935 plan for Broadacre City was a horizontal, low density, automobile-based concept rooted in the belief that America's vast and largely undeveloped land resources should be utilized as man's immediate environment. Although the proposal is lavish in terms of land density, requiring a minimum of one acre of land for each dwelling, the two square miles which comprise the city are carefully divided by a rectilinear street pattern which gives form coherence to the entire composition.
A. County Courthouse, B. Airport Terminal, C. Sports facilities, D. Office building, E. Stadium, F. Hotel, G. Hospital, H. Light industry, J. Small farms, K. City park, L. Motel, M. Heavy industry, N. Shopping center, P. Railroad, R. Orchards, S. Residential area, T. Interdenominational temple, U. Research park, V. Zoo, W. Schools.

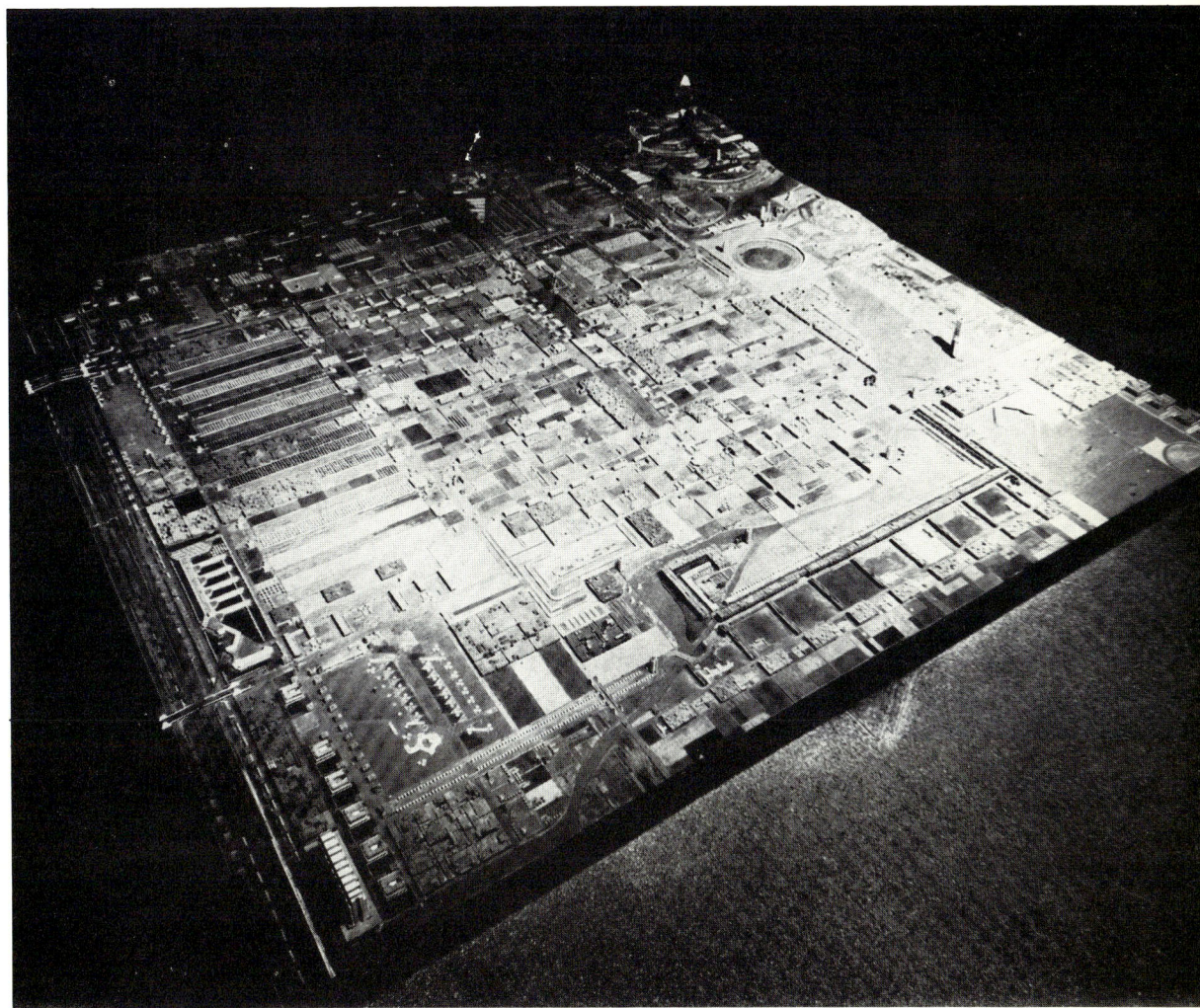

Model of Broadacre City, Frank Lloyd Wright's totally new urban pattern, an imaginative but economically hypothetical vision in terms of land, space and time.

The degree of comprehensive design found in Broadacre City is unmatched—the forms of boats, cars and helicopters totally integrated with those of buildings.

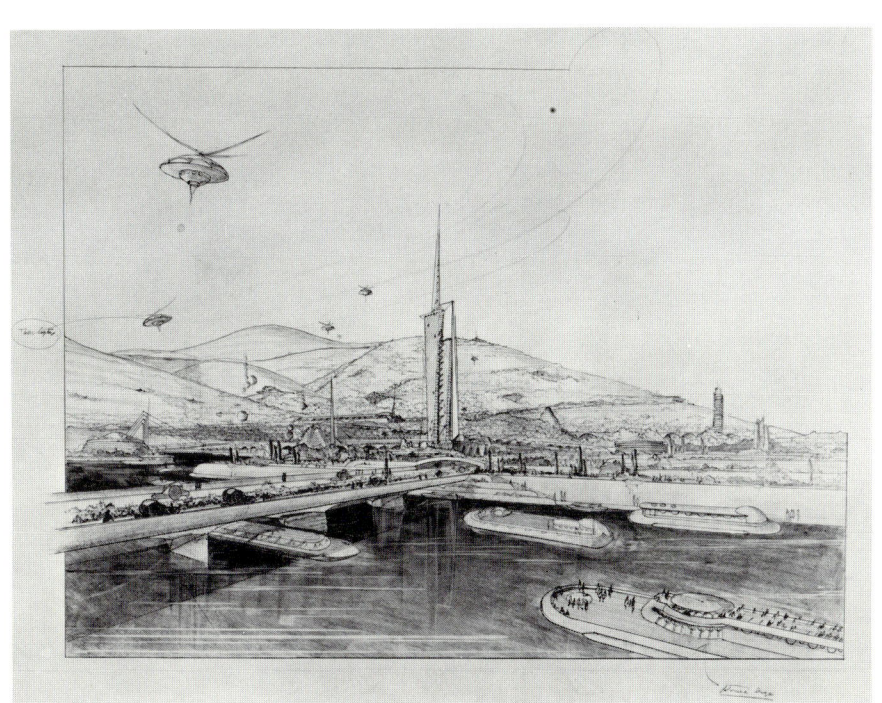

4. *Reston* Reston, Virginia, located about twenty miles from Washington, D.C., is often identified as the first satellite new town in the second half of the twentieth century. Robert Simon began to think about building a model community for 75,000 people in the 1950s, but was unable to buy the original 6,750 acres until 1961 and to have the first neighborhood completed before 1967. The design has undergone many changes during the process of conception and implementation. In its initial stages the development was influenced by the Garden City concept; by the time Lake Anne Village, the first neighborhood, was completed Simon lost control of the town to other financial interests and the community began falling under the spell of typical suburban growth — so much so that the sculptured space of Lake Anne Village is now obviously different from the rest of the town.

Pages 73-87

The early sketches of the community included well-defined neighborhoods and a system of all pedestrian walks within green wedges clearly separated from automobile circulation, suggestive of the Radburn theme — the idea that in the architecture of the contemporary town, human scale must be present. But neither this theme nor its idealistic implications appears in the partially completed work. Despite the merit of individual architectural elements, the spatial composition and location seem to be primarily suburban in concept. They have been arranged neither as a part of an overall metropolitan plan nor to provide a living environment for low-income families degraded in the city slum.

Unlike Howard's garden city concept of basic concern with the problems of the city, Reston concentrated mainly on creating an environment for those who could in any case afford the suburban life. Although some places of employment for the residents are being provided, Reston is basically a "bedroom" town. With the noted exception of one high-rise apartment, the concept is horizontal.

Reston, Virginia, designed in 1962 by Whittlesey and Conklin, is the first post-World War II attempt in America to stem the uncontrolled sprawl of formless suburbia.

The first "village," Lake Anne, of this satellite town designed for a population of 75,000 people and being developed largely without government assistance, 1965.

Lake Anne Shopping Plaza—Whittlesey and Conklin, architects, 1965.

opposite: Reston's only high-rise apartment tower, 1965.

Strong forms of Reston's golf club, by Charles Goodman, 1964.

All pedestrian space enclosed by powerful geometry. Well-defined stonescape next to water's edge—a very distant echo of San Marco's Piazza, 1965.

right and opposite page: Reston would not have been possible without new legislative measures that permit a higher percentage of public space than allowed in suburban areas.

opposite: Juxtaposition of playful sculptural forms.

right: Street furniture for children.

below right: Colorful forms of Charles Goodman's rowhouses, 1964.

A highly original sculpture playground—an integral part of the pedestrian plaza at Lake Anne Village. The "Sun Boat" and the "Lookout" play-sculpture by Gonzalo Fonseca.

Sunday afternoon mid-summer leisure activities turn the central lake of Reston's Lake Anne Village into a pond for sails— "agrarian urbanism."

Town-country social activities not usually associated with suburban living patterns.

right and below: Lakeside townhouses cluster designed by Chloethiel Woodard Smith, 1964.

opposite: Charles M. Goodman's geometric townhouses, 1964.

Double orientation of the lakeside cluster permits easy access by water as well as by road.

Schools within easy access by foot from the residential neighborhood centers. Lake Anne Elementary School by Caudill, Rowlett, Scott, 1966.

opposite: Reston's crescent garden apartments designed by Cohen, Haft, and Associates, 1968.

Experimental housing for a great variety of income groups has lately become one of Reston's chief preoccupations. Golf Course Island Cluster by Louis Sauer.

Within a totally rational and human approach, the planners and the architects were able to shape a synoptic community environment.

Reston provides many spots for passive recreation and meditation—places for solitude as well as spaces for social interaction.

The walks, pathways, foot bridges and streams all provide healthy and natural places of movement, social contact and recreation.

Model of Town Center as it will appear in 1980.

5. *Columbia*   Columbia, Maryland, located between Washington, D.C., and Baltimore, Maryland, was conceived in the 1960s by James Rouse as a balanced community containing large numbers of individual low-cost houses. The principal concern here seems to be the organization rather than stemming of the formless suburban sprawl. Provision of an overall structure of public facilities and amenities is the overriding design idea. This concept was developed by architect-planners Hoppenfeld and Finley with an interdisciplinary team of experts.

This planned suburb, when completed, will house a population of 150,000 on its 15,000 acres. Columbia will consist of ten separate villages, each with its own communal facilities and containing between 2,500 and 3,500 families. The basic unit of each village is a neighborhood of 500 to 600 families. The town center, when completed, is expected to contain an office building, a large enclosed shopping mall, a theater, several restaurants, and a transportation center. A major interstate highway dissects the town and provides a link with other centers of this highly suburbanized region.

This recent suburban experiment expresses a revolt against the preoccupation of the architecture of the first half of the century with individual buildings and the creation of intimate private space at the expense of social, urban concern. As in all revolutions, one extreme of the morphological cycle was replaced by another—concentration on social public space rather than on man's immediate environment.

The individual family shelter in Columbia is unimaginative, dull, and its space is lacking in scale, proportion, and responsiveness to modern family life. It is divorced from the macrostructure and form of the community. Limited to traditional dimensions, it is not expressive of or conducive to the dynamic, moving, exciting and multidimensional quality of twentieth-century urban life.

Pages 88-95

Plan of the new city of Columbia, Maryland, designed in 1964, clearly defines each residential village which in turn contains a number of individual neighborhood units, each with its own community center.

The communal places and pedestrian movement corridors around the residential clusters are imaginative and express full appreciation of the need for variety and contrasts in outdoor planning.

Downtown Columbia faces Lake Kittamaqundi, and the lakeshore at this point has been developed into multi-level plazas.

The stores and shops at Wilde Lake Village Green face a landscaped square. Also a part of the village center is a community hall and youth center, a library and recreational facilities.

The social identity of the Columbia community is focused upon its central services, parks and lakeside plazas.

Pergola-covered walkways, wooden foot bridges, and a great variety of paving textures and colors make walking in this satellite town a recreational experience.

B. THE VERTICAL CITY

1. *La Ville Contemporaine*

That automobility and telecommunication have made the dense centralized city obsolete is the belief of the proponents of the horizontal city concept.

On the other hand, the pioneers of the vertical city movement profess that the vertical city offers unmatched variety and choice of spatial experience; tension, drama and excitement; juxtaposition of space and man and mass; economy in time and technology; and unlimited opportunities for personal contact.

Le Corbusier's La Ville Contemporaine is the first twentieth-century concept which totally accepts the vertical city with its technological base—the automobile, the elevator, and the reinforced concrete and steel skeleton frame. This 1922 prevision of a modern city with sixty-story buildings, elevated freeways, density of twelve hundred per acre, automobile and air travel is in dire contrast to the romantic "city in the country" concept of the garden city movement. Scorning the "universal waste land of garden cities," Le Corbusier proposed a garden in the city concept, with towering buildings set in a spacious park.

Page 97

Le Corbusier foresaw the threat to the central city of horizontal megalopolitan expansion of the satellite spider web. He predicted that if this process were to go unchecked the great centers would turn into great urban ghettos—into places of crime and human misery. In lieu of uneconomic horizontal scatterization he proposed continued massive urban renewal of the old city and the building of new, great vertical cities away from metropolitanized regions.

Le Corbusier saw in modern technology a great liberating force for the slum dweller. Unlike many other architects of the period, who feared industrialization and urbanization, he saw twentieth-century science as a means of achieving total control over environmental space. He rejected natural building materials, preferring the synthetic, unmovable, fixed ones, and he viewed architecture as being governed by strict logic, geometry, and mathematics.

In the center of La Ville Contemporaine, Le Corbusier placed a multi-mode transportation megastructure. The downtown consisted of twenty-four 60-story skyscrapers covering only five percent of the land, with a total capacity of 400,000. The heart of the city was to be

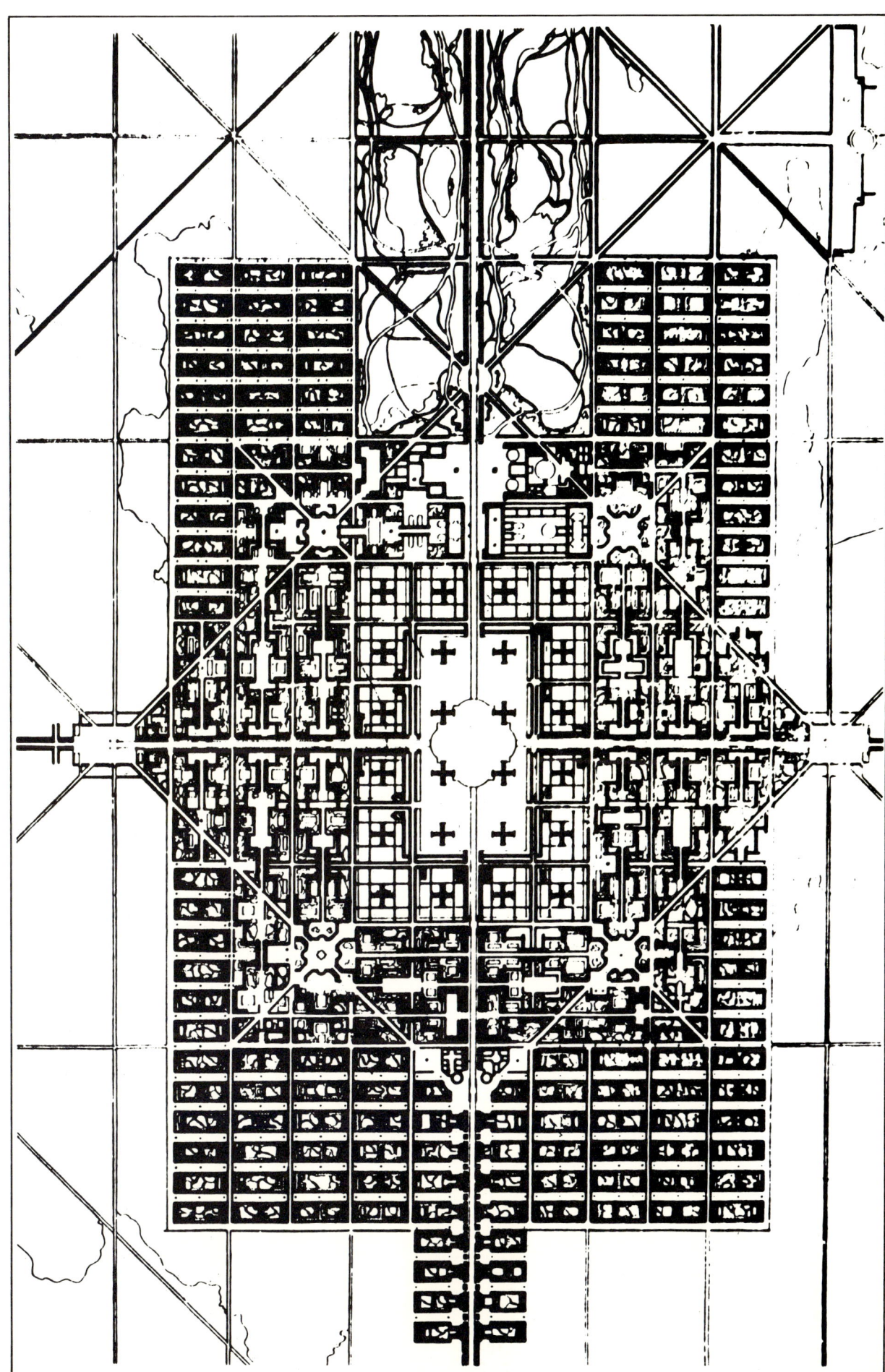

surrounded by continuous eight-story apartment slabs for 600,000. On the outskirts he placed individual houses for 2,000,000, spaced within a gridiron pattern.

The plan reflects a desire to create a total man-made environment employing all available achievements of science and technology with an objective to decongest the city and to clearly define space, utilizing the new dimensions of urban systems.

2. Chandigarh

The world is urbanizing at an astronomical rate. Wars, industry, and educational development absorb available resources. City building efforts are generally limited to rebuilding and expanding existing centers of population, not to constructing great new cities. New cities of Chandigarh, in India, Islamabad, in Pakistan, and Brasilia, in Brazil, are rare exceptions.

The original planning for Chandigarh was the work of the great Polish architect Matthew Nowicki and the outstanding American architect-planner Albert Mayer. Nowicki's brilliant concepts were abruptly interrupted by his death while planning this city. India then turned to Le Corbusier.

The design of a great city on the virgin land of a continent fraught with expectations of modern urban life, on a site flanked by the towering and verdant Shiwalaks, offered an unlimited challenge. It was also an opportunity to apply for the first time some of the lifelong theories of this undisputed master of modern architecture. Furthermore, India gave Le Corbusier a free hand to translate its aspirations into a meaningful urban form.

Despite these ideal conditions, the final plan, developed in collaboration with Pierre Jeanneret, the English architects Maxwell Fry and Jane B. Drew and Indian planners soon after the turn of the mid-century failed to meet even the most rudimentary requirements. Instead of embodying the virile visions of his city of tomorrow, Le Corbusier's Chandigarh, as finally developed, is a misapplication of the garden city. The plan lacks scale, variety and multidimensional quality. The scale of a small town is applied here to a city of 9,000 acres and half a million people. The basic unit of the composition is a rectangular block three-quarters of a mile long by one half mile wide, 240 acres in size and housing about 15,000 people. The urban movement systems—the pedestrian, the cyclist, the bullock cart, the motor car and the commercial vehicle—are intermixed and allowed to use basically the same circulation pattern.

The lack of multidimensional integration of urban systems is further confused by inarticulate programing of urban functions and undefined spaces. Perhaps the greatest weakness of the concept is the

The Secretariat building, with its powerful forms and articulations, is but a building block in the dynamically superimposed composition of spaces of the government center. The center was designed in totality by this virtuoso architect and reflects the spirit and strength of its immediate environment.

opposite: Of Le Corbusier's many visionary city plans, the only one which he had the opportunity to implement is the great capital of Punjab in India—Chandigarh. Architecture and city planning in his government center are adroitly and sculpturally integrated, creating an orchestrated whole. The design of the government scheme was originated in 1952.

dichotomy which exists between the geometric rectilinear shape of the plan and the strong plastic forms of the rivers, the two seasonal torrents on the east and the west which bound the site but which have been largely ignored in the composition. Also, the city has a strong beginning at the foot of the mountains but no finity, formlessly spilling into the fertile but endless plain.

The architecture of the government center, on the other hand, shows the virtuosity of Le Corbusier in full orchestration. The monumental trinity of the High Court, the Legislative Chambers, and the Secretariat is extremely well integrated and exudes strength and incomparable freeing of significant tension across space and communion with the natural environment.

The architecture of the parliament building, the Legislative Chambers, clearly reflects in its shapes the epic power and inspiration of the Shilawaks mountain range.

The real spatial drama takes place within the buildings. The internal juxtaposed and interweaving spaces of the Court of Justice create a revolutionary movement and exciting and fascinating environment.

Chandigarh represents a milestone in the movement of modern architecture to find its virile roots in local culture and environment.

Le Corbusier's architecture and city planning combines his artistic and sculptural qualities with his thorough comprehension of twentieth-century technology, administration and economics.

Tension and drama of the space between buildings is accentuated and heightened by strong sculptural shapes strategically placed.

opposite: Rhythm, contrast, repetition and variety of architectural music on the surfaces of the Court of Justice building.

107

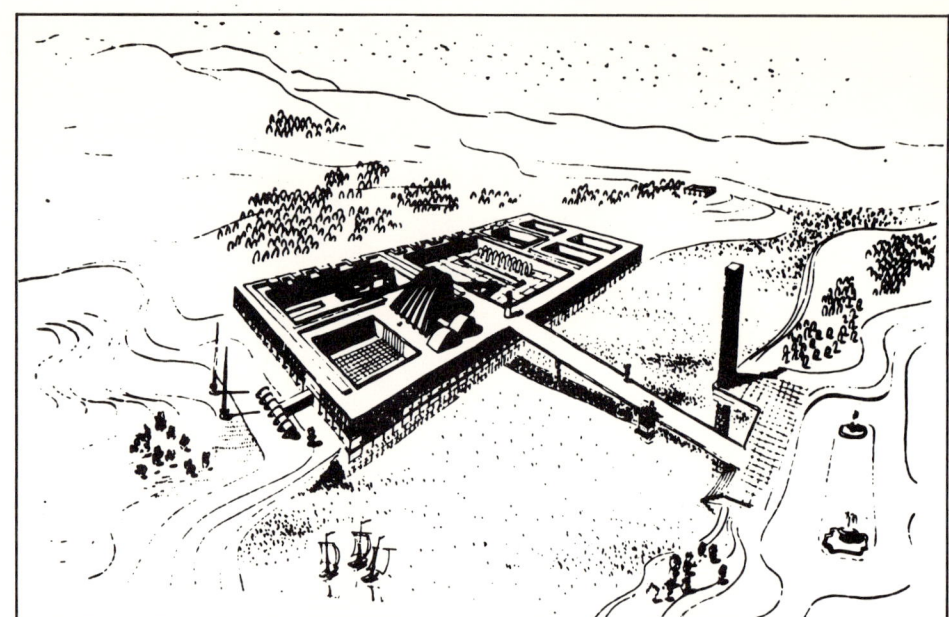

Nowicki's government center clearly evokes the great Moghul spatial organization.

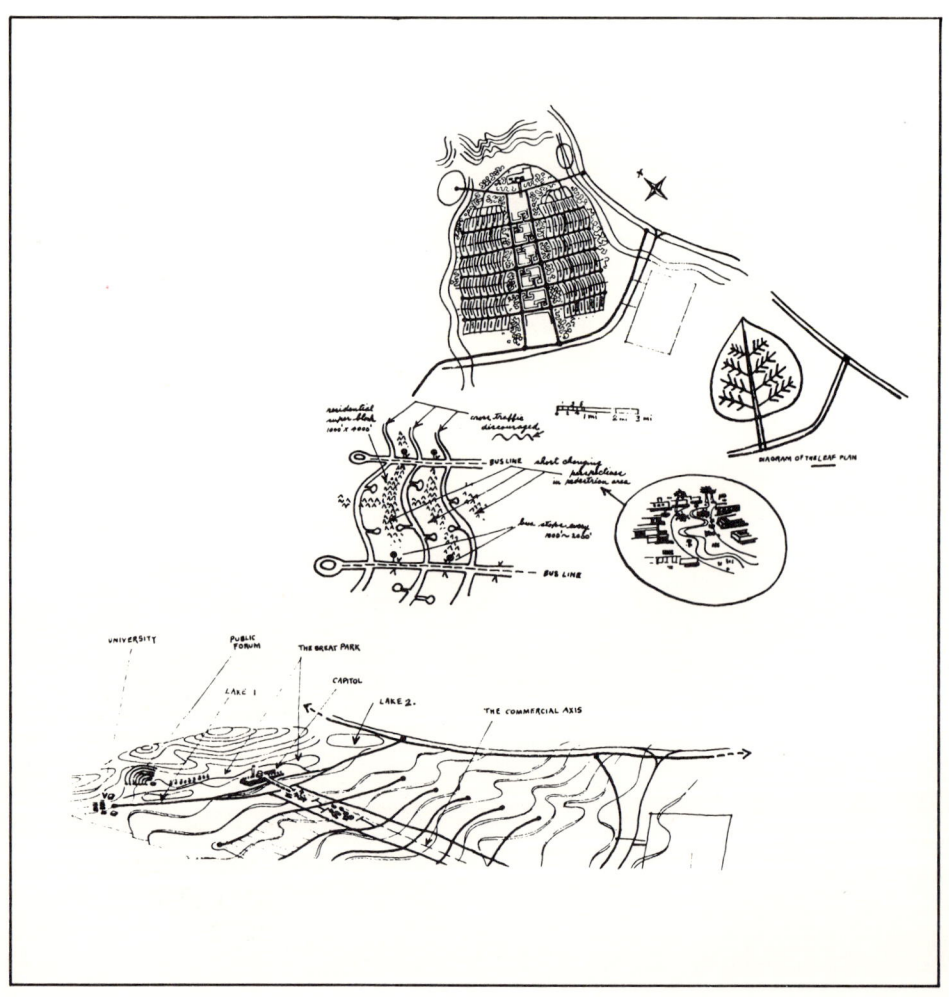

Original plans for Chandigarh by Matthew Nowicki in collaboration with Albert Mayer show designs different from that of Le Corbusier, yet in some ways showing even stronger roots in Indian culture and history.

Sketch of proposed civic center in which Nowicki integrates the European spatial tradition with the richness, texture, and patterns of Indian work.

Upper level buildings of the government center indicate a primary concern with expressing the potentialities of mid-twentieth century technological discoveries.

109

3. *Islamabad* Pakistan's capital city of Islamabad is located in a natural setting not too dissimilar to that of the capital of Punjab, Chandigarh. Nestled against the Margalla Mountains and covering the northeastern part of the Potwar Plateau, the new capital's location at first sight recalls that of Chandigarh. However, the similarity between these two new capitals stops there.

Islamabad is a new city built around the ancient city of Rawalpindi situated on the famous Grand Trunk Road, the international highway from Calcutta, India, to Kabul, Afghanistan. Thus, the cultural and historical continuity expressed in the mosques of Rawalpindi are carried into the twentieth century in the development of this vibrant new city.

The basic planning scheme for Islamabad is the work of the Greek city planner Constantinos Doxiadis, with the assistance of Pakistani planners and architects. As if the basic unit of composition of Chandigarh were not mammoth enough, Islamabad's residential sectors are each one and a quarter mile square. Each sector is designed as a more or less self-contained urban unit, subdivided into smaller residential neighborhoods served by community centers, schools, mosques, playgrounds, and other communal facilities.

The enormous National Park nestled between the hills and the new city contains a large lake around which are being built the chanceries and residences of the foreign missions. Besides the embassy enclave, the National Park will contain the new University of Islamabad and the Atomic Research Institute, both designed by Edward Durell Stone.

Between the Rawal Lake and the Margalla Hills is the heart of Islamabad, the government center, the work of the Italian architect Gio Ponti. These crisp, white Secretariat buildings, with lush Mogul Gardens will, in the near future, be complemented by a Stone-designed government complex consisting of the President's House, the National Assembly and the Cabinet Secretariat and Foreign Office building. The President's House, situated in a complex of three hills, will stand atop a 2,000-foot elevation commanding a panoramic view of the city and will become the central terminating element of the monumental Capital Avenue.

Islamabad expresses the rich sociophysical potential of building a new city in an environment deeply imbued with history and tradition.

Pages 111-126

Edward Durell Stone's Atomic Research Institute building completed in 1970. Located in Islamabad, the new capital of Pakistan, it is an elegant example of continuing the great Moghul tradition in contemporary vernacular.

Model of the Atomic Research Institute in Islamabad by Edward Durell Stone.

Stone's University of Islamabad, now under construction and located near the new capital.

Model of the proposed Grand National Mosque to be located in the new capital of Pakistan and designed by the Turkish architect Vedat Dalokay — winner of the 1969 international competition.

Arcade of the recently completed Atomic Research Institute in Islamabad. Slender and elegant columns, domes and richly landscaped courts, together with the judicious use of fountains and gardens, are in total harmony with the natural environment.

Modern apartment structures in this new city also use extensively delicate, lace-like, white concrete screens to provide rooms and balconies with protection from the sun. The white arched roof also gives an oriental touch to this building. The view from each apartment is across the plains to the glittering Rawal Lake.

External arcade of the Atomic Research Institute in Islamabad by Edward Durell Stone, 1970.

Housing of the atomic reactor and the internal arcades. Exquisite use of color in contemporary architecture.

The Shahrazad Hotel in Islamabad by the Italian architect Gio Ponti. Completed in 1964, it was the first major structure to rise in the new capital.

Free-standing tower rising from the extensive Moghul-inspired gardens of the Atomic Research Institute in Islamabad is a powerful symbol of the aspirations and ideals of the new nation.

The plan of Islamabad is the work of the Greek city planner Constantinos Doxiadis in collaboration with Pakistani planners and architects. The city lies nestled against the majestic background of the Margalla mountains. Construction of the new capital began in 1961.

Moghul-style garden in the five-wing Government Hostel. The entire complex was designed by the English architect G. W. Brigden and completed in 1965.

The first building of the Islamabad government center is the Secretariat complex completed in 1968. Designed by Gio Ponti, the well-proportioned composition of white buildings is set in multi-level Moghul gardens with terraced pools and an extensive and well-designed system of fountains. The entire composition rises robustly against the Margalla mountains in harmony with the natural environment.

opposite: The moving, dynamic quality which pervades the space is the result of the adroitly handled sculptural mass of the buildings which, though monumental in scale, are not oppressive and create human and pleasant architectural spaces.

The Shahrazad Hotel in Islamabad, Pakistan, by Gio Ponti, 1964.

Gardens of the Shahrazad Hotel with traditional terraced pools of water, with the Margalla mountains in the background.

Neighborhood shopping center in a residential sector of Islamabad containing shops on the first floor and dwellings above.

Designed by Pakistani architect A. F. M. Hashim, this residential shopping center was completed in 1968.

A downtown office building in Lahore, Pakistan, designed by Edward Durell Stone evinces strong ties with the traditional environment, 1968.

Dome over the interior courtyard—the central organizational element.

4. *Brasilia* The new capital of Brazil is perhaps the most significant new city. Unlike Chandigarh, Brasilia was, from the start, conceived as a composite hierarchy of integrated but clearly identified urban systems. Lucio Costa, designer of the basic structure of the city, did not design its buildings; they were executed by design teams under the direction of Oscar Niemeyer. During all the stages of planning, design and implementation, teams of experts in all fields of urban and environmental affairs worked side by side. The result is a sociophysical design brilliantly expressed, unified, and inspiring.

The inherent strength of the design composition was achieved through the recognition by Costa of the environmental concept that the space of the entire city must retain continuity with the original unsculptured larger space. The structure and form of the design idea draws its inspiration directly from the shapes of the natural forms of the larger environment: the undulating hills, the dynamic shape of the lake, all the way to the recognition of the effect that the light of the Brazilian sun would have on the spaces of the city.

The plan, determined by competition in 1957, consists of an extremely bold and simple form of a bow and arrow. The arrow tip is the capitol complex, providing the dynamic and symbolic contact point between the city and the country. The taut spine of the bow is an expressway — a clear statement that the city's basic movement system is the automobile. The point of contact between the arrow (the monumental shaft of space) and the bow (the expressway and its related neighborhood) is the great transportation center dramatized in its architectural form. Movement in space and space experienced through movement are dramatically expressed in total design. Driving on the expressway or walking on the mall, we experience constantly changing, moving and interlocking spaces, with buildings used not to confine space but to define and underscore the contiguous nature of the natural and man-made space. Brasilia offers an inkling of the yet unexplored drama and power inherent in sculpting and experiencing architectural space of the contemporary city.

Pages 128-137

The sculptural form of the Metropolitan Cathedral in Brasilia—Oscar Niemeyer, architect.

Apartment complex in downtown Brasilia.

Brasilia—central commercial area with a view of the lake in the background.

Brasilia was developed as a part of the national policy to open up the country's largely undeveloped hinterland, to locate the government buildings away from traffic-congested Rio de Janeiro, and to design the new capital as a symbol of the aspirations of contemporary Brazil. The plan of the new city was selected through a competition held in 1957, with the Brazilian city planner, Lucio Costa, the winner.

The success of spatial planning of Brasilia is the result of close cooperation between the designer of the basic structure of the city, Lucio Costa, with the city's chief architect, Oscar Niemeyer. The result of this contemporary systems planning, with teams of experts on all facets of environmental affairs working closely together, is a brilliant city form and an inspiring urban environment.

The intricately sculptured space in front of the Presidential Palace welds this immediate area with the rest of the city's environmental composition.

The forms of the concrete arcade of the Presidential Palace are reinforced across space by this strong sculpture by M. Martins.

The government center named the Plaza of the Three Powers consists of the National Congress, (the twin towers), the House of Representatives (the inverted dome), and the Senate (the dome).

opposite: Residential super-block, with a primary school and a kindergarten. Four super-blocks form the basic residential neighborhood unit of Brasilia, each with its own community center consisting of shops, a church, a movie theatre, and recreational facilities.

The highly sculptured Presidential Palace—the work of the doyen of Brazilian architects, Oscar Niemeyer.

Free-standing and powerful in its stark simplicity—the city's historical museum in front of the Presidential Palace.

opposite: Ministry of Foreign Affairs building. Designed by the strong protagonist of well-disciplined architectural forms in buildings, Oscar Niemeyer.

Brasilia's Municipal Theater, designed by Oscar Niemeyer, is located at the crossing of the city's main communications arteries.

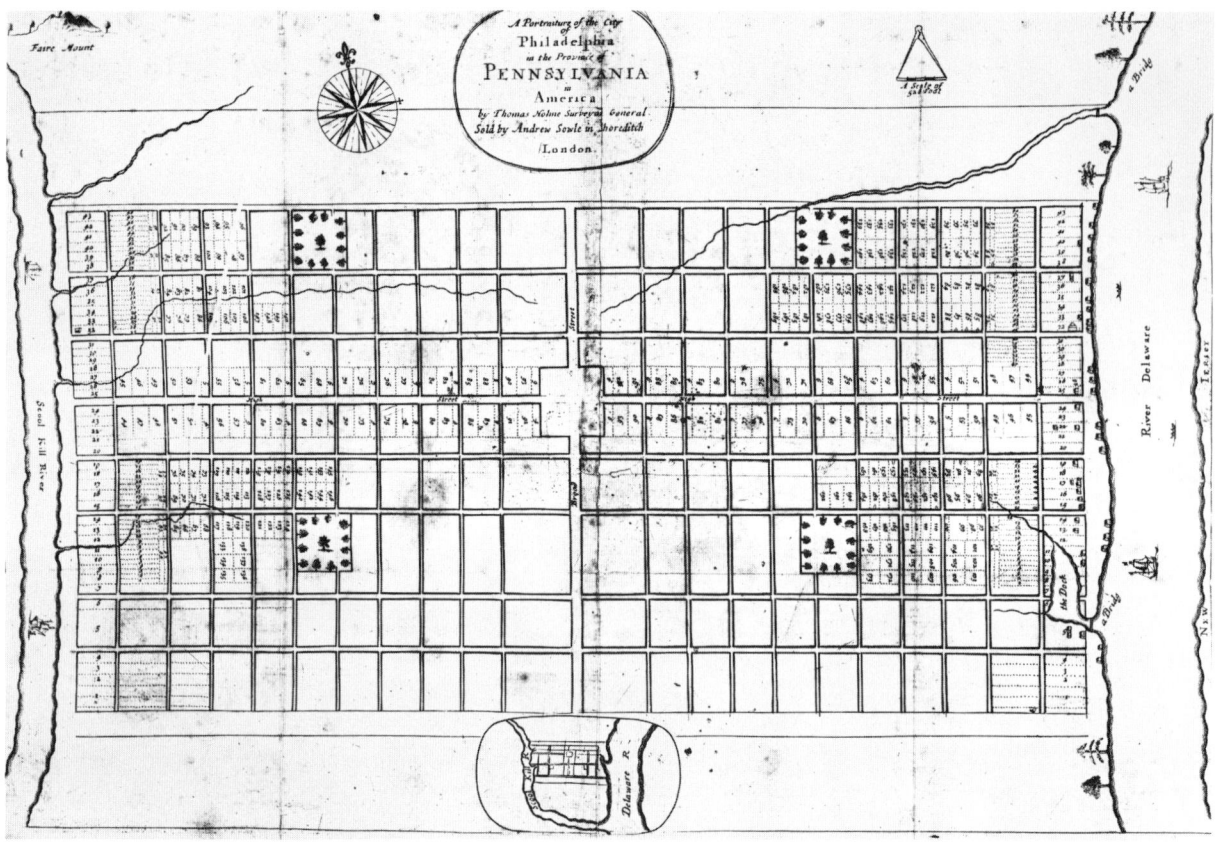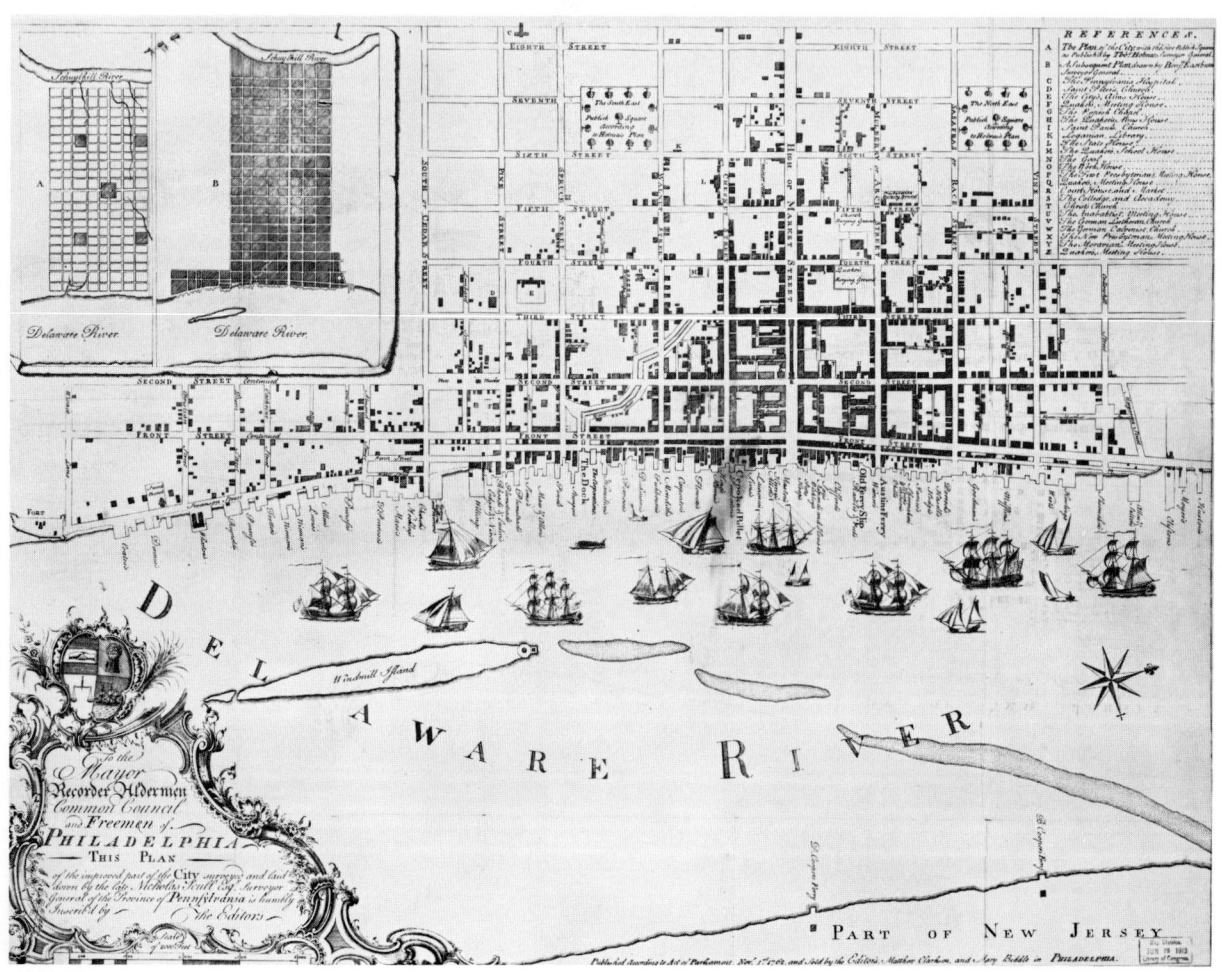

5. Philadelphia

above opposite: Original city plan for Philadelphia, Pennsylvania, laid out by William Penn in 1682. This area, two miles long and almost one mile wide, was brilliantly subdivided on a grid pattern, with each city block of a size which assured ease of movement and human scale. The entire quadripartite plan, with each of the four neighborhoods provided with a communal green, set a basic order which remains to this day.

opposite: During the centuries of evolutionary changes which this city, rich in architectural and planning history, underwent, streets were added to the original plan and existing streets widened, but the basic underlying design idea was carefully preserved. Map of the city prepared by Nicholas Scull in 1762 shows the plan basically unchanged.

The success of spatial continuity in a new city like Brasilia was derived by the designer's ability to place the new structure in an existing non-urban environment, achieving total unification between the man-made and the natural world. Urban renewal, that is, the necessary process of updating the old city to the requirements of today, requires the same principle except that, instead of melding man-made forms with those of nature, the character of the new space must be made compatible with the existing environment and the structure of the new pattern molded with the old. To accomplish historic and cultural continuity, ability to understand and draw inspiration from the existing space is required. Thus, to meaningfully reshape existing urban space, two basic sources of inspiration must be utilized: the rich spatial heritage of the past and the innate spatial opportunities of new technology, new city functions, and new dimensions in architecture.

Architecture as a tool for solving social problems has been employed throughout history. The new dimensions of social patterns in our cities today require equivalent changes in architecture. When whole groups of citizens become aware of the importance of significant urban environment, when they insist on participating in the renewal of the city, when they revolt if this right is denied them, then the process of city design itself undergoes a revolutionary change. Replanning an old, existing city is a never-ending process, with new urban systems added and superimposed over existing ones. This is generally true of all existing major urban centers, and the Philadelphia example dramatically illustrates this new process of urban redesign, encompassing active citizen participation in reshaping the city.

The original plan for Philadelphia was completed by William Penn in 1682. It is known as the first large American city to be laid out on a grid pattern. Since the ground was flat the grid pattern was logical and the small size of the basic block assured human scale and ease of movement. The brilliance of the original design idea is expressed in the way the man-designed pattern was integrated with the natural land forms and space. Just as the layout of Brasilia has a strong one-directional axial composition, the plan of Philadelphia was designed with its main spine, presently Market Street, strongly connecting the Delaware and the Schuylkill Rivers, thus interlocking the space of the city with the existing natural environment. The choice of the quadripartite plan, each quadrangle with a green, gave further order and definition to the spatial organization.

Pages 138, 140, 141

During its almost three hundred years of existence, Philadelphia has undergone constant change, particularly under the significant impact of changing movement systems: first, horse and buggy, then the horse-drawn streetcar, the electric streetcar, the railroad, the automobile, rapid transit and air travel. Yet, the designers were able to maintain

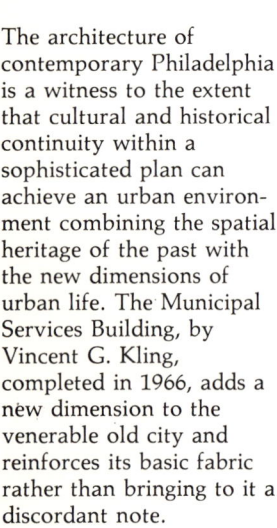

The architecture of contemporary Philadelphia is a witness to the extent that cultural and historical continuity within a sophisticated plan can achieve an urban environment combining the spatial heritage of the past with the new dimensions of urban life. The Municipal Services Building, by Vincent G. Kling, completed in 1966, adds a new dimension to the venerable old city and reinforces its basic fabric rather than bringing to it a discordant note.

the basic form and structure unchanged. Each new urban system added a new scale, a new dimension, and new movement to the original design idea, making it spatially more enriching.

This process was far from being a change that occurred without the knowledge and guidance of architects. Philadelphia has had one of the richest architectural heritages of any city in the United States. Today the sophisticated level of urban design is again due to the high architectural standards that exist in the city. Architects and planners continue to add new dimensions to and to improve upon the original plan. A complex urban system of greenways is being developed, linking the original squares of William Penn's plan, Independence Hall, Society Hill, the waterfront with the new transportation center and the ghetto areas which are being redeveloped with active citizen participation.

In the Police Administration Building the architects Geddes, Brecher, Qualls, Cunningham use a prefabricated concrete window panel over the curvilinear form of the structure. The imaginative plan of the building creates moving and dynamic internal and external spaces which form different mood effects under varying light conditions.

US Treasury Department United States Mint, Philadelphia, Pennsylvania; the world's most efficient, modern coin-production plant, in the historic heart of the city, designed by Vincent G. Kling and completed in 1968.

Chapter II
The Dwelling Group

1. *The Urban Setting*

The history of urbanization is recorded in the rise of housing as the number one problem of society. The most serious housing problems in the world today are in the countries of Africa, Asia, and Latin America, which have the highest rate of population growth. More than a quarter of the world's population lives in urbanized areas and, in the United States, almost three-quarters. About one-third of urban housing in the industrialized countries is obsolete and unsuitable for human habitation and more than half in the less developed parts of the world. As the supply of new, decent housing units drags behind the demand, conditions of overcrowding and ill health are rapidly increasing. In some countries half of the dwelling units have an average of three or more persons per room. The effect of this dire shortage of residential space upon man's development is all too obvious.

Housing is the largest single economic item of national wealth. Construction of dwelling units amounts on the average to more than one-fifth of yearly capital expenditures. The United States alone possesses today over seventy million dwelling units with a total value of around $400 billion. However, although residential occupancy takes up by far the greatest amount of urban land, new yearly housing construction amounts to only 3 percent of all housing, and more dwelling units deteriorate than are being built.

Shortage of decent housing is a great social problem, and the provision of residential space in the quantity and quality necessitated by modern urban life makes residential housing a major architectural challenge. Developments in high-density, low-cost housing in the second half of this century also portray the changing dimensions of architecture.

2. *Suburban Subdivision*

A typical suburban subdivision consists of a more or less prefabricated house on a privately owned, individual lot. Endless repetition of similar elements, generally a rectangular single-family house on a rectangular-shaped lot parallel to the street, creates a deadening monotony and produces mostly unusable, static space. It is also an uneconomical use of land, allowing a general density of approximately fourteen persons per acre. There is no separation of pedestrian and automobile movement systems. Cars have to cross sidewalks and almost 25 percent of the land is devoted to roads and driveways. There is perpetual conflict between traffic and pedestrians, and each house is open to the street, providing little privacy and no communal space.

A space in these familiar horizontal suburban developments is prohibitive in socioeconomic costs. Each dedicated to a narrowly stratified group of society, these houses provide little opportunity for social interaction and only accentuate urban-suburban animosities. Since public transportation is virtually impossible in this sprawling pattern, the whole system is designed around and for the automobile. Journey to school, to work, and to shops is impossible except by car, and the choice of spatial and social experiences is almost nonexistent.

Attempts to bring life to this rigid residential space either result in chaos or are highly mannered and generally unconvincing. Among the most frequently employed attempts to alleviate the monotony and lack of spatial quality is the use of an arbitrary system of curvilinear street patterns, by clustering standardized dwelling units around parking lots or by an endless number of attempts to achieve variety for the sake of variety. Functionally, these variations do not alter the inherent flaws of subdivision design or make modern life and movement within any easier.

3. Courthouse Cluster

Neither the undefined, sprawling, and shapeless suburban subdivision nor its center city counterpart—the vertically stacked, undifferentiated, and equally monotonous apartment tower—offers the spatial experience and choice required of the dynamics of modern urban life. Multidimensional opportunities of sculpting residential space are limited only by the architect's skill and the legal and administrative regulations which govern the development of urban land. Unfortunately, zoning and building regulations are generally not conducive to multidimensional planning, as they are two-dimensional and negative in nature. They specify arbitrary and mandatory setbacks for property lines, what should and should not be placed on the land, and are based on now-obsolete standards of performance. These mandatory prescriptions, unless updated to the requirements of the modern city, often prevent logical spatial development of a community.

The courthouse cluster, with its many sociophysical and economic advantages, is still forbidden in many cities by obsolete legal regulatory measures. The modern courthouse is an adaptation of ancient Mediterranean house-building principles to the demands of the twentieth-century city. Exemplifying logical sculpting of urban residential space, it was first developed by the Congrès Internationaux de l'Architecture Moderne (CIAM) in the first half of the century under

Courthouse clusters integrated with high-rise apartment structures provide variety in living patterns and architectural form and assist in providing the much-needed choice of living patterns for center city residents. This particular example is a proposed residential scheme for an urban renewal area in Washington, D.C., designed by the author, 1964.

the direction of Le Corbusier and Walter Gropius. Undergoing constant refinement and adaptation, it consists of tightly knit and integrated private outdoor living areas with blocks of combined single family houses. Grouping of houses not only achieves economy in the use of land, permitting densities as high as fifty persons per acre, but allows a far freer and more logical street pattern, privacy, and separation of man and the motor car. Its relatively high density makes its application economically feasible in or around the urban centers.

The courthouse cluster may be used in an all-horizontal development or in combination with high-rise apartments. Land saved through this concept can be devoted to communal facilities and amenities not possible in the suburban pattern. Automobile parking may be combined and located along a highway axis or placed below ground, as has recently been done in residential development of major urban centers. While the old city pattern was based upon a pedestrian scale, the automobile age requires a larger basic residential unit—a neighborhood. The compact urban cluster is as applicable to private ownership of each dwelling unit as it is to rental or condominium use.

Page 144

4. *High-Rise Cluster*

Design of urban housing necessarily raises the question of space standards—what are the minimum housing conditions conducive to man's development in the modern city? What is the minimum desirable ratio of persons per room or the proportion of people per acre? What is the minimum size of a room, and when does space become so overcrowded and dense that it stops being habitable? These questions cannot be answered in absolutes since they are all relative. The average ratio of persons per room in dwelling units in the United States is more than one room per person. When compared with this national average, the rental dwelling units occupied by one-third of all Black American families contain a minimum ratio of three persons per two rooms and in some instances of slum dwellings contain a proportion of three to four persons per room. There is no question that these rooms are overcrowded and most of them unfit for human habitation.

However, it is much more difficult to measure the degree of overcrowding of residential land by such a highly theoretical and rather arbitrary measure. The height of the building, the articulation of mass and the sculpting of space, the provision of available nearby communal and transportation facilities all determine whether or not a housing complex is overcrowded. It is a question of design.

High-rise housing in the centers of cities has until now been restricted to individual apartment blocks or towers, and the question of density was determined on the basis of the size of the lot not covered by the building and the distance between the buildings themselves. As long as they provided easy access to public transportation and the open land was adequate for children's play and adult recreation, they were judged satisfactory.

Pages 147-149

When the automobile became the basic mode of transportation, not only of the suburbanite but of the urban apartment dweller as well, it gave an impetus to a high-rise cluster design.

The high-rise cluster in the renewal areas of cities is a new concept of urban housing—where continuity and variety of spatial experiences are paramount. If we consider a particular example, Columbia Plaza in Washington, D.C., a cluster designed by Keyes, Lethbridge and Condon, we see a highly skillful use of urban residential space. This cluster is surrounded by modern freeways, and the shapes of the composition reflect a transition between these high-speed corridors of movement and the internally defined living space of the Plaza. Basically, the building occupies 100 percent of the lot area, but this mass is hollowed out from above, from below and from the sides, so that the space of the composition is not divided into a series of compartments like the traditional twentieth-century apartment patterns. City space flows continuously from below to the top and from inside to outside. This composition has no front and no back in the ordinary sense, as it is a freestanding element open on every side to all parts of the city. Some buildings rest on colonnades, further heightening the sense of the contiguity of space. Public areas, first-floor stores, banks and other community facilities are connected with the Plaza by glass partitions. The Plaza is open to the sky and the curvilinear mass of row housing is depressed to permit viewing of the surrounding Potomac River, but only through a series of well-defined internal views.

Study of the plans and sections of the cluster reveal the ingenuity used in the relationship between internal and external space of this composition. The multilevel automobile parking is vertically connected with the open Plaza, the streets, and the apartments above. This example of variety within a unity is impossible to comprehend from any single view. To experience it, a person must view it from a thousand different points, each point different and each offering a different impression and experience.

The Watergate residential complex, due for final completion in 1971, is a co-operative with the price of apartments presently ranging from $44,000 for a one-bedroom unit to $190,000 for a penthouse apartment. All apartments are provided with generous balconies, many of which command a panoramic view of the riverfront or of the Federal city. All parking is below ground, and ownership provides many amenities and conveniences. The success of these expensive apartments is largely due to their central urban location and the total architectural environment achieved by the designers. The predominant significance of this experiment lies in the fact that now that the economic feasibility of this development has been proven, there is a likelihood that similar cooperative-type ownership will in the near future be provided in the center city for other income groups as well.

Pages 150, 151

Columbia Plaza, Washington, D.C., a high-rise residential complex by Keyes, Lethbridge, and Condon. Surrounded by urban highways, this residential island provides a dynamic, varied, and exciting living environment. The plaza, above which the apartments hover, contains shops and communal facilities, and all automobile parking is restricted to below-plaza levels, 1968.

overleaf: Two views of Columbia Plaza.

147

Watergate residential complex, located on the Potomac River waterfront in Washington, D.C., next to the John F. Kennedy Center for the Performing Arts, is a new form of luxury urban living in the nation's capital. It also signifies a significant reversal of the post-World War II trend of urban exodus to suburbia.

This luxury high-rise complex, designed by the Italian architect Luigi Moretti, consists of three curvilinear apartment blocks, a hotel, and an office building, set in well-designed multilevel plazas with landscaped courts, fountains, and waterfalls. Final completion date, 1971.

5. *Modular Cluster*

Architects, the building industry, and government have so far failed in developing a system for providing decent, sanitary housing in quantities demanded by the lower income urban population. This major problem has in recent years occupied the attention of the younger, more socially conscious generation of architects. Dissatisfied with the inability of present building methods to produce the required numbers of new dwelling units to meet the demands of the society, these architects propose the application of mass production techniques as the only feasible method for meeting this enormous challenge. Instead of conventional building methods employing only individual prefabricated elements, the modular housing cluster envisions the dwelling unit itself, the whole apartment, as being manufactured and only assembled on the site into desired groupings, vertically, horizontally or combined. Thus, the whole "house" becomes the module, reflecting mass megalopolitan living requirements and the application of modern technology to the creation of a family shelter.

The architectural possibilities for sculpting residential space at this scale are almost unlimited. The first actual construction of the all-prefabricated modular housing cluster occurred in Moshe Safdie's Habitat, at the 1967 World's Fair Exposition in Montreal.

Page 153

The original project envisioned a cluster of twelve-hundred apartments with the basic module being seventeen feet wide by thirty-eight feet long, and weighing between seventy and eighty tons. The prefabrication process of this unit deserves close attention. The enforcing steel cage of the cell is picked up by an enormous travel lift and taken to a unit mold. While the cage is still attached to the travel lift, concrete is poured; after the concrete has set, the mold is removed, and the lift continues on its way with the enclosed cage. The suspended cage is then moved onto a production line where the interior is completed. When finished, the entire module is hoisted into its place on the twelve-story, highly articulated, steel-framed "mountain." The variety possible in this approach was apparent in the fact that Habitat, when finished, contained fifteen different types of apartments, ranging in size from one to four bedrooms.

Although providing high-density living in a twelve-story-high structure, each apartment contained at least one roof terrace, exposed to sun and rain, making gardening feasible. The complex and highly articulate mass of the building also allowed a maximum of privacy and natural light not available in vertically stacked, tower apartments with antiseptic, and generally useless, balconies. The high degree of integration between movement systems, vertical and horizontal, pedestrian and automobile, with streets going under, over and through the cluster, permitted the public to experience space entirely modern in spirit. The inherent excitement of architecture as applied to solving man's social problem—housing—immediately caught the public's imagination and became a symbol of the Exposition.

This concept is today being applied to redevelopment of central urban areas, particularly to development of housing for low-income families. In the past, urban renewal activities consisted of removing not only the slums but also the slum dwellers and replacing the buildings with luxury apartment towers, thus forcing the poor to move to yet another slum.

Habitat, a modular cluster of prefabricated apartment units, is one of the most revolutionary building projects of the 1960s. When built at the 1967 World's Fair Exposition in Montreal, it became Expo's chief feature in dramatically illustrating the new potential of contemporary building technology and economics in residential urban form.

6. *Housing Megastructure*

The greatest challenge facing man's ingenuity is the integration of formerly separate systems (transportation, recreation, employment, housing) into a workable interwoven urban organism.

The city of the past, with its individual buildings placed in a clearly discernible street pattern accentuated by dominant structures of open spaces, has long outlived its form. The city of today demands a total integration of space and mass, of movement systems, and of buildings. High concentrations of populations in urban centers demand the minimizing of excess and unnecessary movement and require integration of as many miscellaneous functions of the city as possible into huge, large-scale housing megastructures.

The city of tomorrow may well contain much more than one street level. Large sections of central urban space may be occupied by these megastructures from ten to one hundred stories in height. The roofs of these multidimensional, colossal clusters will then provide open recreation space, light and air for man's residential needs. Inner space of these urban mountains will be occupied by functions which do not absolutely need natural light and ventilation—offices, classrooms, shops and theatres—and interconnected vertically and horizontally with the dwelling units on the outside of the buildings' envelopes. Today's city already contains many windowless buildings placed, however, in a street pattern of a bygone era. Mechanical conditioning of environment permits exploration of underground and inner above-ground space not possible before, thus permitting a more economical utilization of natural space and making enormous housing densities possible without overcrowding.

An example of a modern, large-scale public housing project devoted to the needs of the urban poor is the proposed scheme for the La Puntilla Section of San Juan in Puerto Rico. Designed by a young architect, Jan Wampler, this megastructure would contain five hundred low-rise and five hundred high-rise dwelling units, schools, churches, community halls, and recreational facilities. These communal facilities were consciously placed in the center of the single huge structure to provide a meeting ground between the extremely low-income poor and the slightly higher income group. Within this mass housing there are envisioned eight large open plazas and fourteen small ones. The first floor of this megastructure would contain only public facilities vertically connected through stair towers with housing above. Although this concept adds little to social interaction between various strata of socioeconomic groups, it does attempt to provide an environment not so radically changed from the previous hillside cluster of tarpaper and wooden shacks as to enable the inhabitants to adjust to this new environment.

A utopian megastructure completely unintegrated with the existing environment is the "City Module Megastructure" proposed for Oakland, California, by Pinney and Ong. The project consists of six levels of streets, each contained within the compression rings which interconnect the sixteen structural pylons supporting this "hilltown." The housing of social groups is envisioned as being structured horizontally along the streets, as well as vertically between the radiating pylons. The superblock upon which the structure would be located contains thirty-eight acres of land. The housing megastructure would contain 1,000 dwelling units, with a variable density of between thirty-four and ninety persons per acre.

The structure is physically connected with the rest of the city through eight major pedestrian entrances and four corner automobile entrances. The center of the structure contains parking, shopping, and community facilities organized around a central interior plaza open to the sky, while the structure itself sits on a huge square.

The design idea was to provide a large-scale structure within which people themselves could design and organize their immediate residential space.

The proposed megastructure fails to achieve a spatial continuity between the new structure and the existing space. Instead of achieving the mutual compatibility with its environment, this structure produces a jarring, discordant note, further adding to the already existing chaos. Megastructures, to be successful, must themselves be totally integrated into the basic structure of the city.

An example of a comprehensive urban "new town in town" concept is the Fort Lincoln New Town in Washington, D.C., designed to achieve maximum possible integration and interaction between various socioeconomic groups and between blacks and whites. It is a forerunner of the type of large-scale sociophysical redesign of the old urban neighborhoods which will provide each residential area with a unique social and physical environment.

Planning and design for the proposed commercial, communal, educational and residential areas was done by Keyes, Lethbridge and Condon in association with David A. Crane and with Edward J. Logue as the principal development coordinator for the project.

Pages 156, 157

A recently completed, large-scale moderate-income housing complex by Burger and Coplans in Oakland, California, was financed and built by an all-black investment group. This highly successful sociophysical design was the outcome of a well-integrated, interdisciplinary design team effort.

Pages 158, 159

Plan for the Fort Lincoln New Town is a unique concept for injecting the experience gained in new towns into the redevelopment process of major urban areas. Designed to achieve maximum residential integration, racial and economic, it is a forerunner of future new-town in-town sociophysical reconstruction of the old cities.

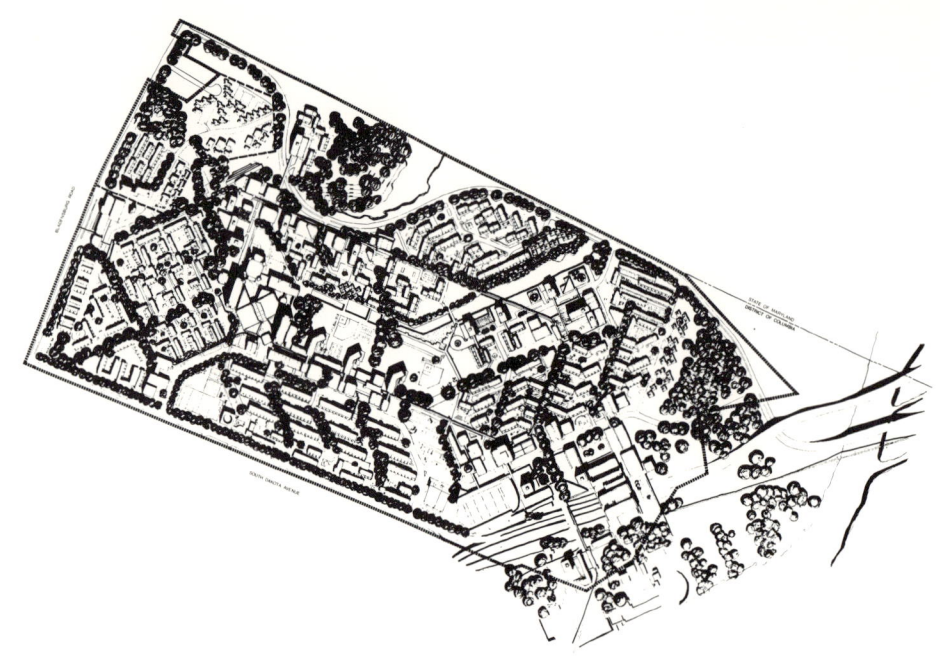

The proposed urban center of Fort Lincoln, designed in 1967 by Keyes, Lethbridge and Condon, was conceived to house the town's shopping center, offices, apartments, educational and communal facilities. The scale of the proposed center of this in-town residential neighborhood is indeed urban.

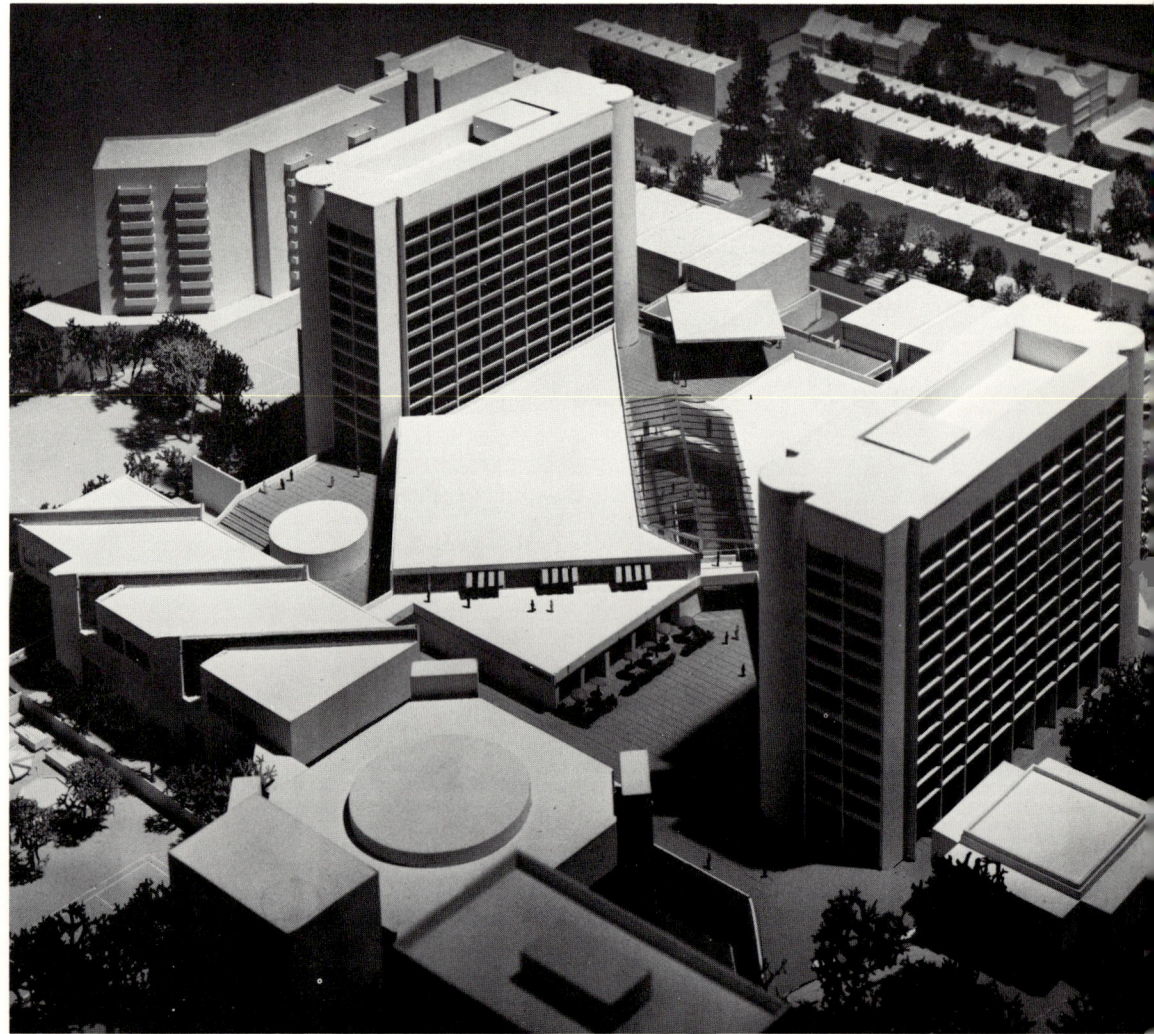

One of the central elements of the town's center would be the school located in the midst of the urban complex, with its own nucleus, the glass-enclosed, multilevel plaza interconnected by moving stairways. This space was consciously designed to provide maximum opportunity for social urban interaction.

View from existing green at the crest of a residential area looking south toward the town center, showing the performing arts theatre and commercial and office space with parking below.

157

Each group of rowhouses is clustered around an intimate landscaped area with off-street parking nearby but not intruding upon the communal-social areas.

The nucleus of this highly articulated plan is the community center, with its own buildings and outdoor play areas. The plan is unique in its easily comprehensible human scale and the clarity of the separation between pedestrian and automobile spaces.

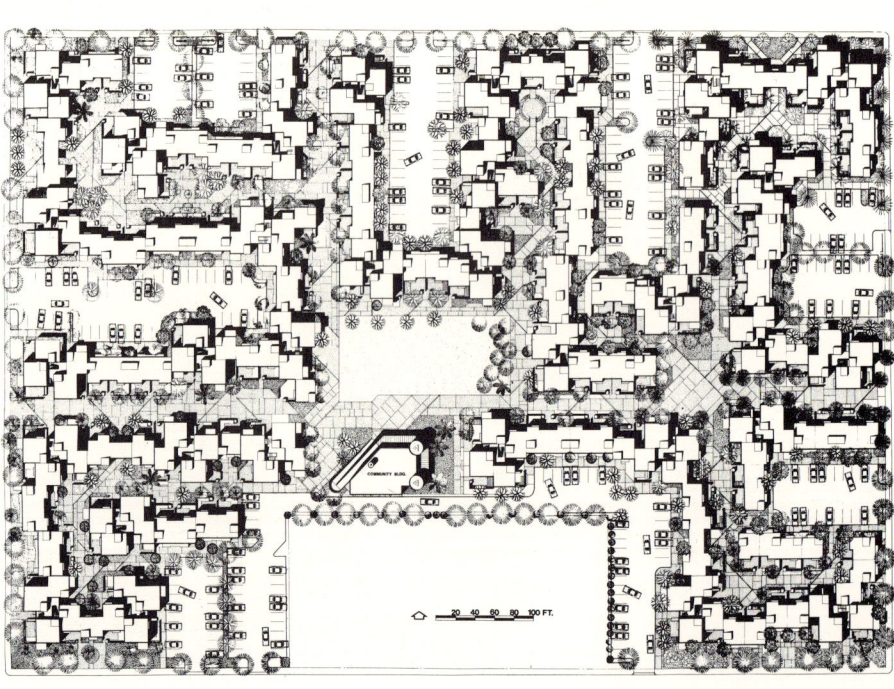

An urban moderate-income housing neighborhood in Oakland, California. One of the first large-scale all-Black residential projects in the United States, financed and built by an all-Black investment group.

Designed in 1965 by Burger and Coplans, the forms of the rowhouses provide variety and dynamic quality seldom found in mass residential architecture. The Acorn urban renewal project was completed in 1968.

A new township in West Berlin, named in honor of its planner and architect—Gropiusstadt—designed by The Architects Collaborative in 1966, Walter Gropius, partner in charge.

Plan of Gropiusstadt, West Berlin.

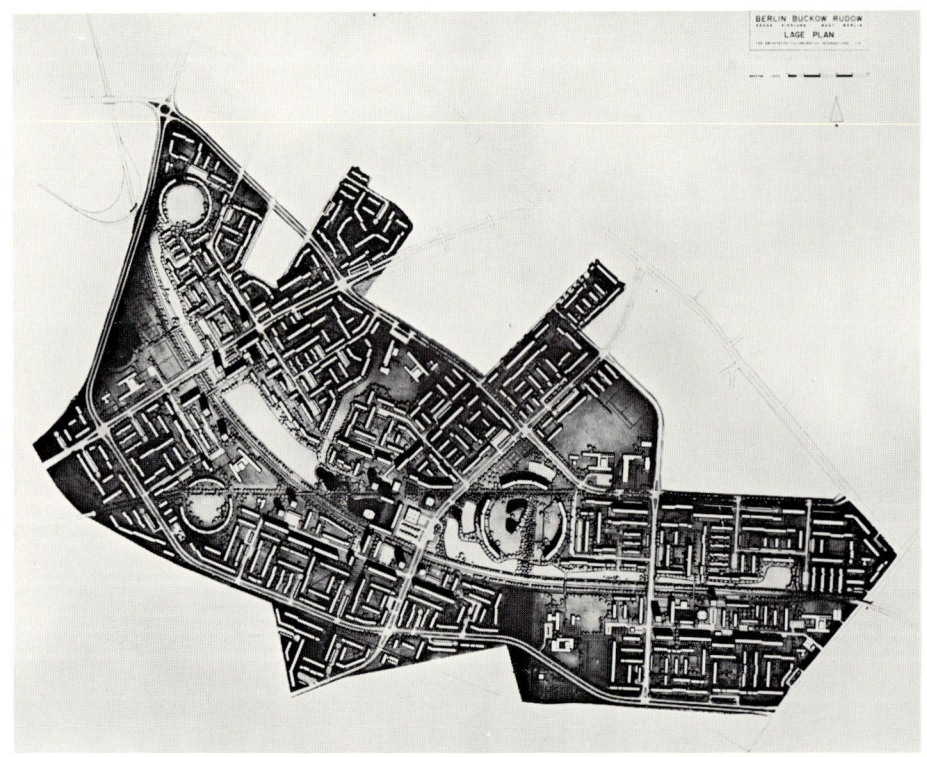

This self-contained residential 650-acre township, when completed, will house 44,000 people in 16,400 dwelling units.

Chapter III

Transportation Complexes

1. *Architecture of Motion*

The monuments to man's movement through space are the architecture of motion. The railroad era was responsible for such significant architectural achievements as the suspension bridge and the great railway halls. By the twentieth century the railroad era had reached its zenith and had produced many grand central terminal spaces— meeting places for people in motion.

Pages 164

The automobile age not only changed the perception of architecture but also the whole concept of architecture and city planning. It also produced its own inventions and monuments. The highway is perhaps the classic example of a clear definition of space devoted to motion. The highway ribbon brought new scale and new curvilinear pattern to our lives.

The points of articulation where the superhighway connects the secondary street pattern of a city or crosses natural or man-made space can be particularly dramatic in spatial movement. The highway ribbon as a cloverleaf intersection integrated into a suburban pattern or in the form of a bridge is highly illustrative of the moving, dynamic quality of twentieth-century life and architecture.

Page 165

The interstate highway system freed the regional planner from the constraint of broken continuity between urban centers. It also brought millions of automobiles into these centers, congesting the streets designed for another movement system and radically changing the design of urban structures themselves.

After all available horizontal space in the city was taken up for storing the automobile, the parking garage emerged as a new building type. The design of the multistory parking structure ranged from such dramatic buildings as Paul Rudolph's parking garage in New Haven to city-wide attempts to integrate parking structures in strategic locations within the total automobile-movement system of a city. However, the vertical growth of the center city and the realization that city space is too valuable to be devoted entirely to the storage of the motor car pushed the parking garage below the surface of urban land. Today's modern city requires adequate parking provisions for each specific building type, and the hitherto unoccupied space above urban freeways is now being devoted to air right structures: housing and office buildings constructed above the channels of movement instead of on land.

Pages 168, 169

An example of total integration of urban highway space with housing is the proposed air rights scheme for San Francisco by Burger and Coplans. The highway is depressed below the street level and partially covered with cantilevered, slanting, terraced apartments. Circulation across the highway is provided by bridges carrying pedestrian and local street traffic. Parking garages are integrated into the first floor. Housing for low-income families, utilizing hitherto unused space, is economic and integrates movement systems within the new urban form. An adaptation of the scheme for luxury apartments envisions both parking and freeways below ground and completely covered by plazas and pedestrian promenades with dwelling units built into the hill and served from parking and plaza by incline elevators.

Pages 170, 171

The use of air rights marks the beginning of the evolution of city-space from the traditional dimensions of width, length, and height into the multidimensions of space and time. The two-dimensional pattern of urban land development disappears and is replaced by city megastructures interconnected with many horizontal streets and vertical and diagonal movement channels.

One of the earliest of the great American central terminal spaces. This 1871 drawing of the Grand Central Station in New York was designed by John Snook. Revolutionary nineteenth-century building technology ingeniously applied to spanning great architectural spaces.

The cloverleaf intersection with its biological form has become an inherent part of American suburban environment—The Eastshore Freeway near Hayward, Alameda County, California, 1957.

The Verrazano-Narrows Bridge, between New York City and Staten Island, is the largest suspension bridge in the world. Opened in the early 1960s, the bridge itself enhances the already epic urban environment.

The automobile age changed the pattern of cities by introducing the curvilinear highway upon the rectilinear urban structure. A large highway interchange built in 1964 in Los Angeles.

As the dynamics of intramegalopolitan travel place a greater and greater emphasis upon high-speed travel, the traditional bridge connecting two shores in a straight line becomes a highly dynamic sculptural form in motion. The Theodore Roosevelt Bridge in Washington, D.C., completed in 1965.

The Bixby Creek Bridge on Highway 1 in Monterey County, California, is a superb example of contemporary bridge architecture, 1934.

The automobile brought an entirely new dimension to the urban pattern, and the parking garage emerged in the 1960s as a brutal new building form.

Church Street Garage in New Haven, Connecticut, 1962, by Paul Rudolph. An example of reinforced concrete forms unencumbered by curtain walls, strong and naked in their unabashed virility.

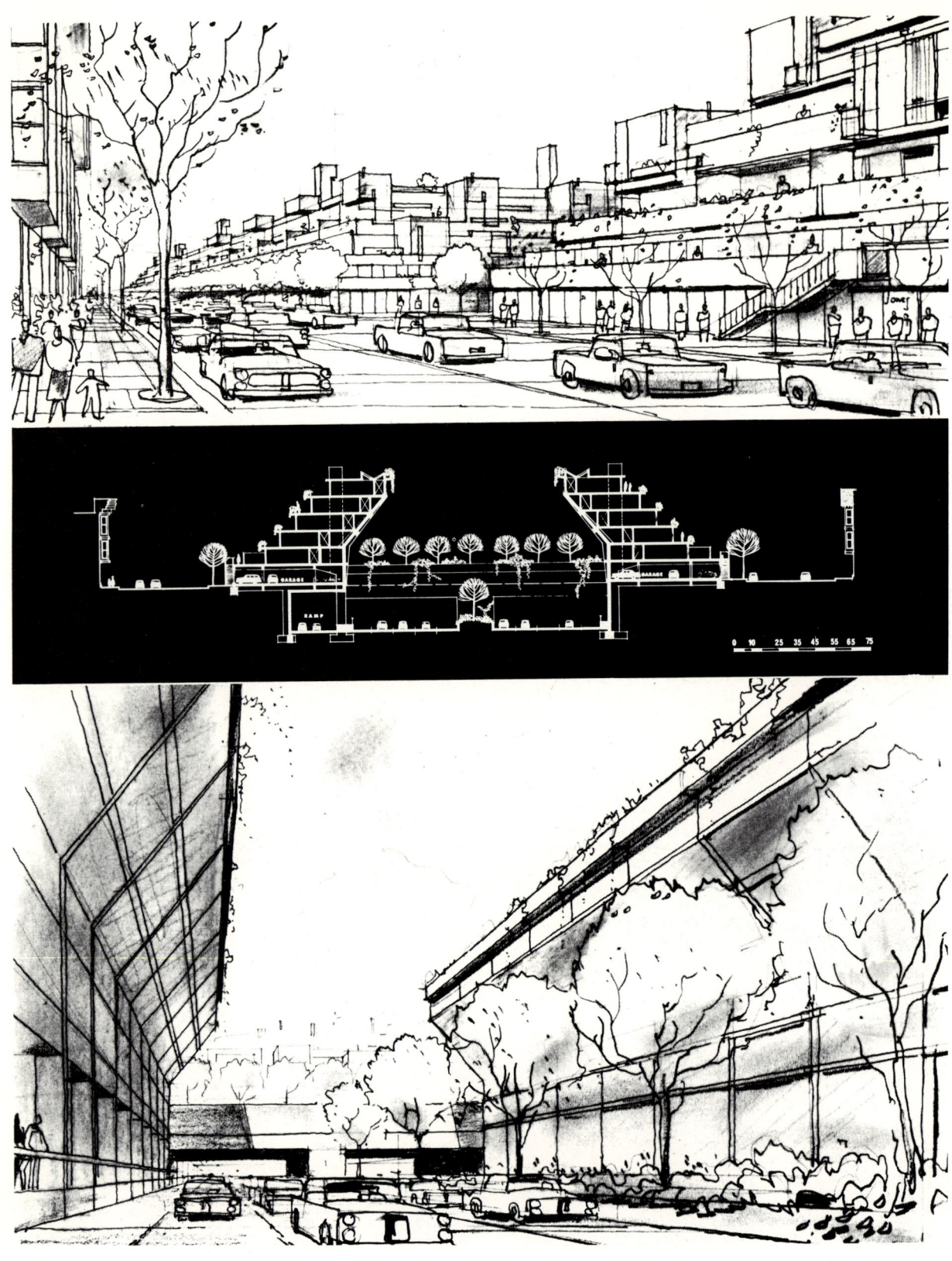

Air-rights housing constructed over urban highways tends to reduce the objectionable elements of the urban freeway and provide new space for badly needed housing in the center city. This moderate-income housing scheme designed in 1966 proposes sixty-foot-high cantilevered concrete walls on both sides of the highway with the banks of the terraced apartments supported by these slanting walls.

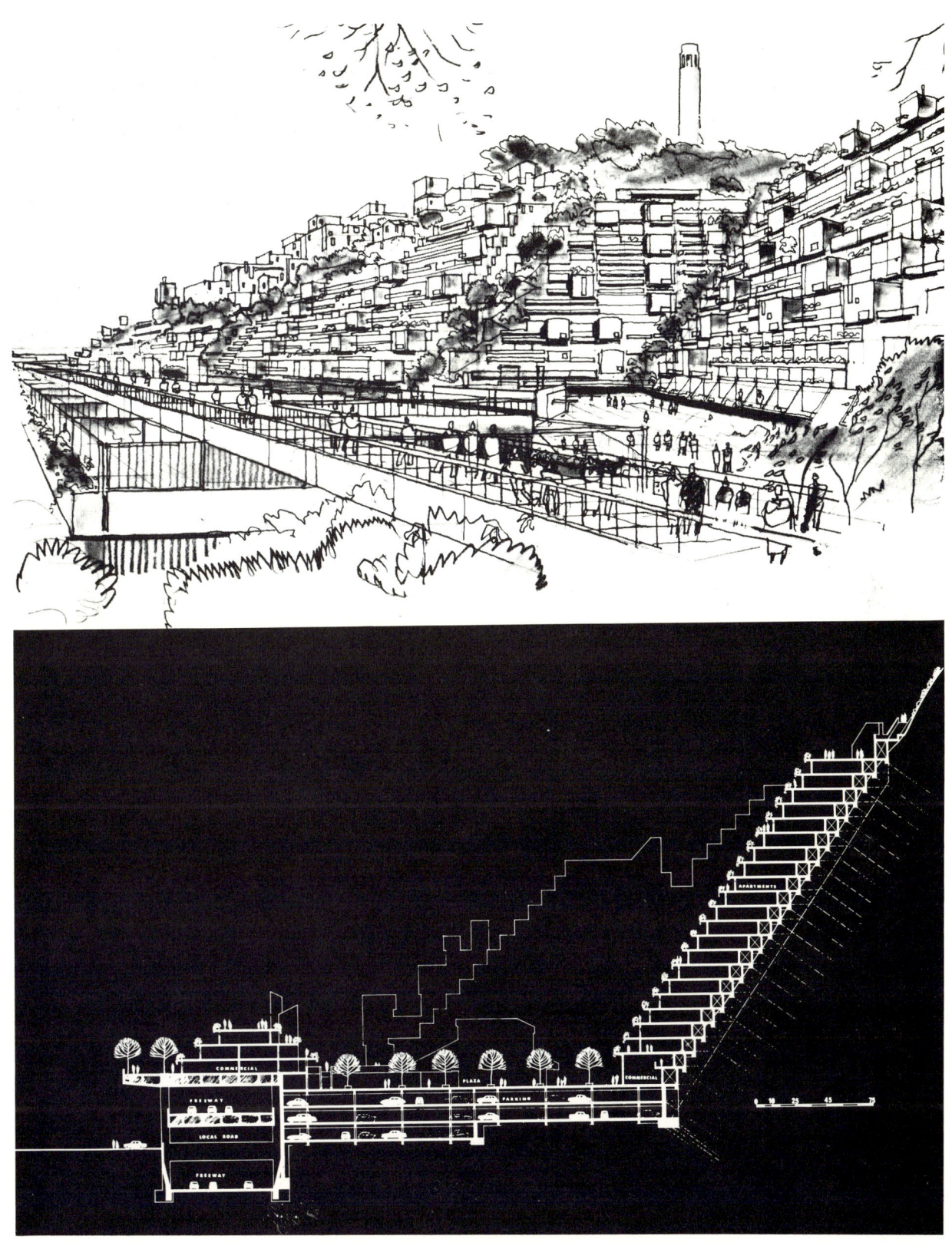

Another version of air-rights living by the same architects, Burger and Coplans, also for a San Francisco urban renewal area, proposes locating luxury apartments along the stretch of the highway running along the base of the Telegraph Hill. Separating the San Francisco Bay-oriented apartments from the partially covered freeway would be a continuous shopping promenade supported by underground parking garages.

2. *Transportation Centers*

The complexity of the modern city requires many movement systems, each serving a specific purpose, type, and scale. The high-speed tube transportation proposed for the Northeast Megalopolis for connecting Boston and Washington by means of below-ground movement would cut this travel time to ninety minutes and assist in decongesting space in this densely populated region. At the other end are the proposed intra-city transportation systems: the moving sidewalk, the incline elevators, or the fully automated, electronically operated versatile teletransportation systems. These systems, designed to replace the automobile for center-city movement, can be housed in narrow curvilinear channels below ground, within the mass of the buildings or above, and would serve as the intermediary movement system for dispersing great numbers of people throughout the city space.

Pages 174, 175

The most recent modern subway system is the one proposed for Washington, D.C. Its architecture, designed by Harry Weese, employs single, simple geometric forms to provide new spaces and new channels of metropolitan movement. Conceived as part of a balanced system of highway, bus, and rail transportation, it attempts to complement rather than to replace existing modes of travel.

Pages 180, 181

In contrast to Weese's subway station, well-integrated as it is into the existing urban structure, is New York City's new bus terminal. The George Washington Bridge Bus Terminal by Pier Luigi Nervi is located at the end of the Bridge, once referred to by Le Corbusier as the city's most outstanding work of architecture. Nervi's structure attempts to serve a dual role: as the entrance gate to Manhattan and as the terminating focal point of the Bridge. Fully aware of the powerful scale and form of the highway arteries, the nearby apartment towers, and the Bridge itself, Nervi selected a form which in its strong, muscular, diagonal shape would be able to create space that would add to the existing drama. The huge concrete trusswork of the roof serves to accentuate the role of this form as the gateway to a major urban center.

Pages 176, 177

Perhaps the most successful recent example of a modern multi-transportation-system terminal is the one proposed for Market Street in Philadelphia. This megastructure in the heart of the city is envisioned as the nodal point of the entire region's simultaneous movement systems. Among the various types of transportation provided for within this complex is a 3,000-car above-ground parking garage. The terminal for all local and long-distance buses is to be placed directly below the garage in this proposed design, which intends to make a clear separation between road transportation facilities (buses and autos), placed at above-ground levels, and rail transportation (railroad and rail rapid transit), located underground. The pedestrian circulation system would be totally integrated into this design, with people freely moving about underneath the streets, divorced from street traffic and from the motorcar. *Pages 178, 179*

Internal transportation within this great center would hinge on the electric trolley spinal line, which would run the full length of the pedestrian mall. The moving sidewalk system would collect people from the underground railroad station, the subway, the bus terminal, and the parking garage and distribute them on the elevated promenade connecting all major department stores. The design of this extensive multilevel center deserves attention as a pioneering effort attempting to integrally combine employment, services, and transportation in a megalopolitan hub.

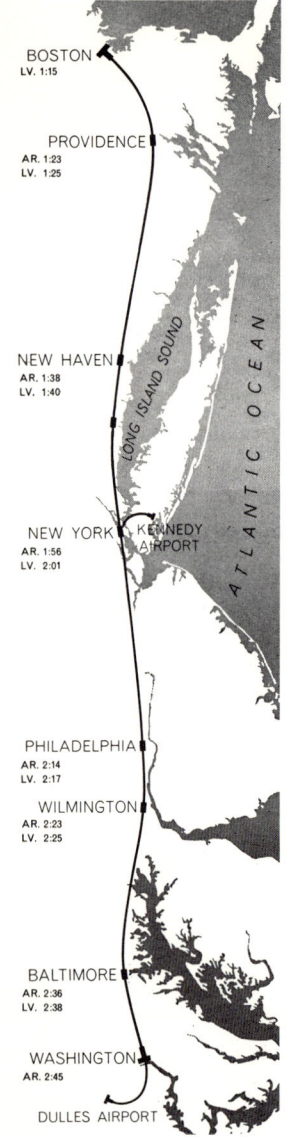

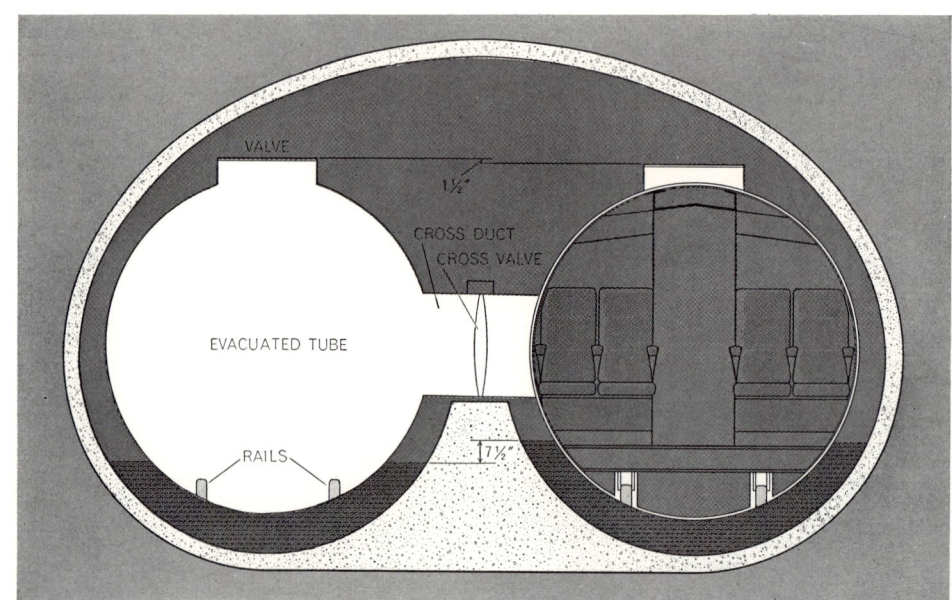

left and below: This revolutionary super-speed mass transit was designed in 1964 by Tube Transit, Inc., for the Northeast Corridor of the United States. The dual tubes would be floated in a cushion of water to insure a smooth ride.

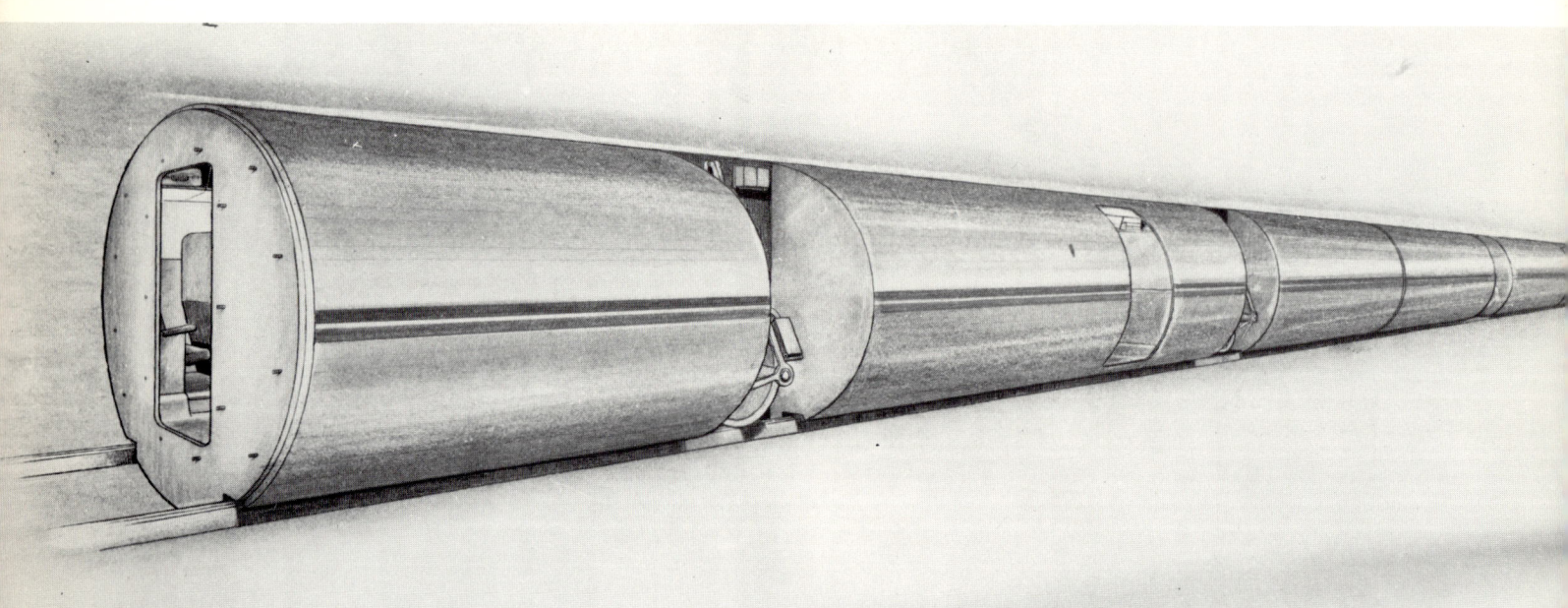

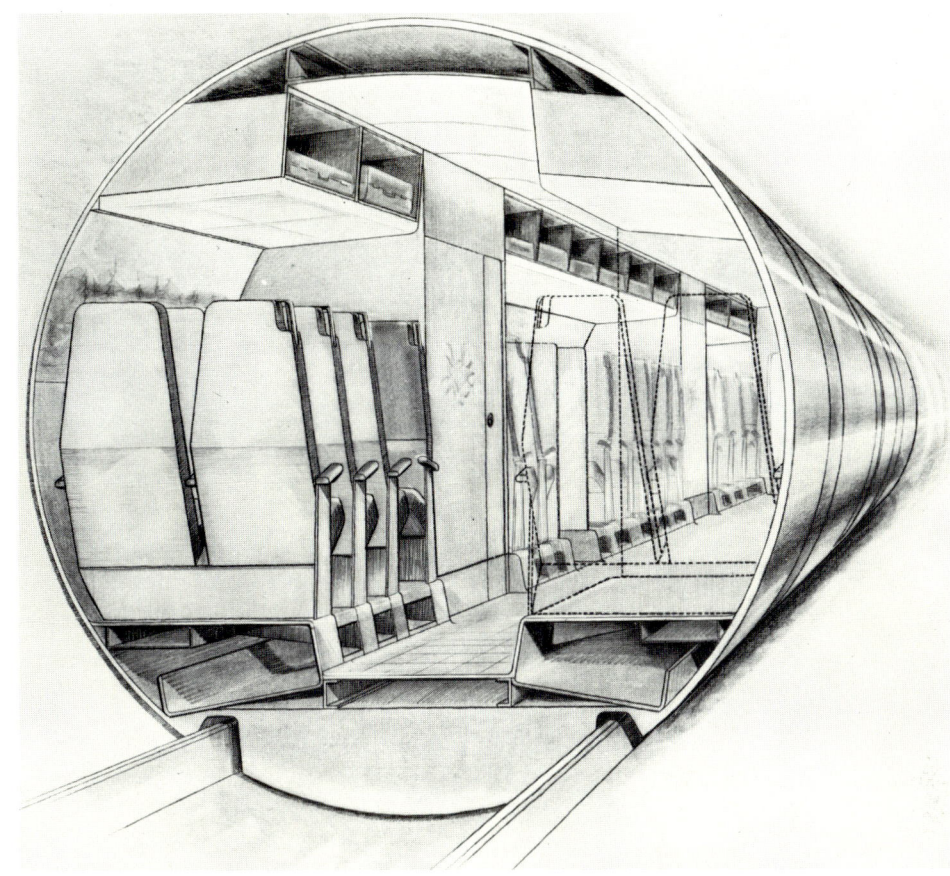

Contemporary version of the pneumatic tube train which was first built on an experimental basis a hundred years ago under Broadway in New York City.

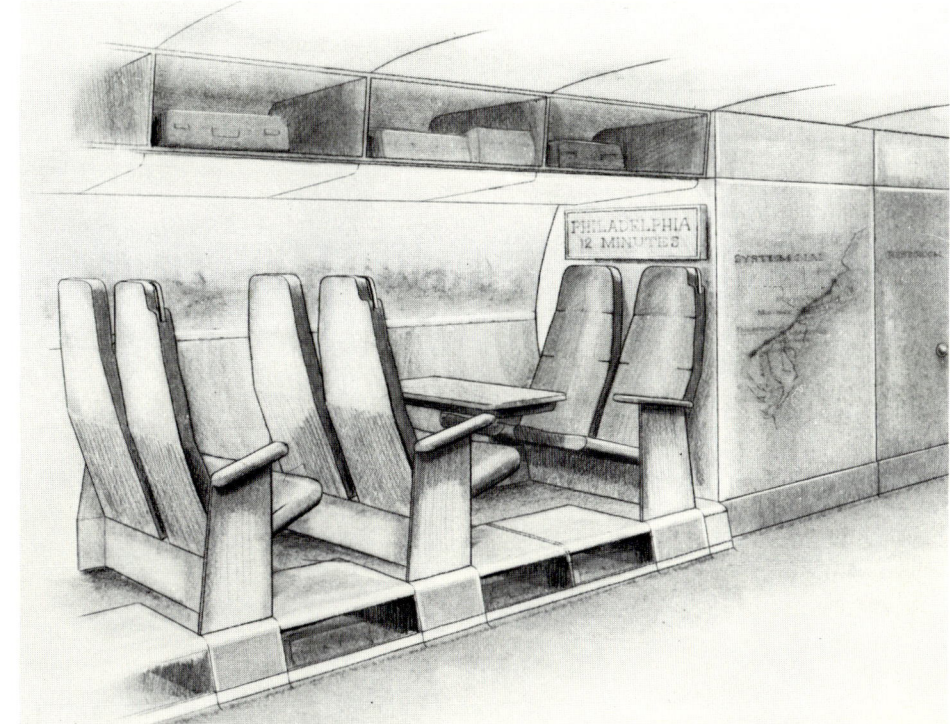

The tubes being concealed completely below ground could be easily integrated into the urban infrastructure, and the system would eliminate ground and air congestion and noise and water pollution.

opposite: The approximately 400 miles between Boston and Washington would be traversed in comfort and safety in this underground tunnel in a mere ninety minutes. The system as designed would be capable of moving 4,500 passengers in a single hour.

Architecture of the gateways to the contemporary city, be it a jet airport, a bridge, a railway station or a bus terminal, is inherently capable of providing a dramatic entry into the urban center.

The George Washington Bridge Bus Station in New York City, designed by the Italian architect Pier Luigi Nervi, 1963, is a moving and vibrant space achieved by expressing the nature of modern travel in strong architectural form.

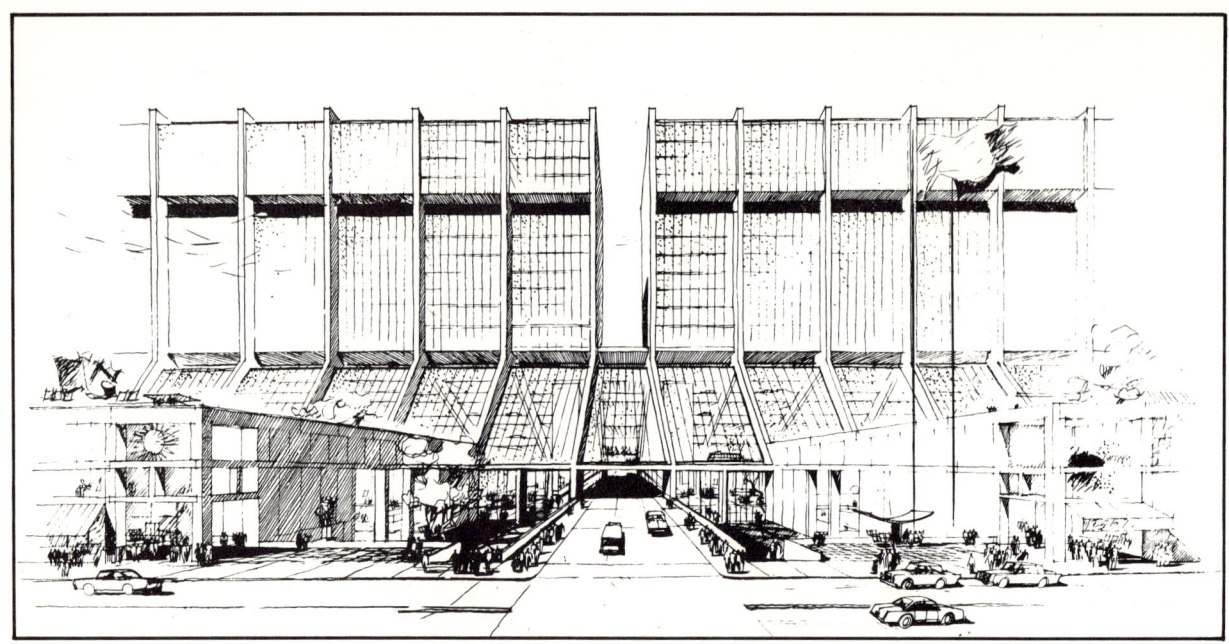

Philadelphia City Planning Commission Study for a complete redevelopment of the center of the city.

Bird's eye view of the Market East study showing the relationship of the proposed design to the existing pattern of the city.

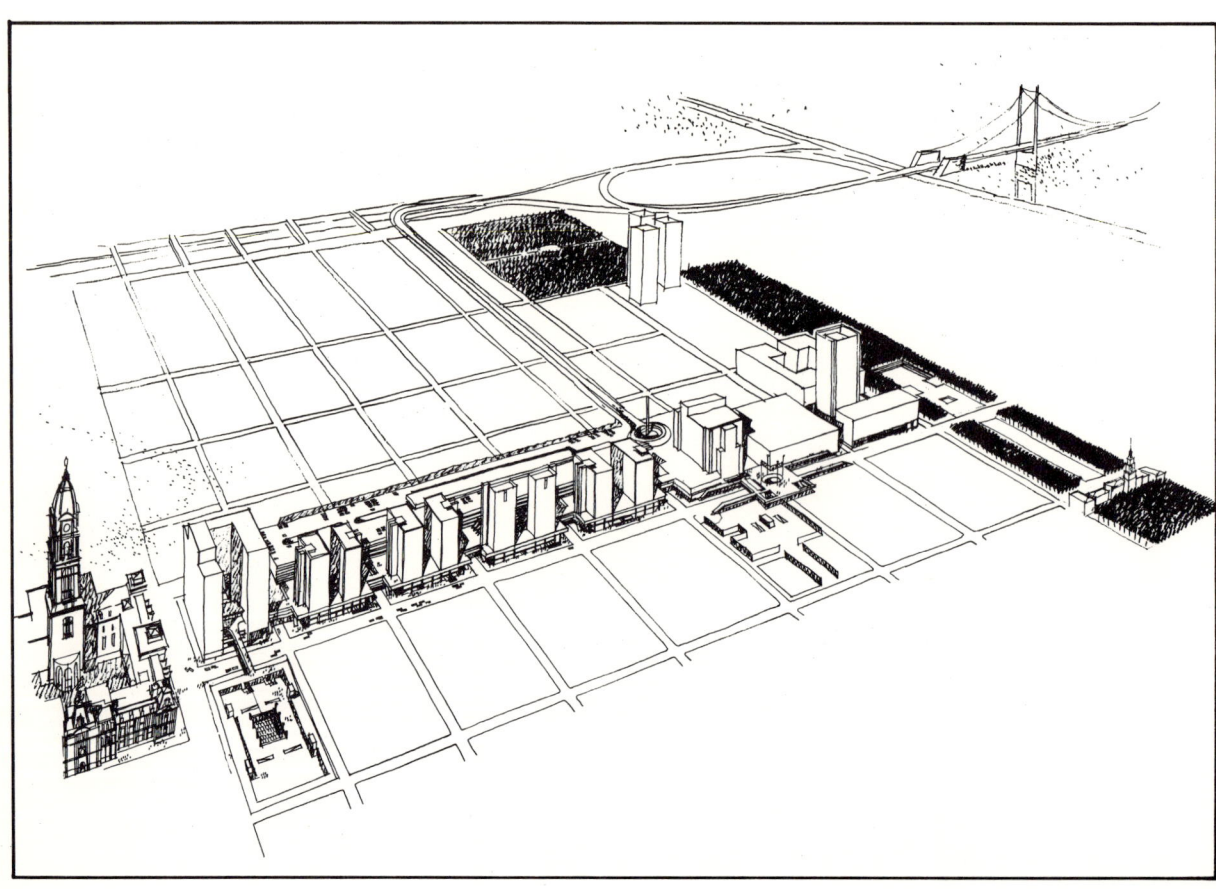

Cross-section of the Market East proposal showing various modes of urban transportation totally in integrated with architecture.

The proposed rapid transit system for Washington, D.C., is conceived to complement rather than replace existing urban highways. In the center of the city the lines would be located below the surface but in the suburbs would be integrated with the highways.

The entire architecture of the subway system, with all its underground and surface stations, was designed in 1967 by Harry Weese. Proposed subway terminal below the enduring Union Station.

In the downtown area the station will be completely integrated into the commercial architectural environment. Entrance to the Farragut Square Station.

Wherever possible the entrance to the subway will be located in the parks and squares of the nation's capital, as in this simple and unobtrusive entrance to the station at DuPont Circle.

3. Movement, Economics, and City Form

Circulation systems create urban land use, value, and form. Transportation networks increase the value of the land and create density of development. Linear systems create linear high-density development. Where they cross they create particularly high land values. The highest land use and value exists in urban centers, where movement channels converge.

Models of man's travel-destination patterns generally correspond to land-value models and are often reminiscent of the actual spatial composition of the city form. The model of passenger trips in Chicago portrayed in three-dimensional form indicates the highest density as being in the center of the city and peripheral density along major converging lines of travel.

Page 183

The effect of movement systems upon land values is direct and extremely significant. Even in this age of telecommunication, the cost of urban land is directly proportional to its accessibility to available transportation, this cost being highest at the center of the city. This is true regardless of whether the urban transportation system is totally controlled by government regulations or by the unregulated market mechanism. The land value model of Copenhagen illustrates land costs and not building costs, yet dramatizes the form-giving qualities of transportation.

The planner must possess an intimate working knowledge of the forces which shape the modern city: economic, legal, and administrative. Attempts to cope with directing city growth and sculpting urban space outside of these natural forces of modern urban life are foredoomed. The lack of success in controlling man's urban macro-environment is to a large degree due to the application of traditional tools and approaches, land-use controls and financing to mold modern urban forms. As urban structures become increasingly more complex, the need for knowledge of the forces which shape the city becomes correspondingly great. To organize and direct these forces in shaping a modern city, the planner must be continually aware that movement systems not only serve the city but create urban land-use, value, and form.

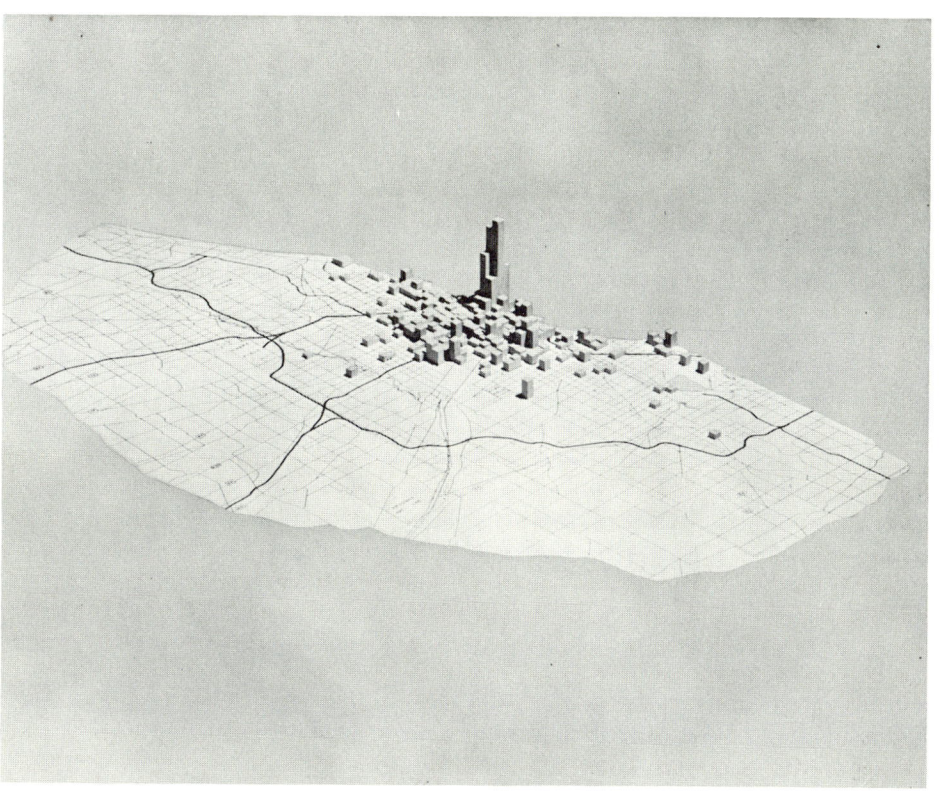

The use of land in a city may be expressed through a three-dimensional model. This model shows the nonresidential floor area contained within the Chicago Loop, 1959. The resultant distribution of almost 1,000,000,000 square feet of commercial and industrial space shows the extremely high concentration of floor area in downtown Chicago.

The destinations of travel trips can also be dramatically expressed in model form. This model shows the relationship between the concentration of floor area in downtown Chicago and over 10,000,000 person-trips to that area on the average weekday, 1959.

4. *Air Terminals* The evolution of commercial air travel in the second half of this century into the major mode of mass passenger movement generated construction of air terminals throughout the world. The design of airports posed a completely new set of problems, their location in relation to the city served being only one of them. The air terminal became a major gateway to the community and, like the railroad station before, its first impression and symbol.

The Municipal Airport Terminal in Memphis, Tennessee, by Mann and Harrover, is an outstanding example of the smaller, all-purpose airport. The building complex is located between two major runways, the main entrance facing a large parking area and connected with the city by a cloverleaf interchange. The original design contemplated expansion of the terminal on both sides of this central axis.

Pages 185, 187

The composition of the terminal is tripartite, vertically and horizontally. The first two floors are enclosed with solid brick walls and, together with an elevated auto ramp which brings passengers to the main level, provide a podium upon which this modern temple rests. The structural system of free-standing, exposed concrete columns supports a roof of hyperbolic-paraboloid concrete shell vaults—a strong visual symbol. The main concourse is spacious, simple, and friendly. The space of this modern "agora" is continuously transformed by the play of light, and the feeling of continuity of space and flight is omnipresent. Until the construction of this terminal in the early 1960s, most airport design was still reflective of the linear railroad station of the past.

As jet travel has unfolded, notable characteristics of airport design have been a tendency (1) to find inspiration in this new medium of architecture of motion, (2) to utilize new structural methods to enclose uninterrupted volumes of space, (3) to dramatize space travel, (4) to reduce the walking distances between the concourse and the gate, (5) to use a systems approach in distributing people and baggage, and (6) to link the airport with as many local modes of movement as possible.

Eero Saarinen, a leading modern architect of the second half of the twentieth century, designed two of the best known international

The design of the modern airport terminal poses a difficult architectural task because of the revolutionary changes which are taking place in air travel. The Municipal Airport Terminal in Memphis, Tennessee, one of the pioneer jet terminals, shows in its plan an unusual degree of foresight for future growth and expansion.

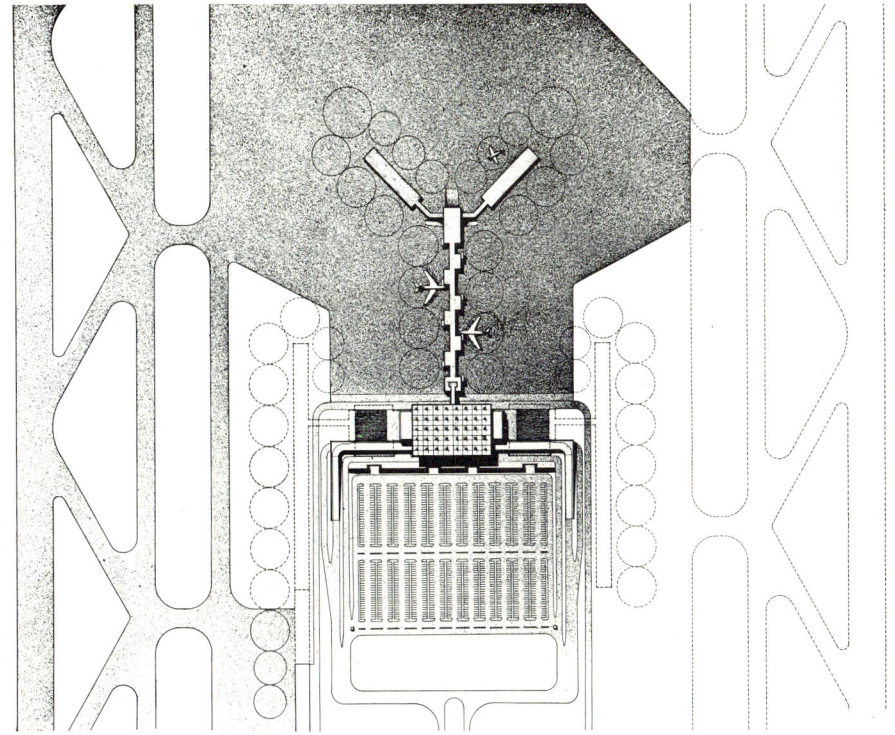

Designed by Mann and Harrover in the early 1960s, this concept uses free-standing concrete columns supporting concrete shell vaults to enclose and organize the internal space of the terminal with extreme elegance and simplicity.

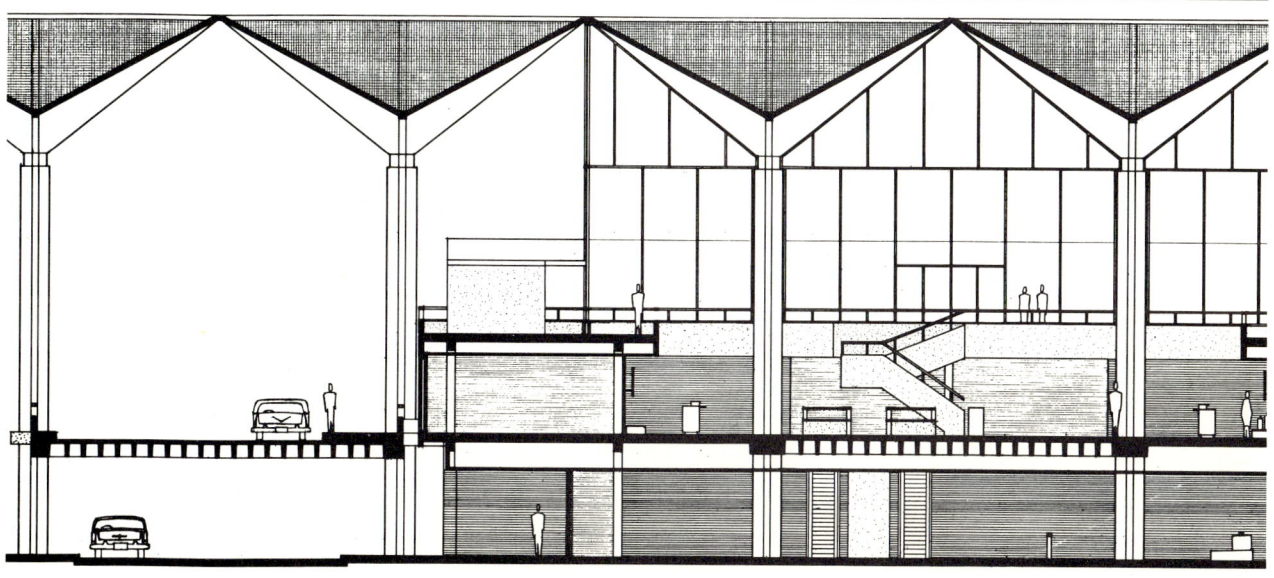

185

airports. The TWA building at the Kennedy International Airport is a magnificent example of sculpting space by using flowing, poured-in-place concrete forms, reminiscent both of the enclosure of a cave and of the expansive quality of flight. The plasticity of this great interior form creates a movement in space which is extremely real and exciting.

The Dulles International Airport near Washington, D.C., was designed by Saarinen after a world-wide survey of the pattern of operations of large air terminals. After a study of the effects of these spaces on the traveler, and an examination of the problems involved in transfer operations, Saarinen arrived at the purpose and intent of this transportation complex in a vigorous and highly creative manner. This purpose and intent—the design—was then transformed into a most meaningful structure and space.

Pages 188, 189

This transportation complex has highly distinguishable elements. The basic features are extremely simple: a large, central, enclosed space with a dominant form, a vertical control tower, a pattern of runways, landscaped approaches, and parking platforms. These few elements are used to form a unique space and to define and control this oasis within the presently natural landscape. The homogeneous quality of this space is unmistakable. This center outside a center, the gate to Washington, divorced from the city by Virginia's rolling countryside, today provides a refuge from frenetic urban tensions.

It is, however, more successful as a point of departure than as a place of arrival and the entrance gate to the federal city. From the lower levels of the massive podium the intimately scaled openings in the base of the temple and the interior spaces act strongly upon the curiosity of the urbanite, inviting him to enter. Upstairs, the simplicity of the enormous interior is at once apparent as the eye becomes accustomed to the now magnetic natural light that enters between the eurhythmic and elegant structural supports, creating a magnificent space. The feeling of this great volume, with lights streaming through the large expanse of glass, creates a truly awe-inspiring universal space—indigenous of temples.

The external form of the Memphis Municipal Airport by Mann and Harrover fully expresses the voluminous soaring space within.

At night, the terminal building becomes transformed into a terminal temple and forms of the hyperbolic-paraboloid vaults become the dominant elements of the composition.

The Dulles International Airport, serving the Metropolitan Washington area, is one of the best designed airport facilities in the world. Through the extensive use of jet-to-terminal luxurious buses, the passenger is able to board a plane with a minimum of walking, and the terminal itself becomes a space related to man as well as expressive of the revolutionary nature of jet travel. The internal and external separation of incoming and outgoing passengers is also handled with great dexterity and forthrightness.

opposite: Designed by Eero Saarinen, the basic structure of the terminal building consists of a clear span roof suspended from the eurythmic and soaring concrete columns evocative of the power found in the great ancient temple. The terminal was completed in 1963.

5. The Mega-Terminal

The phenomenal growth of air passenger travel made the single terminal, however large, impractical for transferring air passengers at the major airports. In the United States more than 150 million people are being carried yearly by commercial airlines, and it is expected that by 1980 the number will approach 400 million. The Los Angeles International Airport alone is expected to handle over 80 million passengers yearly by 1980. The problems of the future airport require a complex systems approach to design and have already resulted in the nucleated air megaterminal—the large airport consisting of a series of modular, interconnected terminals.

The systems approach to design involves detailed analysis of each movement to determine which system it belongs to and to find out its place within a specific sequence of that system. Only when all systems have been analyzed can the interaction of one system on another be determined. The airport system operates within the metropolitan transportation system and interlocks with the broader system of universal air travel. Thus, the airport system consists of a movement sequence of physical nodes at which change occurs—for example, the point at which the airborne traveler becomes a pedestrian.

The Houston International Airport by Goleman, Rolfe, Pierce and Pierce, is the newest example of the linear multiterminal concept. The site of this airport is mammoth, approximating the size of the whole new town of Reston. The complex, when completed, will consist of a series of 400-foot square terminals, each with a central underground station of a continuously running, battery-operated, electronically-guided internal movement system. Each terminal will have its own entrances and underground parking facilities and also four circular satellite passenger holding areas with baggage handling and service operations below. The interterminal transportation system will serve only those passengers who will be transferring from one terminal to another, going to a hotel, or getting to the outdoor parking areas.

Pages 191-193

The expansion of existing airport megastructures also seems to encompass the multiterminal concept. The Newark Airport expansion program applies the Houston concept to an elliptically shaped scheme. The internal movement system consists of moving sidewalks and stairs. Outside circulation consists of three roadside levels and two apron levels integrated into a split system.

Pages 194, 195

The changing mode of travel is also radically affecting the design of terminals for seagoing vessels. In particular the recent increased demands for winter cruises, another expression of the new leisure activity patterns, require all new port facilities. The Miami Passenger Terminal by John Andrews is an example of the changing form of the modern passenger port facility.

Page 196

The plan of the Houston International Airport consists of a linear multi-terminal complex connecting the satellite circular flight station with the city's transportation system. Each terminal is self-sufficient and contains its own entrances and underground parking facilities. First stage of construction was completed in 1969.

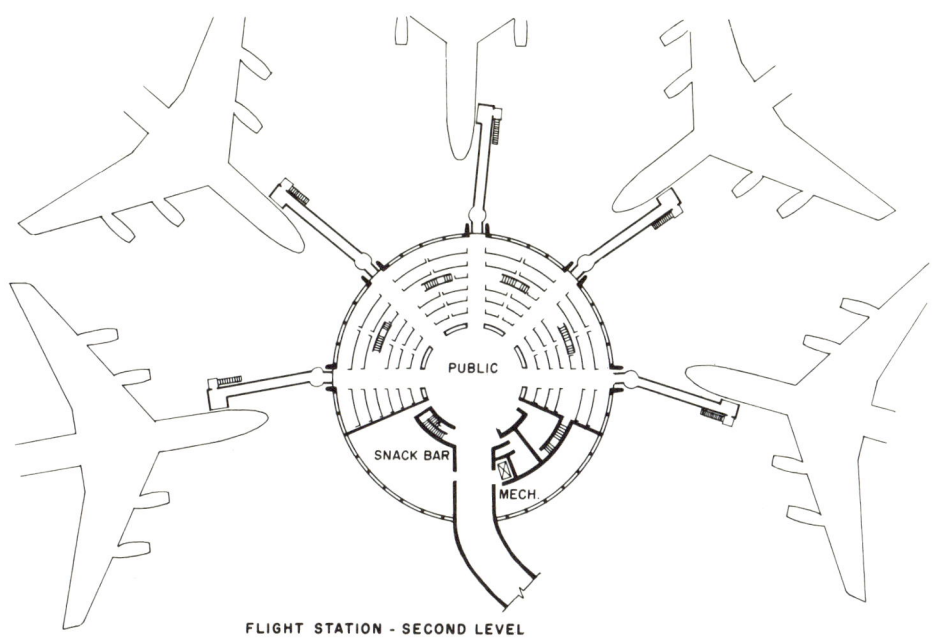

FLIGHT STATION - SECOND LEVEL

The central movement spine which interconnects the individual terminal buildings consists of a tunnel which contains a continuously running, electronically guided internal transportation system designed to transfer passengers from one terminal to another.

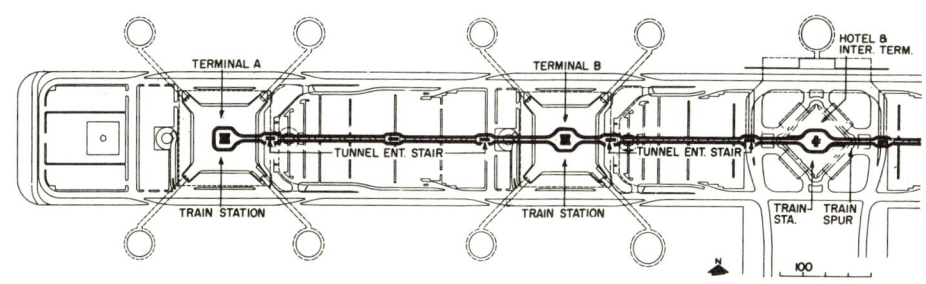

The central terminal building includes a large hotel. Designed by Goleman, Rolfe, Pierce and Pierce, the Houston International Airport is the most recent example of a multiterminal complex.

The mega-terminal airport of the future does not have to capitulate human scale. The individual terminal of the Houston International Airport designed by Goleman, Rolfe, Pierce and Pierce, is a self-contained space clearly articulated and strongly expressed.

opposite: The virile, brutal form of the individual flight station with its overhead connecting terminal evinces the sculptural, architectural potential of the supersonic age.

The Newark Airport expansion program includes a semi-eliptical tripartite, mega-terminal complex with basically the same circular flight station as the Houston International Airport.

The internal movement system of the Newark Airport scheme consists of moving sidewalks and stairs and the external system of clearly separated departure and arrival ramps. Design completed in 1966.

Among the unique features of this airport terminal is the level and intensity of artificial lighting. The designers went into a study in depth to assure that the internal spaces of the terminal would be illuminated in such a way as to create the maximum of architectural mood effects.

Tourism is fast becoming one of the main industries of many developing countries and its revolutionary recent growth has given rise to changing patterns of movement and a renaissance in ship travel.

The Miami Passenger Terminal, designed in 1968 by John Andrews, is a recent example of a contemporary passenger port facility.

Model of the multiterminal port facility expresses similar nucleation concept found in modern airport terminals.

Chapter IV

Places of Work

1. *Poetry of the Skeleton*

Places of employment form the very essence of central urban spaces. The central business district of Manhattan, in an area of less than eight square miles, provides employment for almost two million people. More than one-third of these workers are employed in a small, three-square-mile area.

The skyscraper is the well-known symbol of a megastructure—vertical assembly of high-density employment. The modern office tower was the product of the Chicago School of Architecture towards the end of the nineteenth century. The architects of the Chicago School developed the modern office building, using the new construction methods of the metal skeleton frame and new vertical transportation system, the elevator.

These new dimensions of architecture immediately fired up the enthusiasm of the architect for exploring them in skeleton construction, form, and space. As early as 1920 Mies van der Rohe in Germany produced all concrete skeleton glass office building designs, which, in their futurism, explored some of the potentialities of skyscraper construction. Working with rectangular, irregular sites, Mies portrayed in these designs articulation of spaces which only today are being realized. The central feature of these designs was a vertical elevator and stair tower, which, together with cantilevered concrete floors, sheathed in fully transparent glass curtain walls, has had tremendous poetic impact.

Pages 198, 199

The great attraction of the vertical form did not escape even the protagonist of horizontal architecture, Frank Lloyd Wright. However, Wright was more interested in exploring the possibilities of internal spatial composition than in the skyscraper as an element of urban form. He also shunned skeletal construction. The office building for the Larkin Company in Buffalo, built in 1904, is basically one enormous vertical space articulated by gallery floors and vertical piers and organized around a central volume. The use and expression of the skeleton construction, so important to the architect of that period, is consciously shunned by Wright in order to achieve a self-contained space, entirely separate from the space outside.

The Johnson Wax Company office building at Racine, Wisconsin, by the same architect, built immediately prior to the outbreak of the Second World War, exemplifies the same "paleolithic" treatment of space, but this time employing curvilinear and circular rather than rectilinear shapes. As in the Larkin Building, the natural light is brought in only from above, the enclosing brick walls remaining unpierced and uninterrupted by windows. The verticality of the space

Model of Mies van der Rohe's project for an office building on Friedrichstrasse in Berlin. Glass as the enclosing curtain around an office building was a revolutionary idea in 1919 when it was proposed in this uncompromising expression.

The uninterrupted and undulating use of glass was again suggested by Mies van der Rohe in this 1920-1921 model of an all-glass skyscraper building. This fully epic expression of the poetic potential inherent in the glass-enclosed skyscraper has never been more ingeniously conceived.

The great interior space of the Johnson Wax Company Administration Building by Frank Lloyd Wright, Racine, Wisconsin, 1936-1939. The free-standing elegant "lily pad" concrete columns are lighted from above through glass tubing which filters the light. The resultant space is filled with sophisticated vibrancy.

is implied rather than real. The form is horizontal, and it is only the free-standing, slender, elegant columns which give the space its vertical quality. These "lily pad" exposed concrete columns are basically self-supporting. They are used to articulate space and to provide an indirect lighting effect reminiscent of a forest environment—an extremely dramatic and poetic moving space.

In 1950 Wright added to this office complex his first high-rise structure —the deep-rooted, free-standing Laboratory Tower. The cantilever principle of the "lily pad" columns was here applied to the entire building structure, each floor being cantilevered from the main structural stem which houses all vertical elements: elevators, stairs and utilities. Every other floor is recessed, thus not only allowing space to flow vertically within the building but also expressing this movement on the exterior of the wall.

Pages 200, 201

Wright's design of these places of employment showed beyond doubt the great potentiality of spatial expression and drama inherent in the office building.

The exterior of Frank Lloyd Wright's Johnson Wax Company Administration complex, with the office tower added in 1950. The construction of this tower consists of a deep-rooted central utility shaft from which the floors are cantilevered with every alternating floor independent of the glass tubing which, together with the brick spandrels, forms the exterior envelope of the building.

2. *Skyscraper and City Space*

The modern city grows vertically as well as horizontally. New York City is a prime example of vertical growth resulting from the dynamics of the market mechanism and the skyrocketing of land values in the center of the city.

The first modern office megastructure is the multiblock complex of Rockefeller Plaza built in 1932, a seventy-story structure employing express elevator systems and the most advanced building technology of skyscraper construction of the first part of the twentieth century. Its contribution to modern urban design and to handling large-scale city-space is outstanding.

The World Trade Center in Manhattan, by Minoru Yamasaki, consists of two 110-story towers and underground parking facilities. Growth of individual megastructures at these heights and densities, directed by the will of economic forces, creates fantastic problems for directing and coordinating the growth of the city and reshaping the multitude of existing urban systems. The architect-planner, working with these powerful forces, is hard put to continuously update these systems.

The Lower Manhattan Plan of 1966 accepts the inevitability of uncontrolled vertical private development in the heart of the city and attempts to bring order to the molding of urban space by controlling the design of the movement systems rather than the mass of the buildings. The work of a design team, the plan proposes an intricate system of pedestrian, automobile, service and parking systems—the public structure for unifying uncoordinated private development. The pedestrian system would also include compatible, slow-moving vehicles—open-sided minibuses.

Pages 203, 204

The Island's perimeter expressways and parking areas, as envisioned in the plan, would be depressed, replacing the existing obsolescent piers with parks, open spaces, and some residential development above. Unlike so many uneconomic and futile plans for sculpting city space through administrative and legal controls of buildings, alone, this concept offers development control within a framework of publicly owned spaces and movement systems.

opposite: Overall view of model of the World Trade Center looking west, shows main plaza entrance at Church Street.

The World Trade Center features two 110-story towers, tallest buildings in the world, which soar 1,350 feet above a spacious plaza of almost five acres.

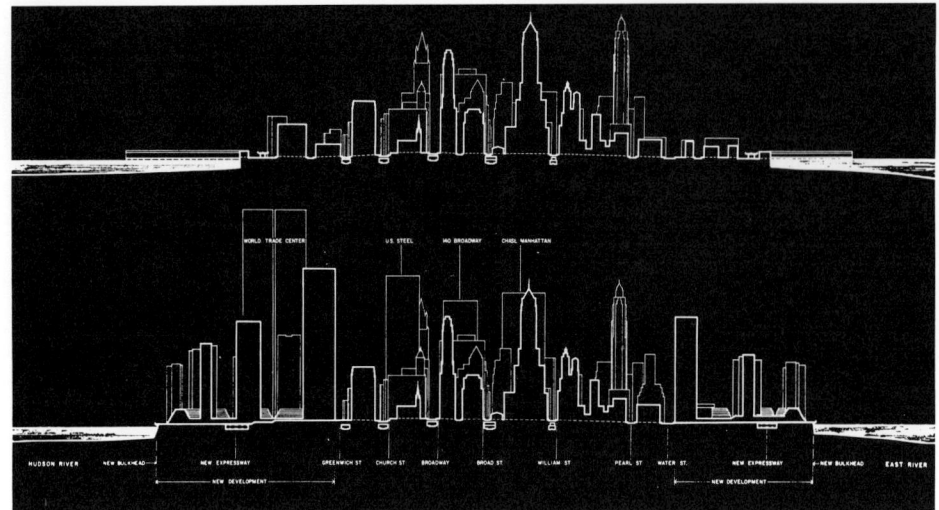

Proposed redevelopment of the Lower Manhattan area of New York City, 1966.

The plan envisioned replacing existing piers with parks and open spaces and depressing the island's perimeter expressways below the new developments.

The future of the skyscraper as a free-standing individual structure is foredoomed. Its weakness lies in the separation between the all-private and all-public aspects of the city structure. Its further incompatibility with the integrated multidimensional modern city life is the skyscraper's single tenancy—an all-office building filled and emptied twice a day five days a week, the remainder of the time standing empty and useless. Such segregation seems incompatible with the integrated nature of modern urban systems. The future "skyscraper" will, in all probability, be an integral part of the multi-use megastructure containing many "streets," levels and organically integrated mixed uses. Thus, the upper floors of such megastructures might well be residential, the lower zones commercial, and the intermediate institutional.

3. *Public Office Space*

Control over the changing form of the city is not limited to the design of its movement channels. The public building is an important element in the framework of the public urban structure. As the rate of urbanization magnifies, the role and responsibility of government and the need for government megastructures increases, and with it the opportunity for setting high levels of design excellence.

The Toronto City Hall by the Finnish architect Viljo Revell, completed in 1965, is a dominant structure in height and shape. The two concave office towers and the central, circular council chamber are as unrelated to the city space as is Le Corbusier's government complex in the city of Chandigarh. This segregation of the space of the center from the surrounding environment is a conscious attempt to oversymbolize and overdramatize the role of government in a modern city. It was accomplished by enclosing and separating the space of the center with solid masonry walls placed on the rear of the office towers, thus squelching the otherwise dominant direction of the arcs towards the city—the only feasible relationship. The monumental scale of the plaza and of the entrance ramps is oppressive. Instead of being the center of the city's activities, all innate functions of city life are excluded from this megastructure. The space envisioned as a lively and dynamic center of urban activities is now static and repelling in spite of the moving forms above.

Page 206

The Toronto government center is an oversized piece of sculpture and illustrates a less than skillful use of psychoarchitectural environmental variables with the resulting small degree of relatedness of this space.

The new Boston government center by Kallman, McKinnell and Knowles contains little dichotomy in its hierarchy of architectural principles. Although the bulk of the building is much heavier than that of the free-standing Toronto Towers, it is an architecture of space and motion and not of mass. The building achieves much more than a solution of the immediate architectural environment. It is a statement of a spatial system built for growth, expansion and change, fully capable of reflecting the intimate relationship with the city's past, present, and future framework. This highly versatile and articulated building fully retains its perceptual proportion to the rest of the city and to man in spite of its monumental scale.

Page 207

Great voids form outdoor terraces, decks, and platforms which penetrate the building, bridging space between the vertical cores. The cores contain vertical movement, and service arteries form the nuclei of the mass of the building. These cores feed, interconnect, or separate various functions as required. The voids between elements provide expansion potential for the growth of any functions housed within the system. The center is also intimately tied into the city's complex movement systems.

The Toronto City Hall, designed by the late Finnish architect Viljo Revell, opens towards a central plaza, which in wintertime serves also as a public skating ring. The use of the plaza as a public gathering place assists in offsetting the monumental scale of this government center, 1965.

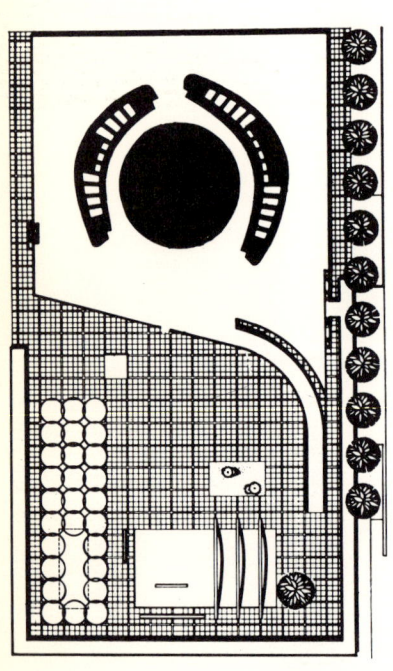

206

The Boston Government Center by Kallmann, McKinnell and Knowles, completed in 1969. Its great urban design significance lies in the fact that the building's basic contribution is in providing a cultural link between the city's historical past and its contemporary and future space.

The proposed addition to the Parliament Buildings in Wellington, New Zealand, by the British architect, Sir Basil Spence. This bold design of significant form, completed in 1965, when built will consist of a ziggurat-type circular building with the ministerial offices above the main reception rooms surmounted by the Prime Minister's suite, cabinet room floors, and a viewing deck on top.

The United States Embassy in Athens, Greece, designed by Walter Gropius and his associates in The Architects Collaborative, completed in 1961.

The architects' intention, in Gropius' own words, was "to find the spirit of the Greek approach without imitating any classical means."

The architectural features are indeed classical, podium, quadrilateral plan, interior plan, and exterior columns, but handled in a completely contemporary manner.

209

National Geographic
Society Office Building in
Washington, D.C., by
Edward Durell Stone,
completed in 1965.

4. *Commerce and Culture* The National Geographic Society Headquarters in Washington, D.C., by Edward Durell Stone, is a dramatic example of a trend towards making office buildings the center of cultural urban life as well. Use of ground floors of public buildings for educational and cultural functions is one of our untapped urban resources.

Pages 210, 211

The proposed Federal Reserve Bank in Minneapolis by Gunnar Birkerts maintains an uninterrupted cultural plaza by suspending the entire building in a bridge-like fashion from two vertical towers.

Pages 212, 213

The office building in Lahore, West Pakistan, and the U.S. Embassy in New Delhi, India, both by Edward Durell Stone, carry on the great Mogul building tradition in a modern vernacular.

Page 126

Interior Discovery Hall—Reception Area of the National Geographic Society Building, with fountains, pool, and revolving globe.

above and opposite: Models of the Federal Reserve Bank Building in Minneapolis, designed in 1968 by Gunnar Birkerts. This unprecedented revolutionary structure consists of catenary suspended-bridge-type design applied to a contemporary high-rise office building. The advantage of the design is that it provides clear spans of 265 feet, enables the entire site to be developed as a community plaza, and permits the building to be built in two phases, the final stage consisting of the upper six floors.

213

The Headquarters Building of the American Institute of Architects, Washington, D.C., designed in 1970 by The Architects Collaborative.

A perfect and compatible companion to the Octagon House, the proposed AIA Headquarters Building emphasizes, in the words of its designer, Norman C. Fletcher, principal in charge, ". . . action, involvement and service to the profession rather than catering to a dead monumentality."

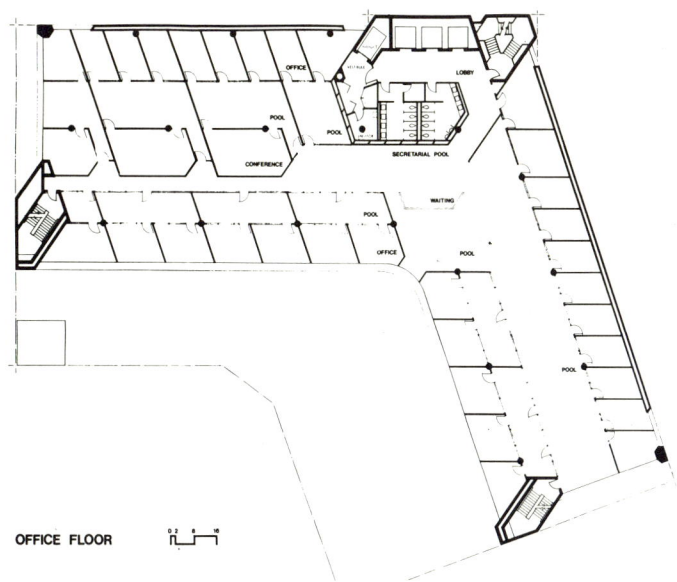

Floor plans of the proposed AIA Headquarters Building in Washington, D.C.

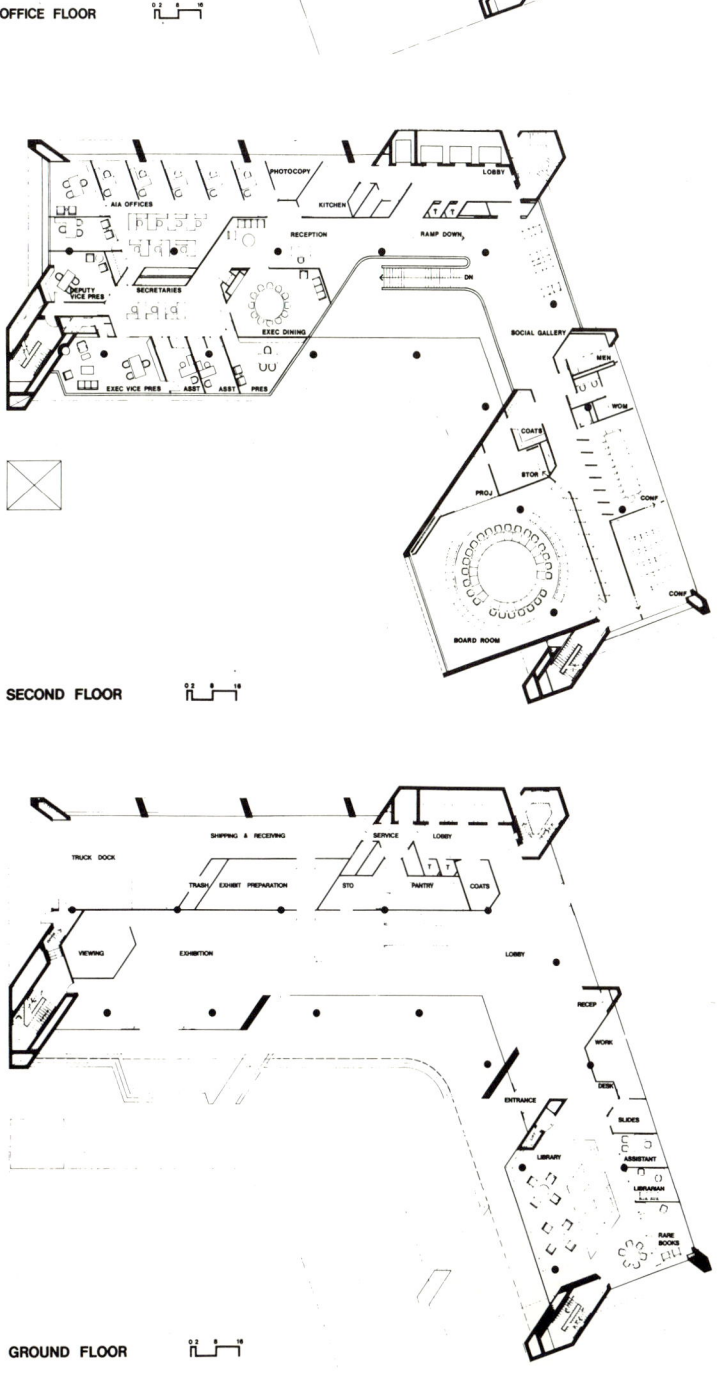

215

Office Building of The Architects Collaborative, Cambridge, Massachusetts, designed as its main headquarters by this architectural firm and completed in 1966.

The exterior of the building consists of sand-blasted concrete columns and wall panels with bronze-colored plate glass.

Interior of one of the studios of The Architects Collaborative headquarters building.

217

Tower East Office Complex, Shaker Heights, Ohio, designed by The Architects Collaborative and completed in 1967.

Interior of the reception lobby,
Tower East Office Complex,
Shaker Heights, Ohio.

Interior of an executive office,
Tower East Office Complex,
Shaker Heights, Ohio.

Chapter V

Places of Learning

1. *Kindergarten to Junior High*

Mass education, automation of the educational process, and the constantly changing goals of formal learning to prepare the student for the demands of modern life have revolutionized the design of the schoolhouse. While even a few years ago all that was necessary was a good teacher and a classroom, the school has now become a complex teaching laboratory. The most significant change that has occurred in school design is the matter of scale and perceptual proportion. The community elementary school, the giant urban high school, or the university city are recent phenomena requiring a new approach to design on the part of the architect-educator team. Some of the most exciting psychoarchitectural spaces can be found today in school buildings.

Everyone is aware of the skyrocketing upward curve of graduates from high school through college and the graduate school. However, the concomitant advances in quality and multiplicity of education are less well known. In order to keep the educational process abreast of man's dramatic progress in the automated and computerized industrial complex and revolutionary systems of communications and transportation, the modern school plant contains a vast gadgetry of cybernetic inventions and audio-visual machinery. This attempt to programize and mechanize the process of learning and teaching is dramatically portrayed in the design of all school-building types. These spaces not only provide for the requirements of the modern curriculum but are in and by themselves significant teaching tools.

The revolution of the modern schoolhouse underwent several changes in the second half of the twentieth century. As both the size of the student body and of curriculum offerings increased after the Second World War, the trend was at first simply to repeat in a horizontal composition the old elements: the classroom, the gymnasium, the multipurpose room. By the 1960s the sprawling trend reached such proportions that to move from one end of the school to another became impossible in terms of both time and distance. The pattern of the 1970s is multidimensional, and although the size of the school continues to increase, the architectural answer is generally found in a centralized solution and in integration rather than segregation of activity areas.

An example of such centralization, which necessarily requires a certain degree of symmetry, is the Southside Junior High School in Columbus, Indiana, by Eliot Noyes. This educational facility for twelve hundred students, although located on a perfectly level site, portrays the spatial variety possible within a strict organization of rectangular shape. The heart of the school is a two-story communal space which serves as the social meeting place for students and faculty. This "noise center" was designed in recognition of the fact that, in addition to formal teaching space, the learning process requires informal exchange of ideas and personal accidental contact. Immediately below the social hall is the swimming pool. This space is dramatically lighted by overhead skylights and the entrance is located at the intermediate level, providing maximum spatial experiences within it. This area serves as the clear organizing force for all other spaces. The mass of the building is strongly articulated by rhythmical proportions and expressions of the three large volumes of space above the roof line. Natural lighting in all spaces is indirect, assuring concentration and privacy in an all-enclosed educational environment.

Pages 222, 223

Experimentation with educational spaces starts with the design of a kindergarten and elementary school. Even at these beginning stages of education, the question of scale and proportion is being recognized as having a tremendous impact upon the child's ability to learn. As the first place after home where the child learns to perceive space, the design of an elementary school is finally beginning to receive the attention that heretofore had been largely denied it.

The Richards Elementary School, also in Columbus, Indiana, by E. L. Barnes is identified with this relatively new spatial movement. Light and space are the dominant elements of the composition. This one-story school has all its spaces lighted by clerestories within the upward-jutting roofs formerly used only in large-scale assembly plants. Four of these enormous serrated shapes are placed over the central communal space and twelve smaller ones hover over the classroom modules which are organized on both sides of the central, longitudinal axis.

Pages 224, 225

Southside Junior High School, Columbus, Indiana, designed in 1968 by Eliot Noyes, was placed on a four-foot-high podium to alleviate the flatness of the site. Projecting fins and sloping tinted glass provide sun control for the upper floors.

The classroom module is organized around an open teaching courtyard. The individual classroom has direct contact with outdoor environment through large-scale window openings in addition to clerestory lighting. The trussed multipurpose space provides a dramatic relief to the normal scale of the side teaching spaces. To enhance the voluminous quality of the space, the architect depressed the floor of this room two feet below that of the classroom level. This space, designed to afford activities which in warmer climates could have been performed outdoors, and generously flooded with natural light, is highly successful. The expression of this light and airy space on the heavy, monumental, and out-of-scale exterior mass of the building seems entirely out of character. A less brutalistic treatment of articulation would have provided a more intimate relationship between the actual internal space and its externally expressed scale— more in keeping with the four-footers for whom it was designed.

An example of a slightly less dramatic, but also less brutal, treatment of space is another elementary school in the same town, the Lincoln Elementary School by Gunnar Birkerts. A square space in a circle of trees, this school seems to provide a more childlike proportion and a more serene teaching environment.

Pages 226-229

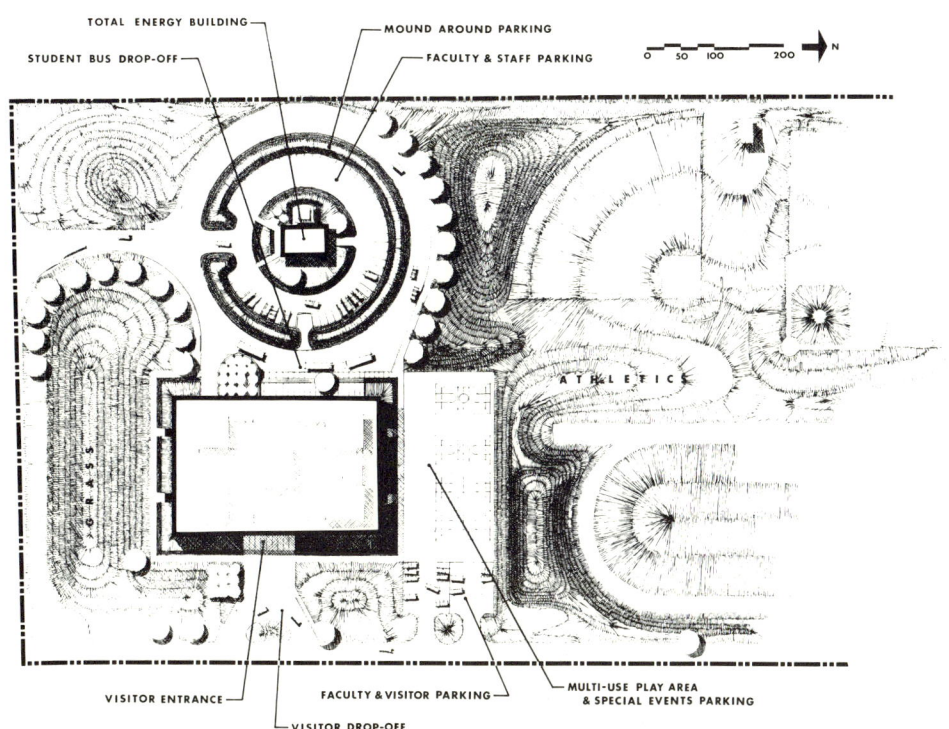

The site of the Southside Junior High School is sculptured with earth mounds, some of which shield parking areas, and depressions which act as recharge basins for disposal of storm sewer.

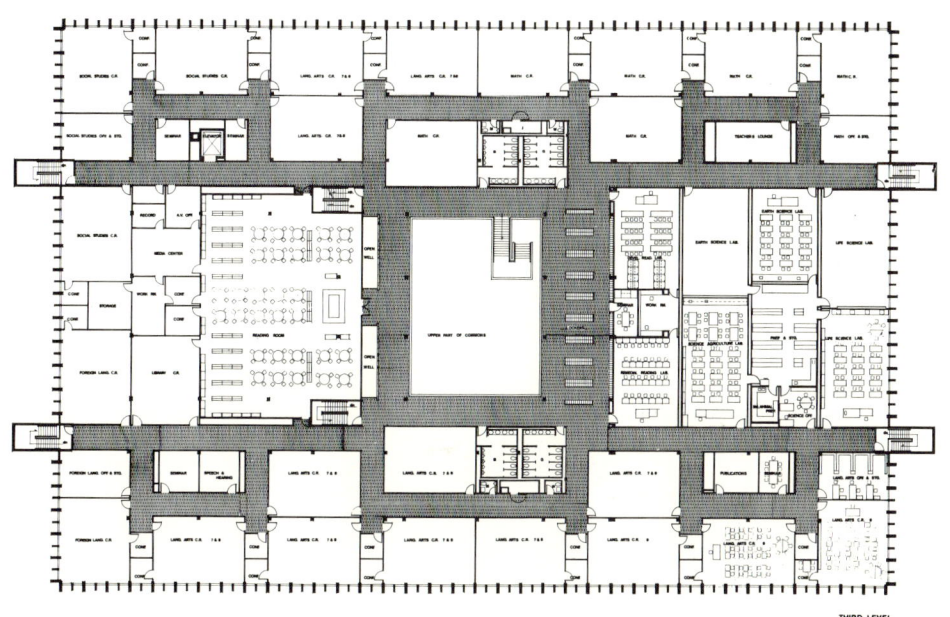

The commons, the heart of the school, is designed to put the student in contact with all major special-purpose areas. All entrances and corridors intersect the commons, making it the main circulation area and a place for social interaction for student and teacher.

The Richards Elementary School, Columbus, Indiana, designed by Edward L. Barnes and built in 1966, is a linear school organized around a central communal space. This cathedral-like space, lighted by clerestory windows is high, imposing, and as much like an outdoor space as possible.

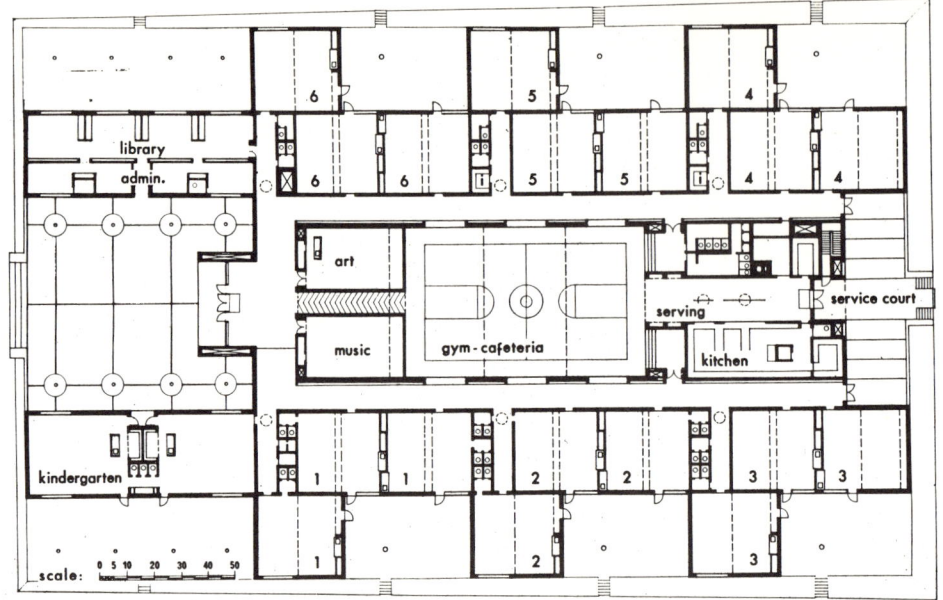

The serrated roofs over the central multipurpose room, as well as those over the banks of classrooms, impart a strong, sculptural silhouette to the skyline.

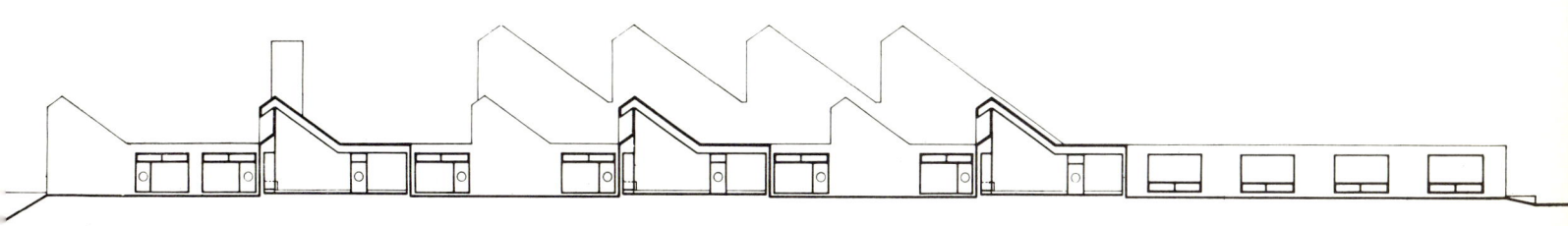

Each grade of the Richards Elementary School has its own nest of classrooms, one an open courtyard and three enclosed. The nest of four teaching spaces was designed by the architect as a means of providing the school with the flexibility required by team teaching.

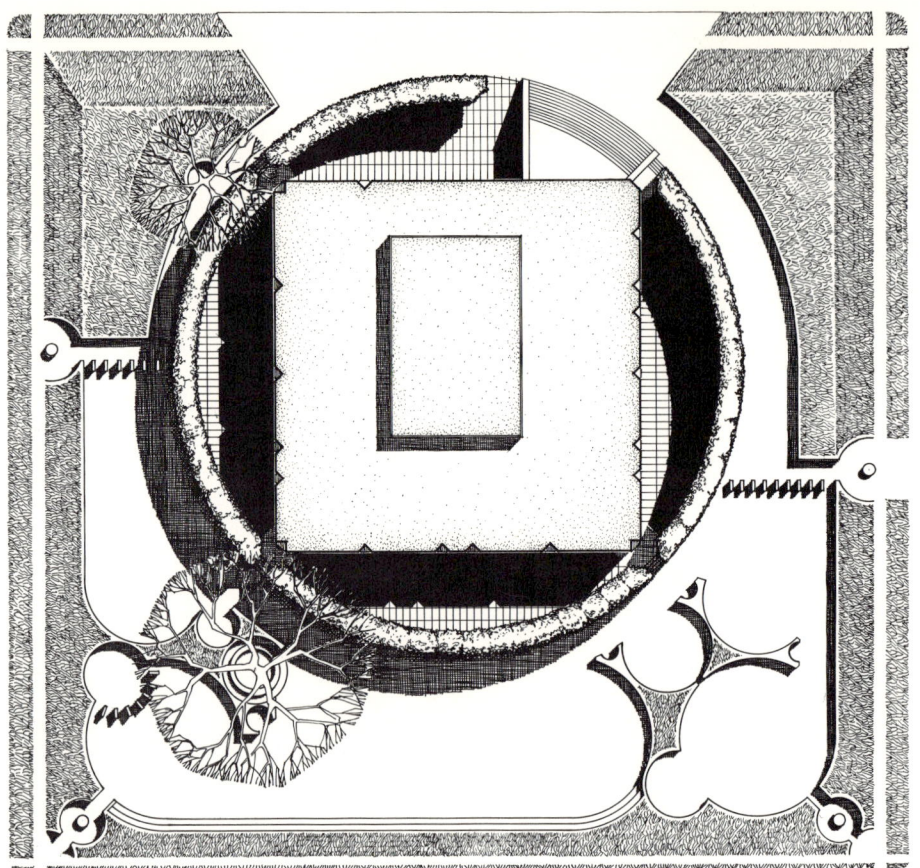

The Lincoln Elementary School in Columbus, Indiana, by Gunnar Birkerts, is a relatively small school designed as an integral part of the downtown city park in which it is located.

Variations in ground level have permitted direct entrances to both floors of this compact school. The architect has heavily planted the site with linden trees in a conscious attempt to relate the microenvironment of the school to the park in which it is located.

The depressed playground provides a natural outdoor expansion space to the internal teaching spaces without separating it from the rest of the city. The interior of the school is organized in concentric rings within a basic square.

The exterior envelope of the school contains a minimum of glass area by using a single window to light two classrooms. Exterior doors are similarly shared, reducing the number of elements to the minimum, and thus giving the building pristine simplicity accentuated by sun effects.

The second-floor corridor of the Lincoln Elementary School, Columbus, Indiana, designed by Gunnar Birkerts, provides the children with a plethora of visual experiences—across the wide parapet they can simultaneously observe the activities within the multi-purpose room and the life in the corridor below.

229

2. *The High School*   Economic development of urbanized areas has in the past been arrested not so much by the lack of decent housing or even by the lack of employment opportunity as by the great gaps that still exist in the post-elementary and pre-university educational system.

Agencies responsible for providing economic assistance to underdeveloped countries have for some time recognized the need for strengthening general and technical education at this level. The International Bank for Reconstruction and Development alone is presently engaged in providing loans for the construction of hundreds of secondary school facilities in more than thirty countries. The small island of Jamaica is currently building fifty of these schools, designed by Caudill, Rowlett, Scott. These predominantly small community schools are an extremely important contribution to the economic and industrial development of the less developed nations. They are, however, extremely simple in concept, design, and function when compared with the problems of the urban high school in the highly urbanized and developed areas of the world.

The city-wide educational systems consist of centrally located great high schools fed by and interconnected with the neighborhood junior high and elementary schools. The large complex of the modern urban high school is the focal point of the entire system and also the central meeting ground for the community's educational problems. During these inner city oriented days, the large cities are becoming acutely aware of the strategic role of the high school in solving the community's social, economic, and racial problems.

The city of Pittsburgh is in the process of phasing out its seventeen existing high schools and consolidating them into five gigantic educational megastructures, each containing 5,000 to 6,000 students. The main advantage of this consolidation is the provision of modern, semi-automated teaching facilities designed to radically upgrade the quality of urban education. The sites for these super-schools are located near the city's problem areas of greatest unemployment, poorest housing, and lowest incomes. The schools will serve to integrate racially segregated neighborhoods and may in themselves become neighborhood centers. The educational system will be closely integrated with other urban systems, i.e., transportation, housing, and employment. Besides the traditional teaching functions, the system will also provide spaces for adult education and community functions.

Each of the five educational megastructures will contain about one million square feet of building area and up to forty acres of urban land. These schools, designed by Hellmuth, Obata and Kassabaum, with some of their buildings located on air rights over rail tracks and future rapid transit lines, will contain many functions previously found only at universities: faculty building, social and science centers,

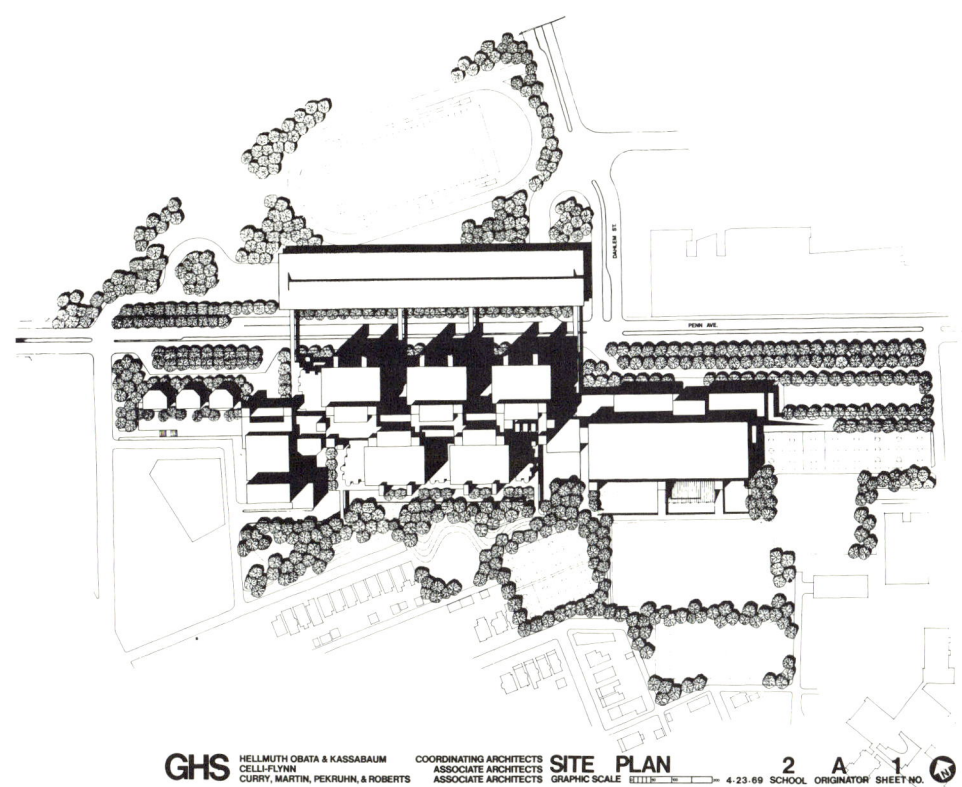

Model of one of the mega-high schools in Pittsburgh, Pa., designed in 1968 by Hellmuth, Obata and Kassabaum, for about 6,000 students. The facilities of this economic teaching plant will be extensively used for inner-city community activities.

The large scale of the project makes it possible to provide an extensive and varied instructional program which would not be economically feasible in a smaller school. In order to assure that the individual student is not simply lost in such a large school, he is made part of a series of small- and medium-sized groups, each with its own spaces and facilities.

art center, administration towers, engineering center, joint educational and community personal services, and entertainment facilities.

The mega-high school will, for administrative reasons, be divided into four units, each serving some twelve hundred students under a separate dean; for each three hundred students there is envisioned a full-time counselor, and for every ten, a teacher-advisor. The organization of these complex spaces exemplifies, through its juxtaposed and varied shapes, the dynamics of the new dimensions of educational space.

Page 231

3. *University Structures*

The college campus today is a veritable experimental laboratory of architectural space; old spaces undergo constant updating and new forms are created to meet new educational demands.

The astronomic demands for college housing in recent years have generated tremendous building activity. Yet the space of the old campus is being respected by even such highly individualistic architect-virtuosos as Eero Saarinen. Commissioned to design college housing at Yale, Saarinen designed a complex which in its scale, texture, and pattern is extremely compatible with the old neo-Gothic structures, yet modern in its form, space, and materials.

Page 233

The university modern science building requires large, uninterrupted, well-ventilated and lighted spaces. The high concentration of complex and varied utilities and the need for utmost control of environmental conditions are frequently integrated in a multitude of arrangements—usually vertical. They have ranged from simple statements as the University of California San Francisco Research Center by Ried, Rockewell, Barnwell and Tarics, a 15-story steel space frame tower, all the way to the poetic application of precast reinforced concrete in the Richards Medical Laboratories at the University of Pennsylvania by Louis Kahn.

Pages 234, 235

The Richards Building was originally conceived by Kahn in 1957, with the stair and utilities service towers serving as structural columns. In order to economically cantilever the floors, he later added structural columns, leaving the service towers as nonsupporting elements. In the final design the circular and square shaped towers are replaced by rectangular elements and the basic square module in the plan becomes more articulated by exposing clearly defined precast structural elements of the floor slabs.

The result is a vertical composition of brick, glass, and precast concrete units in strictly geometric and highly modulated shapes. The composition is ageless, being based upon time-venerated architectural shapes, yet dynamic and modern in arrangement.

Ulrich Franzen's Agronomy Laboratory at Cornell, a thirteen-story, almost windowless all brick-clad tower, is perhaps the ultimate integration of utilitarian and spatial requirements of a college laboratory to date. It is an example of skillfully integrated structural and mechanical systems. Precast concrete floors are used as chases for various mechanical modules and collected on the exterior of the building into vertical supply shafts. They, together with the elevator and stair towers, give the building the monumental scale and form it possesses.

In spite of the increasing use of microfilming and telecommunications media at the modern university, the library plays an ever more important role on the college scene—from a small campus to the large university. Victor Christ-Janer's cubistic library is located in the heart of Lake Erie College in Ohio. This aluminum-clad mass on a rough

Samuel F. B. Morse and Ezra Stiles Colleges, Yale University, New Haven, Connecticut, designed by Eero Saarinen and completed in 1963. The space is in complete harmony with the old campus.

The Alfred Newton Richards Medical Research Laboratories, University of Pennsylvania, Philadelphia, by Louis I. Kahn, 1957-1961. Brutal aesthetics evince the power of ultimate structural determinism expressed in a contemporary, revolutionary form, yet with roots deep in the best traditions of ancient architecture.

Strong, masculine architecture of the doyen of American architects, Louis I. Kahn, in a sylvan setting, united into a significant psycho-architectural environment.

Contemporary architectural cubism of the James F. Lincoln Library, Lake Erie College, Painesville, Ohio, Victor Christ-Janer architect, 1966. The upper elements are covered with aluminum panels, while the base consists of rough textured concrete. Inner space of the library is lighted from above and below.

textured concrete base totally encloses interior space, which is heavily articulated and lighted from above and below. This relatively small space offers a great variety of visual experiences.

Page 236

John M. Johansen's library for Clark University in Massachusetts applies this principle of integrating, with "paleolithic" strength and vigor, the internal space of the library with that of the university environment. This highly masculine attempt at variety has none of the mannerist variety-for-variety's-sake philosophy in it. The conscious disorganization of elements is unified by the central rectangular shape of the stack area and even much more by the movement of space in and out of the building through the strongly manipulated elements. This reinforced concrete structure with nonbearing brick infills is a symphony of space.

Pages 238, 239

Library of the University of Tunis, Tunis, Tunisia, by The Architects Collaborative, completed in 1969.

The architects' design attempts to capture the strong horizontal design of the terraces inherent in the overall campus plan through the reiterated parallel roof lines.

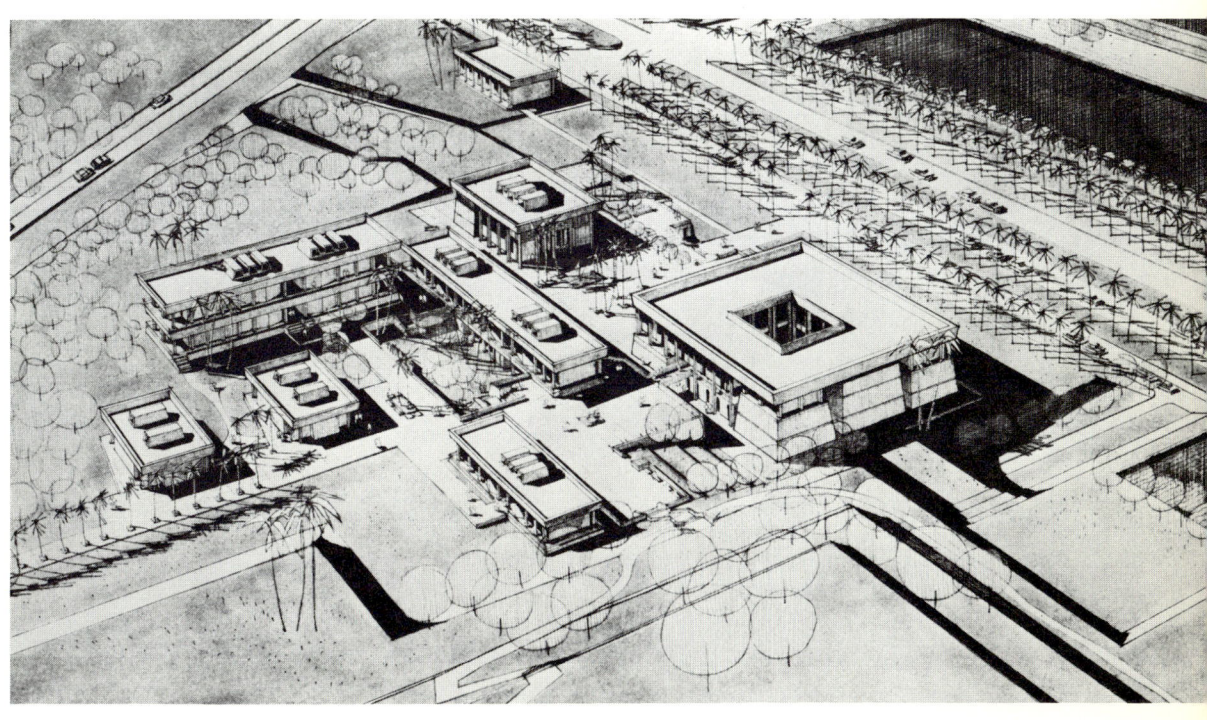

The Robert Hutchings Goddard Library, Clark University, Worcester, Massachusetts, designed by John M. Johansen and completed in 1969. The revolutionary form and space of this three-level "box of books" is raised above a pedestrian plaza. The irregular and seemingly discordant notes of the exterior forms are unified into a piece of architectural "chance music" orchestration. The snorkel-type tubes over the roof parapet are the intake and exhaust ducts.

The interior reading areas of the library are lighted by almost continuous bands of vertical light wells, crossed by bridges at each floor level. The assemblage of the various elements of this complex building is handled with unusual dexterity and clearly evinces the architect's design philosophy that "buildings, and all of our arts, should serve not as consumer commodities but as the means of training man's perception."

239

4. *Campus Design*

College enrollment in the United States will rise to almost nine million students by 1975, according to U.S. Department of Health, Education, and Welfare projections; the enrollment then will be about double that of 1963 and almost four times that of 1950. A large portion of this growth will take place in community colleges not yet built. Planning and design of a new campus requires a systems approach, which is reminiscent on a smaller scale of that which exists in city planning. It also requires extremely elaborate space and program analysis for integrating the flow of students, faculty and paper heretofore applied only to manufacturing production lines. It is again of necessity a team effort, with the computer utilized in analyzing systems and alternatives.

The community college outside of a dense urbanized region is represented by the almost residential scale of Foothill College in California by Kump, Masten and Hurd. Its residential scale, its generous use of wood, texture, and pattern, its spaciousness and its integration with landscape distinguish this small campus.

Pages 242-244

The Bellevue Community College design in the State of Washington by Naramore, Bain, Brady and Johnson, instead of being a campus plan concept of individual buildings separated by space and landscape, is really a single megastructure. It is a linear plan, strong and concise, and is organized around a central space, a "street," with articulated courtyards and minor axes providing a moving experience and a place for interaction between students and faculty. In Eliot Noyes' Southside Junior High School in Columbus the interior communal "noise center" is carved out of a natural environment by the mass of the defining buildings. The compactness of this modular campus allows the rest of the site to remain generally undisturbed, and the linear composition allows ease of future expansion. The academic commons, formed by buildings, offers a wide variety of open and closed spaces, inviting communication among the various academic groups.

Page 244

Louis I. Kahn's Ahmedabad Business College in India is a superb example of combining the traditional strong forms of Indian architecture in creating extremely imaginative modern spaces. His underlying these is the *memento mori*, the timeless quality of architectural space —the idea that even in fullest life, death is always present. Kahn adopted this philosophy that architecture, to retain its continuous quality in time and space, must have its roots deep in the past in order for its space not to become obsolescent within a single decade.

Pages 245-247

All of the forms of the composition have been simplified and to some degree even distorted. The shape of the lake, the central organizational element of this composition, is extremely architectonic and urban. To underscore that the lake is a man-made element, its shape reflects that of the buildings. The lake separates and at the same time connects the educational building and dormitories with the residential-commercial section of the campus. The educational building is the acropolis, resting on the highest mound of the gently rolling terrain, with its modulated plan suggestive of Mogul traditional religious school buildings.

The first design of the educational building had amphitheatre-type classrooms and faculty offices organized around the central space occupied by library and inner court. The later scheme applies a more rectangular order and turns the entire heart of the building into a canopy-covered communal space.

The completed dormitories contain space defined by the strictest geometry of the square, triangle, and rectangle, combined into a single module. The square is the service block, the triangle a hall, and the two rectangles the dormitories. Light and breeze which enter the hall transform the space and give it its primal strength.

Constant search on the part of the architect for spatial, cultural continuity is universal. Just as Kahn built his Ahmedabad Institute, drawing its inspiration from the Moguls, the medieval hilltown concept is recaptured in G. De Carlo's dormitories and commons complex at Urbino, Italy. It is a single structure built into a hill, with the hilltop containing the communal space and magnificent, moving views of the Appenine Hills. The design of this space, using simple materials and forms, is yet another example of the great variety of spatial experiences possible in a harmonic relationship between natural and man-made space.

Page 248

The same approach can be used to bring order where chaos exists. Birkerts' plan for the Tougaloo College in Alabama is a scheme which will accomplish orderly change in time. The existing old plantation buildings will be gradually replaced by a dense, urban space expressive of the changing role of the college. This predominantly Black rural college is undergoing a revolutionary change in its educational structure in preparing the students for modern urban life. The juxtaposed linear composition of the masses which define a great variety of spaces will in time completely transform the entire campus.

Page 249

The classroom nests, with their distinctive regional design and with wood extensively used, are imposing in their simplicity and mellowness, and the entire campus looks most natural in its compatibility with the environment.

Residential scale of the campus is achieved by low and hovering overhangs, use of natural building materials and adroit employment of paving textures and earth sculpture.

Scarborough College, by John Andrews, is a part of the expansion program of the University of Toronto which envisions the future of its downtown campus as a center of graduate studies and of the future undergraduate satellite campuses system. Scarborough, located twenty miles from the city, was designed for a student body of 6,000. It was located on a large wooded hill and its megastructure follows the natural contours of the hill, with its organization, structure, and space well-integrated with that of the larger environment.

Pages 250, 251

The trend toward higher density and centralization of higher educational facilities becomes more intense in planning large urban universities where land is prohibitively expensive and scatterization is functionally and economically out of the question.

The new University of Illinois Chicago Circle campus, by Skidmore, Owings, and Merrill, contains 106 acres of urban land and an eventual student population of 20,000. As such, it is a modern university

Foothill College, Palo Alto, California, designed by Kump, Masten and Hurd and completed in 1962. This plan had an important effect upon the advancement in planning small colleges in the United States.

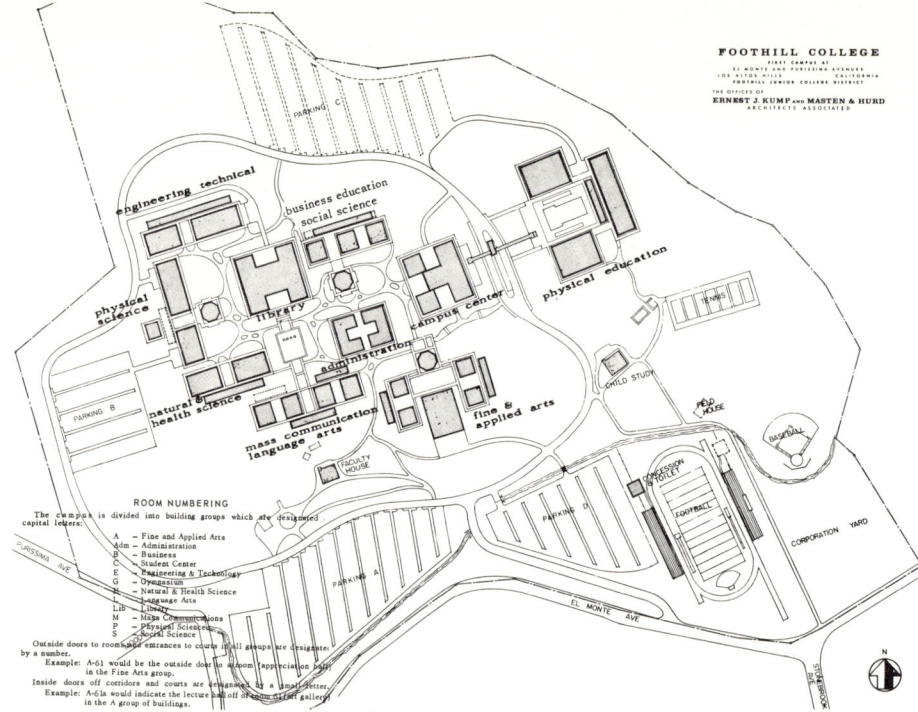

The campus plan of Foothill College, Palo Alto, California, designed by Kump, Masten and Hurd, is divided into building groups with each educational function housed in a separate structure.

Bellevue Community College, Bellevue, Washington, designed in 1967 by Naramore, Bain, Brady and Johnson, is an exciting elaboration of the pedestrian mall concept as an organizing element for a college campus.

Louis I. Kahn's early study sketch of the Indian Institute of Management Campus in Ahmedabad, India, designed between 1964 and 1966, shows the residential dormitories of the college along the lakeside and their powerful forms reflected in the water. All of the buildings in this campus are organized to take full advantage of prevailing breezes for their enclosed as well as open spaces.

Brick arches, with their virile roots deep in the venerable Indian building tradition, form the almost epic spatial order of the central hall of the Indian Institute of Management. Through the combination of traditional building material, brick, with reinforced concrete, Louis Kahn has created a transcendental movement of spatial, cultural continuity.

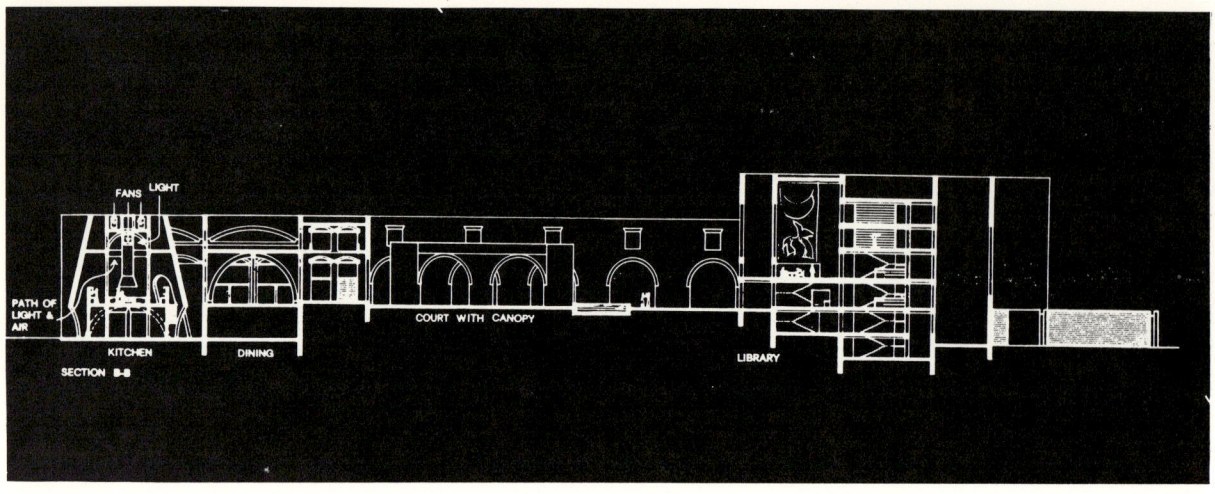

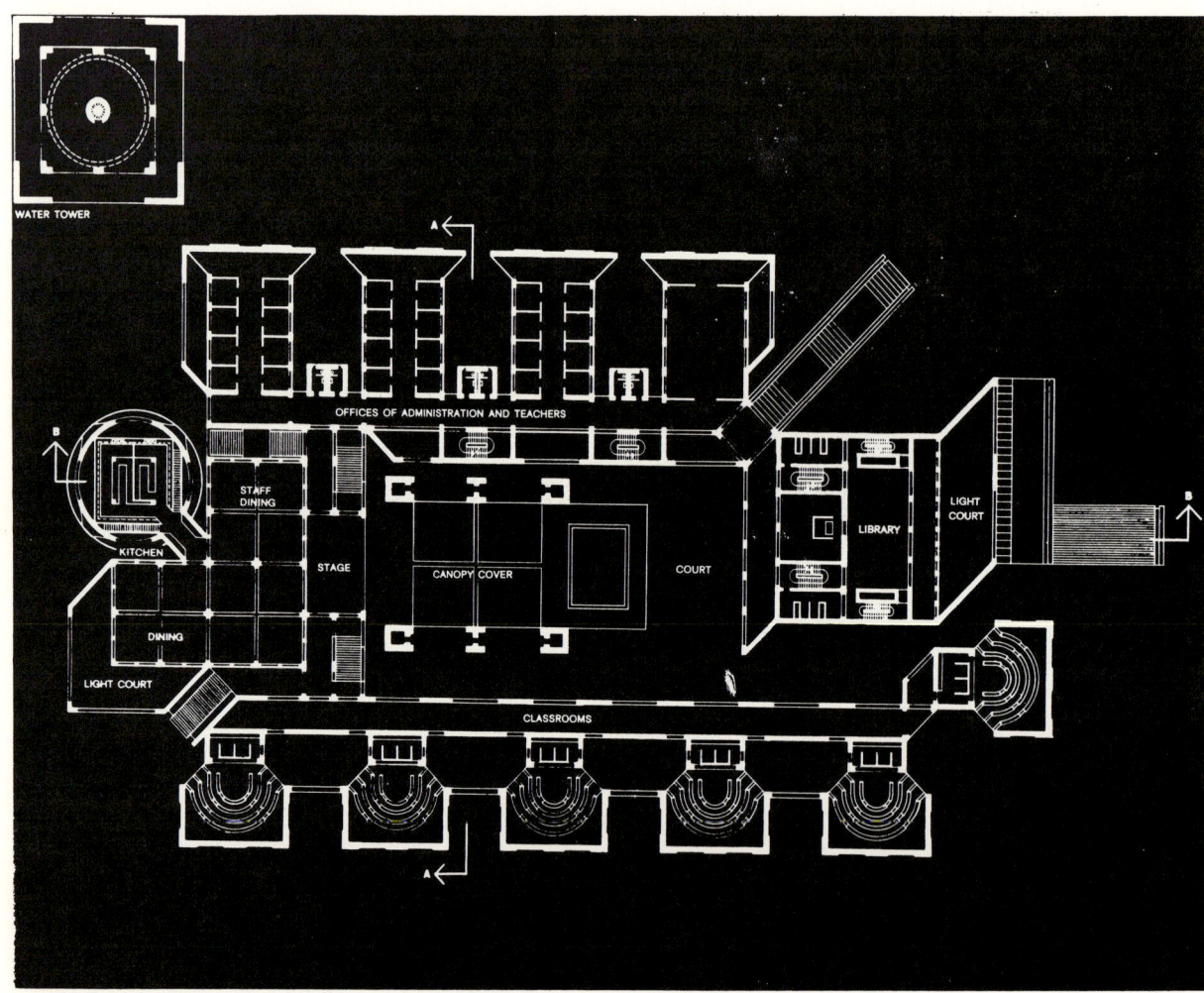

top: Cross section of the educational building, Indian Institute of Management, showing the treatment of internal spaces of the dining area, library, and central canopied court.

above: Plan of the educational building with amphitheatre-type classrooms and faculty offices extending beyond the main wall of the building. Light is allowed into the internal space of the structure through deep arched openings.

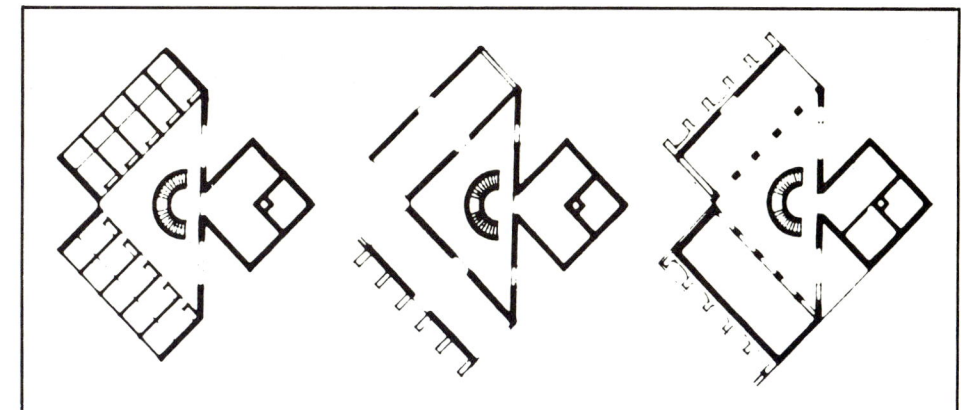

Louis I. Kahn uses the strict geometry of the composite order of the square, the triangle, and the rectangle in the plan of the dormitory units of the Indian Institute of Management in Ahmedabad, India.

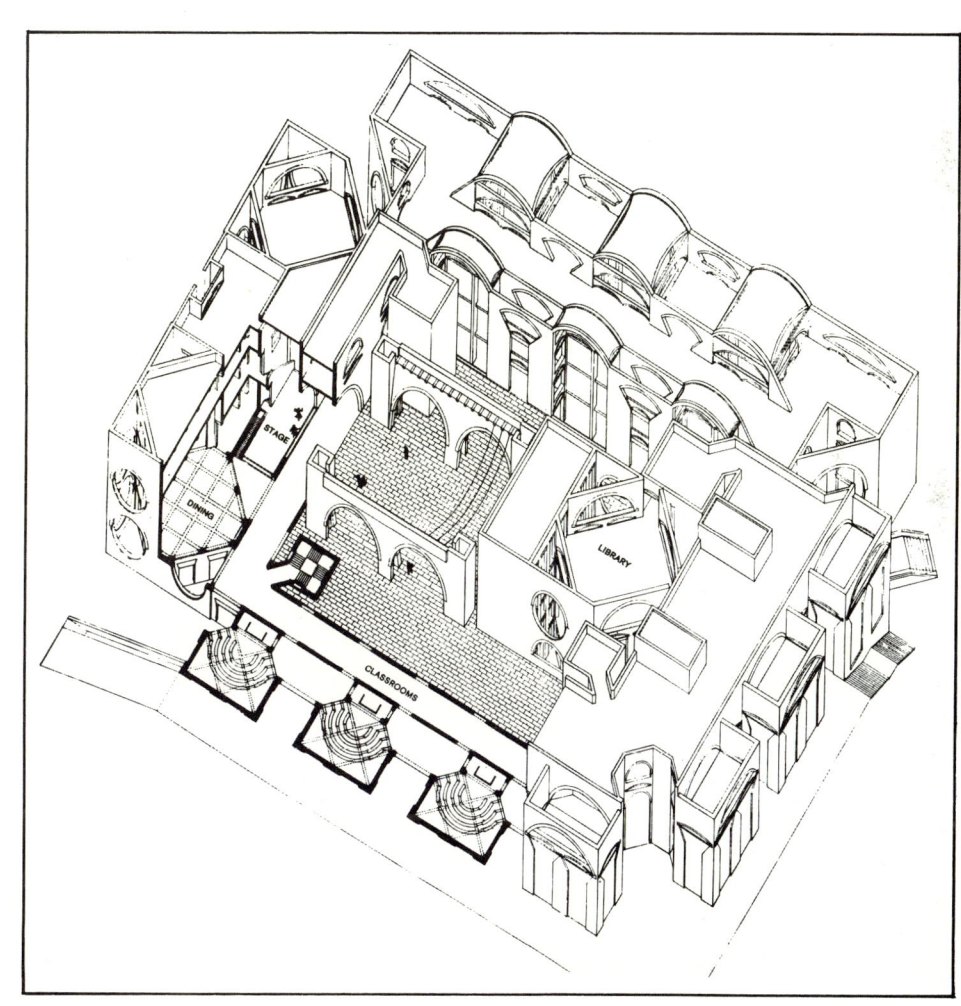

An early architectural study of the educational unit of the Indian Institute of Management, in which concept the architectural environment, in Kahn's own words, is a "building within a building—one given over to the sun, the other to living."

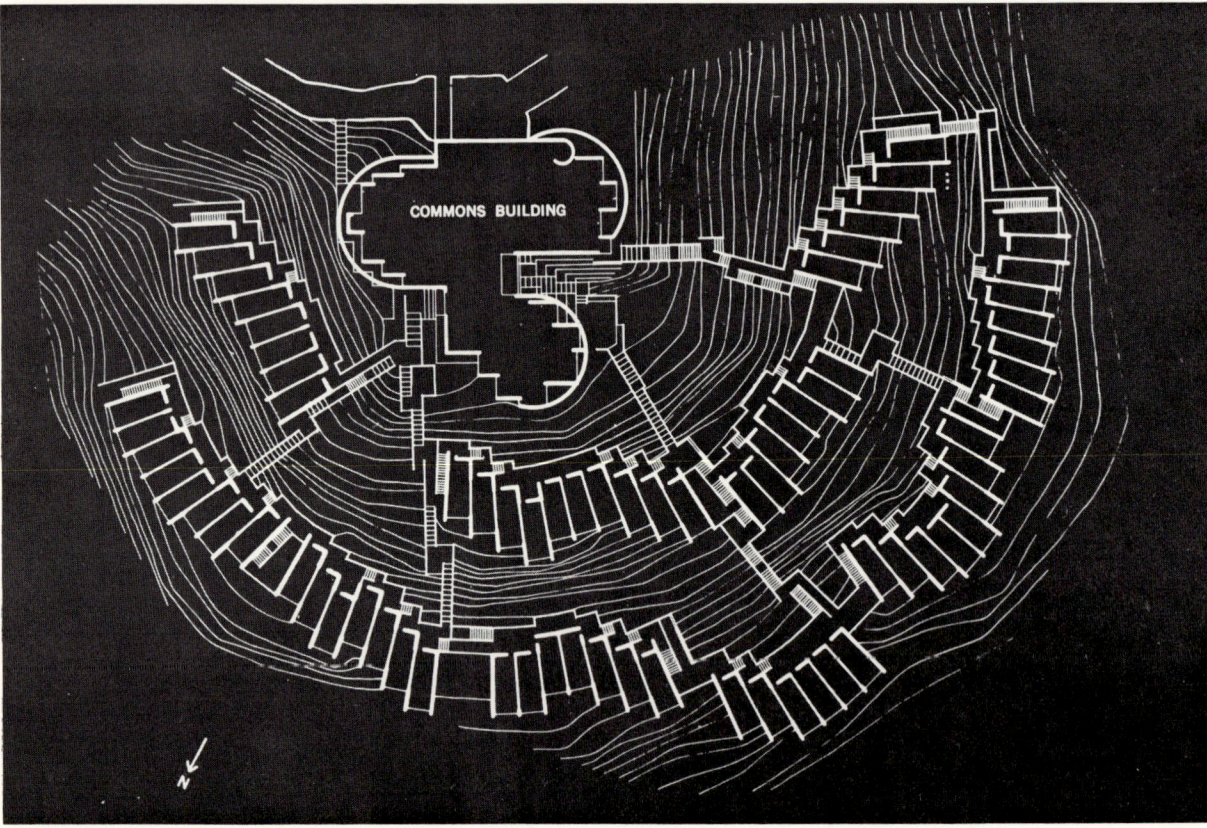

Dormitories and Commons Building of "Libera Universita di Urbino" at Urbino, Italy, designed by the Milan architect Giancarlo DeCarlo and completed in 1964. Built on the Cappuccini Hill, it is based upon the concept of a community of a hundred and fifty students as a single physical organism drawing its inspiration from the hill and the space into which it was placed.

city within a city. The buildings in the first phase are clustered on a forty-acre multilevel site organized around a quadripartite central plaza. The various movement systems originate from this central space and all other forms and spaces are arranged in a combination of symmetrical and asymmetrical plan elements, giving the entire composition some of the movement and ambiguity of the adjoining urbanscape.

Pages 252-255

Another example of a tight and well-organized large university campus is the new State University of New York at Albany designed by Edward Durell Stone.

Pages 256, 257

Model of the Tougaloo College campus near Jackson, Mississippi, designed in 1965 by Gunnar Birkerts. A single-structure higher-education complex for a predominantly Black college, the planning concept of expanding the student body from the present 500 to a future 2,500 is carefully staged. When completed, the present largely obsolete old plantation buildings will be replaced by a comprehensive and unique scheme. Birkerts proposes placing dormitories and staff apartments above educational spaces in a multilayered composition, mostly floating above the sloping terrain. All facilities are housed within the basic 30-foot structural grid which permits emphasis to be placed upon the maximum utilization of open spaces.

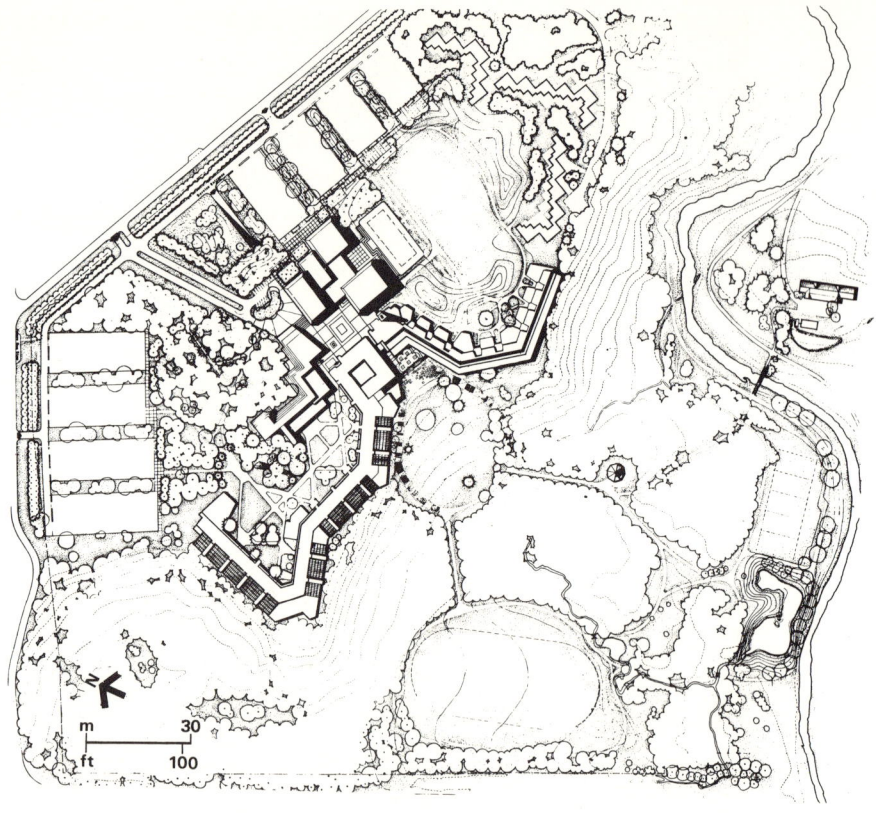

Scarborough College, a satellite campus of the University of Toronto in Canada, is located about 20 miles from the city's center. Designed in 1964 by the Canadian architect John Andrews, the first stage, a single structure, was completed in 1966.

The Scarborough College building is a long, meandering structure built into the hill, with its main entrances provided from the plateau above. Each level of the building consists of glass-enclosed or skylit pedestrian malls which permit the entire college to become an environment unto itself. The short wing contains auditoriums and offices.

The interior pedestrian "streets" of the Scarborough College near Toronto converge upon a central meeting place. Since the Science Wing "street" is a level higher than the Humanities Wing "street," the meeting place serves as a significant vertical transfer space. This skylit internal space with mezzanines is a vibrant place of social interaction.

University of Illinois at Chicago Circle campus, designed by Walter Netsch, Skidmore, Owings and Merrill, completed in 1967. The circular amphitheater of this 20,000-student urban university is a hollow space in the center of the educational forum—the central organizing element of the entire campus. University Library Building in the background.

Overall view of the campus looking southeast showing Circle Forum and Exedrae, with the major elevated walkways and classroom clusters in the foreground. Science and Engineering Laboratory Building in the background. Each of the four Exedrae is a hollow concrete mound with amphitheater-type seating designed as a communal meeting place for students and faculty.

Architecture and Art Laboratories of the University of Illinois at Chicago Circle campus, with tall diamond-shaped skylights lighting the interior studio spaces, turn pure geometry into viable architectural spaces. The architectural studios are contained within a three-story complex connected by corridor stairs.

The Architecture and Art Laboratories Building is windowless. The basic concept of the plan of the building consists of superimposing two or more square grids at an angle, with each of these star-shaped modular spaces containing one architectural or art studio. The building is connected with the rest of the campus by a bridge leading to a raised walkway.

In contrast to these basically rectilinear compositions is the school of Plastic Arts in suburban Havana, Cuba, by Ricardo Porro, organized in an organic, playful and dynamic art form.

Page 258

Fifth level plan of the Architecture and Art Laboratories Building at the University of Illinois at Chicago Circle campus, designed by Walter Netsch, Skidmore, Owings and Merrill. An exotic geometric plan.

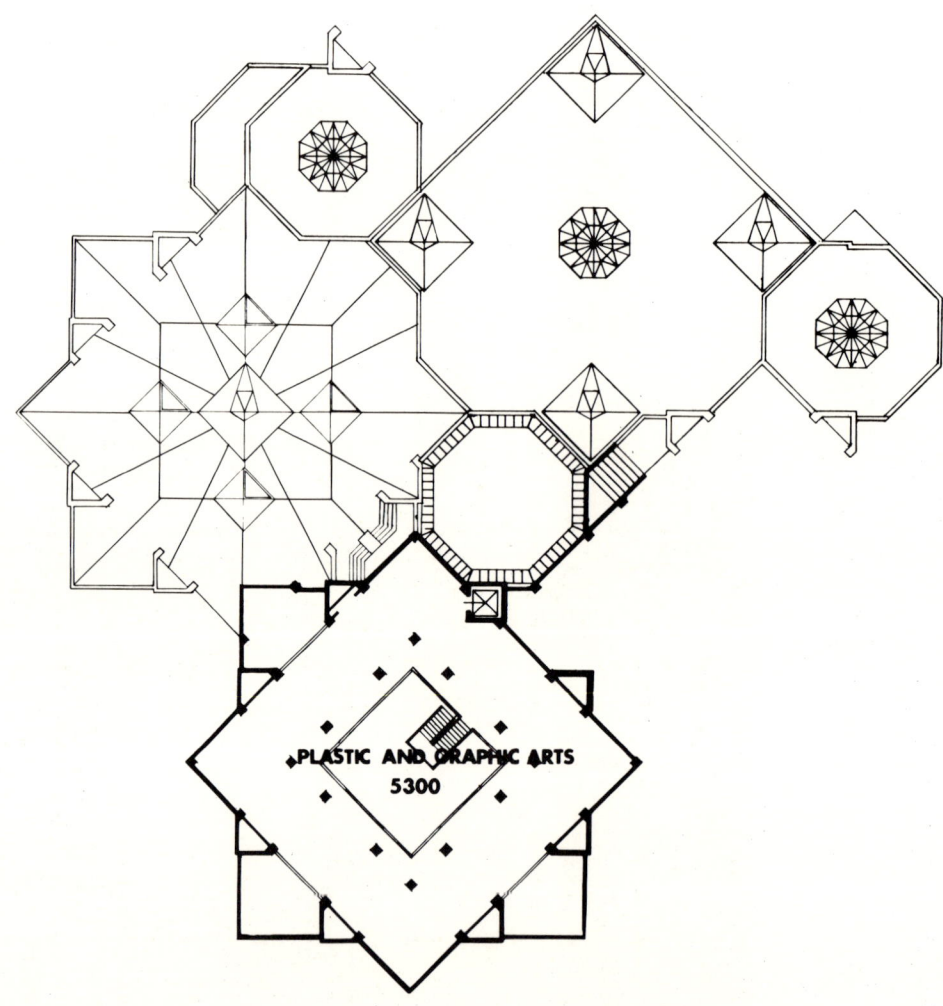

FIFTH LEVEL PLAN

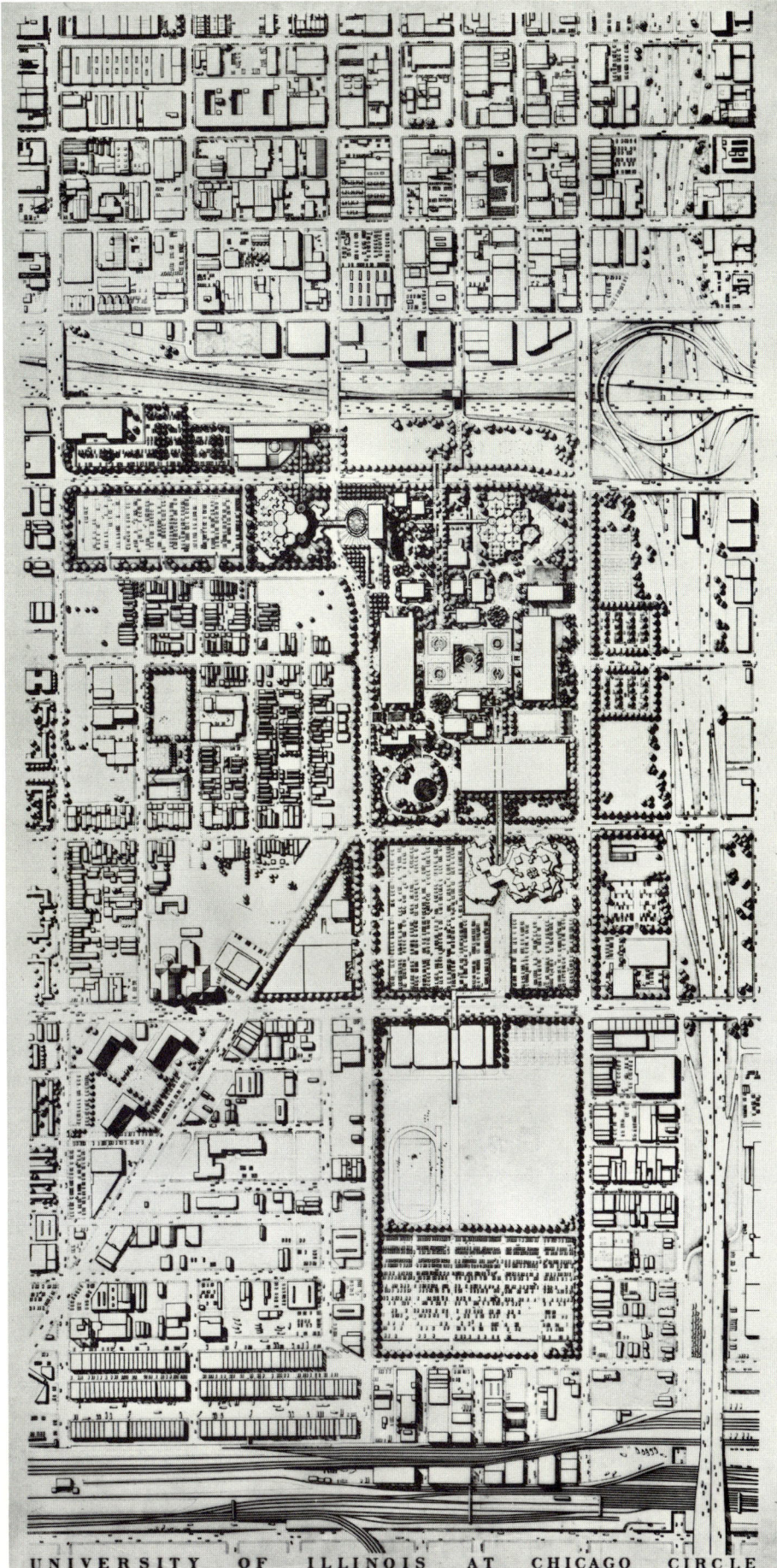

Master plan of the University of Illinois at Chicago Circle showing integration of the campus with the city's main transportation network.

Elegant external arcades of the State University of New York at Albany, designed by Edward Durell Stone. The first buildings were completed in 1969.

Model of the quintipartite scheme of the State University of New York at Albany which comprises the master plan of this new university complex.

One of the four planned educational satellite complexes, the State University of New York at Albany.

The School of Plastic Arts in suburban Havana, Cuba, designed by the Cuban architect Ricardo Porro, is a playfully organized cluster of domes, bubbles and curvilinear movement corridors. Elliptical-domed art studios, snakelike covered walkways converge and recede to form winding streets and plazas. The vital force and "sensualism" of the forms and spaces is rooted deeply in Spanish and African architectural traditions. The architect claims that eroticism in architecture is a "conscious symbol of life and fertility of the creative impulse . . ."

Chapter VI

The Arts, Recreation, and Religion

Urbanized, automated megalopolitan life changed not only the pattern of how people live, how they travel, work and learn, but also brought forth a completely new world of leisure activity and with it the need for new dimensions of space devoted to communal functions.

The traditional forms of urban entertainment, the stadium, the theater, the opera house, the music hall, the zoo, the museum and the picture gallery not only grew in size and importance but became significant spaces of the public urban system.

The stadium, for the first time since Roman days, became the dominant urban oasis of mass human contact and stimuli. The huge reinforced concrete elevated St. Louis stadium by Edward Durell Stone, located in the heart of the city and near Saarinen's Jefferson Memorial Arch, exemplifies the growing recognition that urban renewal must satisfy all needs of the people, including the age-old quest for mass spectator sports. Great strength, spans, and the cantilevered quality of modern reinforced concrete are utilized to the utmost in these mammoth structures. The Jefferson Memorial Arch itself is a symbol of the modern rediscovery of space, of man's quest to recreate himself and his spirit by defining the universality of space with simple forms. This 630-foot-high monument to modern technology at the service of man is the poetry of architecture at its best.

Pages 261-263

The modern opera house is portrayed in perhaps its most extravagant form in the reinforced concrete shell cluster of J. Utzon's Sydney Opera House. The renaissance of the performing arts in the second half of the twentieth century is here dramatized by the use of the form of the space to symbolize a new-found freedom of structural expression at its fullest.

Pages 264, 265

The marriage of the performing arts in such new cultural megastructures as the Lincoln Center in New York City or the John F. Kennedy Center in Washington may be criticized for the monumentality and lack of expression in bringing culture and art to those great urban masses that clamor for it. They are more a desperate attempt to revive the nineteenth-century form in a modern setting rather than to use cultural amenities within a well-located and integrated urban system of culture and recreational activities. In concept, form, structure, and space they reflect little of the modern spirit in urban space-time dimension.

Pages 266-269

The urban museum also has so far failed to be utilized as a dynamic means of education. We are still building such modern temples as the Guggenheim Museum in New York City by Frank Lloyd Wright or huge, static storehouses of artifacts such as the Smithsonian Museums in Washington. There are a few examples of the kind of integration of cultural displays and activities within housing, megastructures, office buildings, and schools which would bring this heritage within daily and intimate and accidental contact with the urban population. The first floor of the National Geographic Building by Edward Durell Stone in Washington, D.C., is an example of the total street-level floor devoted to display of man's achievements in space. Imagine the enrichment of city life if the art of the past and of today were strategically integrated with public urban spaces.

Pages 270, 271

The same would be true if the highly segregated mammoth large city zoo were to be carefully integrated into the existing park system. These points of interest would provide relief from the serious urban activity systems and permit the enjoyment of such fun structures as the Elephant House in London by Casson and Conder. These undulating, heavily textured hand-hammered concrete forms are clearly designed to a scale other than human.

Page 272

The new recreational facilities include such new structures as marine centers, devoted entirely to man's movement through space purely for recreation. These fun spaces permit experimentation with structure, highlighting the potential of structural modular systems. The embryonic design of a prototype Marine Shopping and Recreation Center by Neill Smith contains a translucent roof of basket-like wood lattice domes supported on laminated wood columns that spring from the platforms like giant ship masts.

Pages 273, 274

Perhaps the new dimensions of leisure space in architecture are most dramatically expressed in the experimental structures of the most recent world exhibitions. Montreal's Exposition in 1967 produced such large-scale structures as the twenty-story high "skybreak bubble" by Buckminster Fuller, the all-aluminum cantilevered space-frame Dutch pavilion, and West Germany's steel mesh and heavy fabric suspended construction.

Page 275

The Jefferson Westward Expansion Memorial, St. Louis, Missouri, the epic soaring arch structure which symbolizes not only America's past—the opening of the West—but also points the way to the future. With this design Eero Saarinen won the 1948 architectural competition, and the construction of the arch was completed about 20 years later.

Busch Memorial Stadium, St. Louis, Missouri, designed by Edward Durell Stone and built in 1965, reflects the baseball culture which has developed into ancient-game proportions in the United States during the second half of the twentieth century.

These displays of man's ability to conquer space add important dimensions to the form of the future city. It is these expressive and dramatic structures which will assist in providing sculptured points of interest in the megacity of tomorrow. They will serve the dominant role which the Gothic cathedral served in the medieval urbanscape.

The essence of religious space lies in its contrast with the surrounding environment. The modern church in a rural and suburban setting is capable of evoking emotions similar in content if not in form to the church building of the past. The diagonal and vertical form

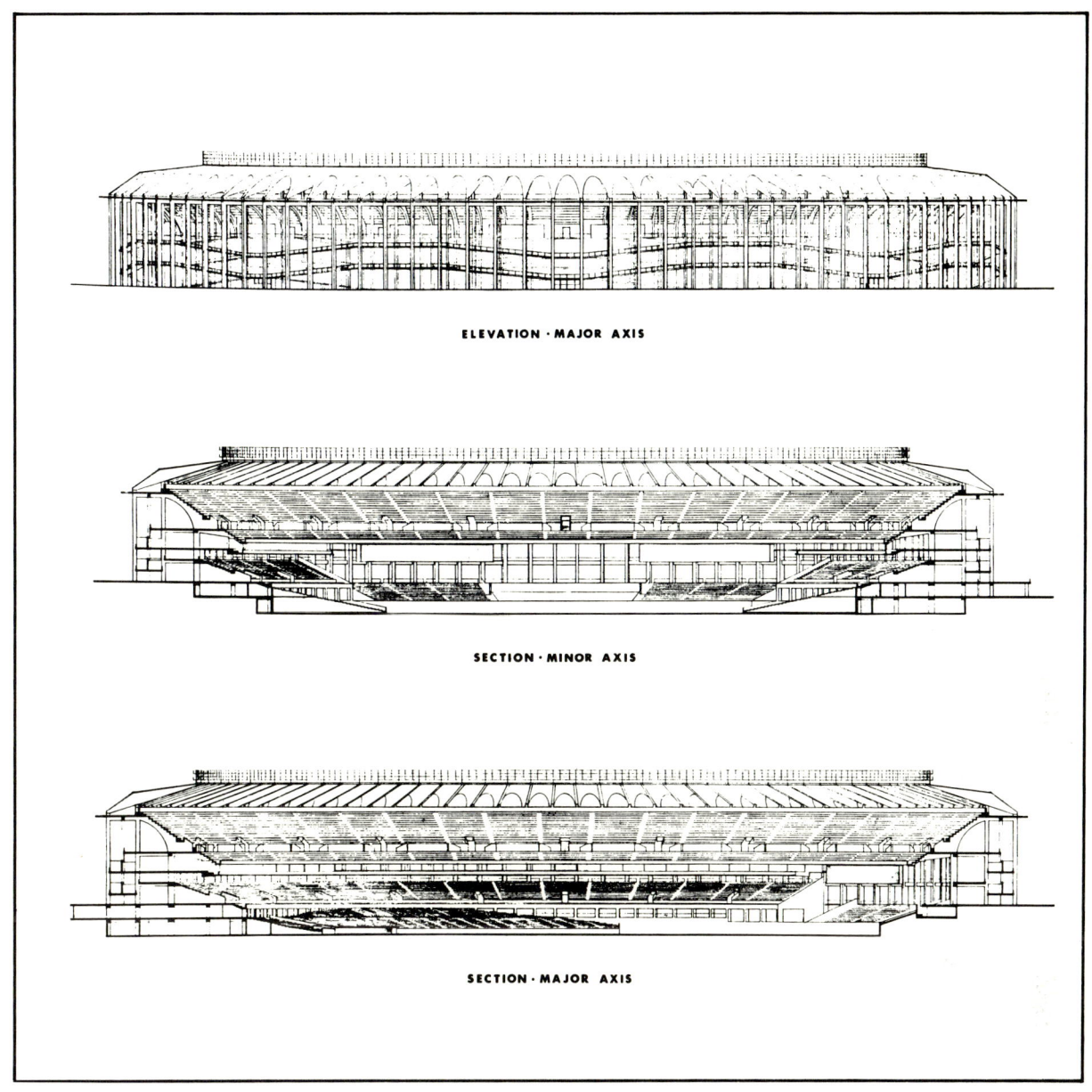

The enormous reinforced concrete structure elevated above the ground level, in the midst of an urban renewal area and surrounded by flashing highways, stands in naked contrast to the Jefferson Arch in the background.

of Wright's Unitarian Church in Wisconsin, built in 1947, or the Beth Sholom Synagogue in Pennsylvania, built in 1959, are basically suburban spaces of worship. Another outstanding example of modern church architecture is the great masterpiece of Le Corbusier, the dynamic space of Ronchamp Chapel. None of these suburban churches, however, provides an answer to the type of religious space which would be indigenous to and provide spatial context for the great megastructures of the future city.

Pages 280, 281

As the mass of the city, the movement systems, and the space itself have become more compact, more integrated and more dynamic, there has emerged an ever-increasing need for places of contemplation, of recovery of the spirit, of worship. In such an environment, competition in scale and mass is futile. The religious space must become the refuge, the

Once the building is completed and the first performances take place, the true test of this romantic expression of the new-found freedom of building technology will occur. The revolutionary nature of this building originated with the international competition, and with the desire to express in this building the hopes, aspirations, and dynamics of Australia.

264

With its gigantic reinforced concrete shell sails, the Opera House has been under construction on the edge of the Sydney Harbor for over eight years. The Danish architect, Jorn Utzon, won with this design the 1957 international competition.

The structure is not only extravagant in its form but also in the way the project cost was estimated. Originally estimated to cost under ten million Australian dollars, the actual cost rose so astronomically that in 1966 the estimate reached fifty million dollars. At that time the project was handed over for completion to a different group of architects and Jorn Utzon resigned.

The Lincoln Center for the Performing Arts in New York City, completed in 1966. In the background is a superimposed design of the Fordham University Lincoln Square Campus, Perkins and Will, architects.

View of Lincoln Center, showing clockwise from lower left, New York State Theater; Metropolitan Opera House and Vivian Beaumont Theater; Library and Museum of the Performing Arts; and Philharmonic Hall.

Model of the John F. Kennedy Center for the Performing Arts in Washington, D.C.; designed by Edward Durell Stone, the complex is due for completion in 1971. Monumental expression of today's dynamics of urban cultural life seems out of step with dignified static forms and spaces.

Model of the interior of the Opera House of the John F. Kennedy Center.

268

Model of the interior of the Theater of the John F. Kennedy Center. This early study of the space for late twentieth-century cultural recreation relates little to the heterogeneous and gregarious central urban life of today.

The Solomon R. Guggenheim Museum in New York City completed in 1959. Frank Lloyd Wright began designing this building in 1946. A building more at home in the prairies than with its venerable avenue neighbors—a conscious reminder that America begins but does not end with the New York skyscrapers.

Interior of the Solomon R. Guggenheim Museum with its cavelike space and illusion of continuous spiraling movement. It is a dramatic space with great theatrical quality that induces spontaneous action.

above: The Elephant and Rhinoceros House in the London Zoological Gardens in England, designed by the British architects Casson and Conder, and completed in 1965. Its exterior consists of hand-hammered, striated reinforced concrete walls and truncated metal roofs; monumental in its scale and texture.

right: The cross section and plan of the Elephant House indicate the space as being highly articulated and evince skillful functional separation of movement patterns between visitors and inhabitants.

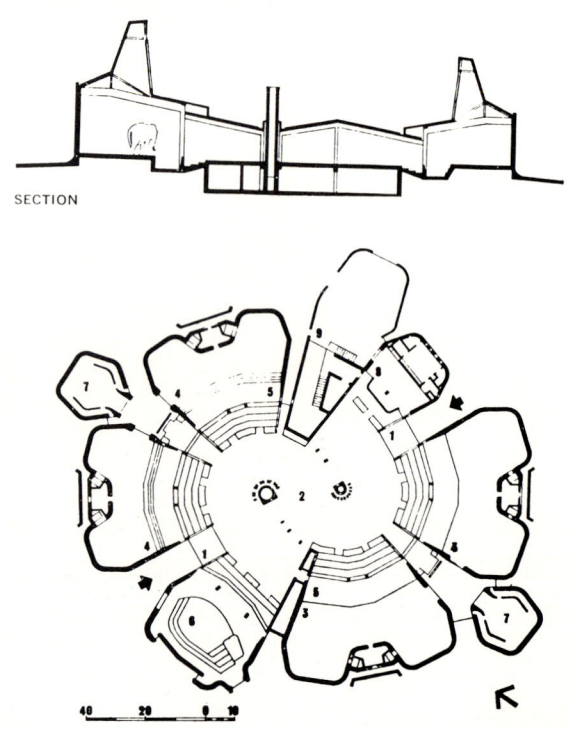

SECTION

PLAN

A marine shopping and recreation center, designed in 1968 by Neill Smith, exemplifies the poetic potentiality of wood as a building material in public buildings. Structure is the dominant element of this design, which echoes the sense of adventure and the ceaseless energy associated with the ocean.

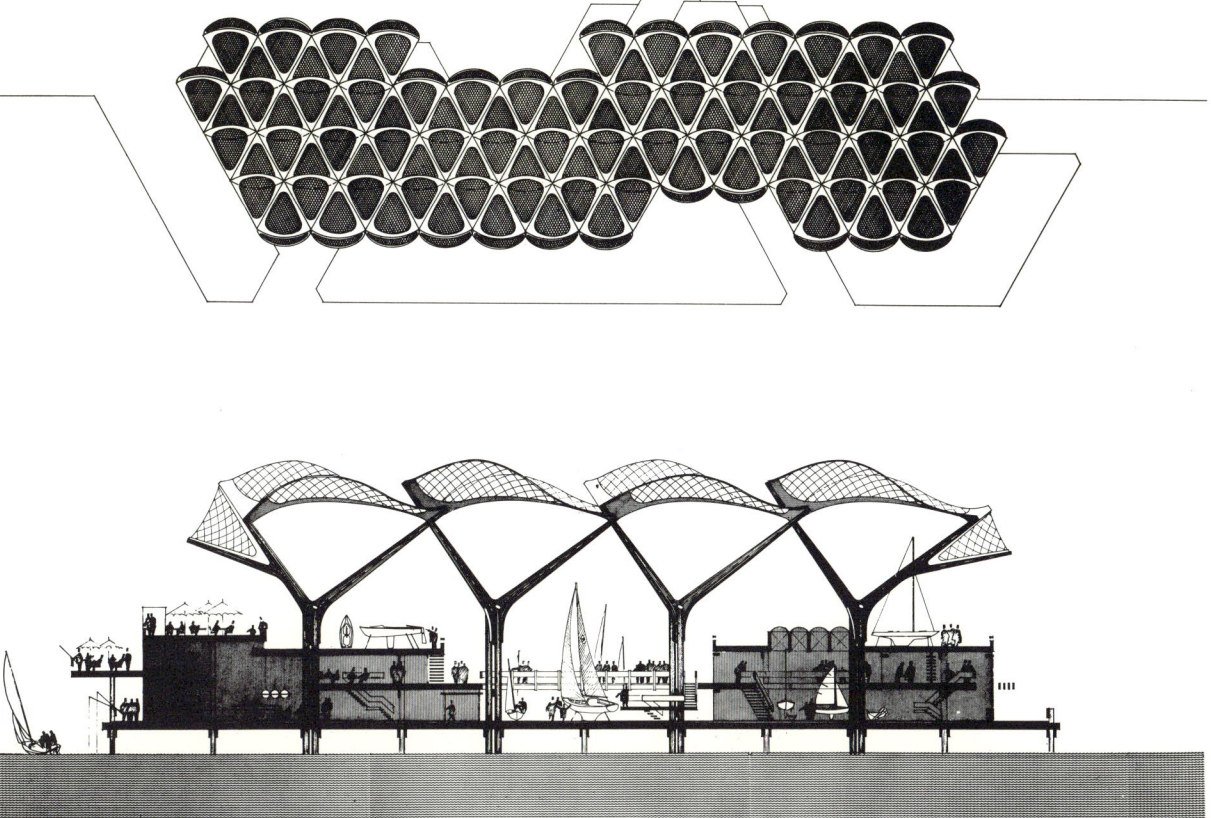

The inherent simplicity of the wood lattice dome and its modular potential is seen in the roof plan and section of the proposed marina center.

The floating canopied space is defined by laminated wood columns supporting a translucent roof consisting of wood lattice triangular plastic domes.

274

United States Pavilion at Montreal Exposition of 1967, designed by R. Buckminster Fuller. Fuller's early experimentation with the tetrahedron unit as a modular component of dome structure is carried here into spanning enormous distances, with minimum materials, least weight, and greatest economy.

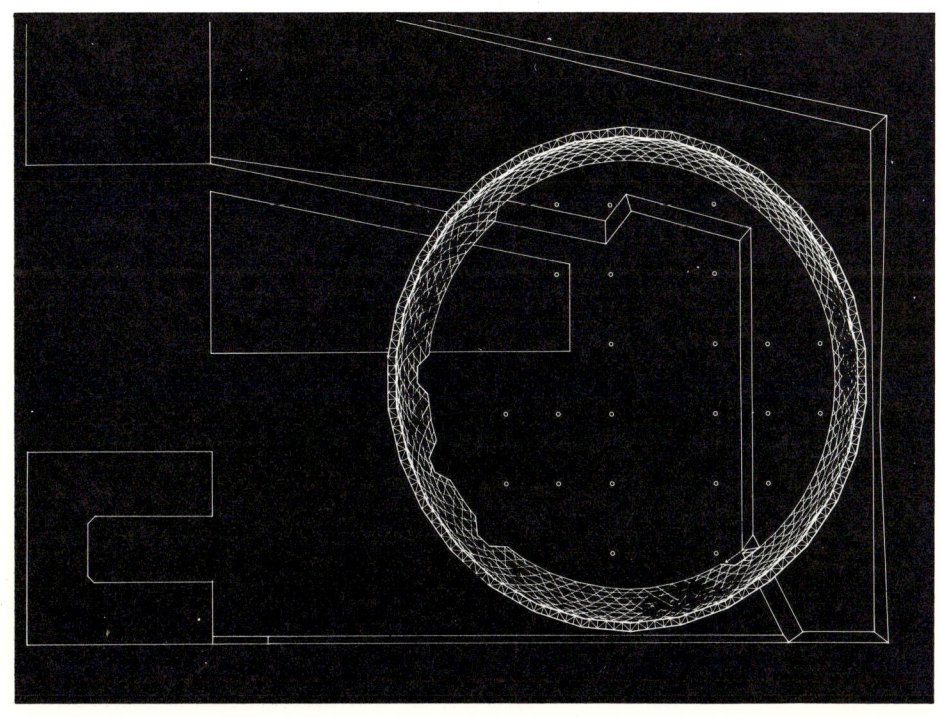

275

The Krannert Pavilion in Indianapolis, the new home of the Indianapolis Museum of Art, due for final completion in 1971. This elegant, simple, contemporary-classic museum building was designed by Richardson, Severns, Scheeler, in association with Wright, Porteous, and Lowe.

The interior of the building is as simple, straightforward, and successful as the exterior, clad in indigenous Indiana limestone. The windowless wing on the right is the Clowes Pavilion designed to display a magnificent art collection. Below the museum is a 1200-seat outdoor amphitheatre.

The Sports Center in Norfolk, Virginia, designed by Pier Luigi Nervi and completed in 1971.

Massive and dynamic concrete flying buttresses support the dome.

Model of a 4,000-bed tourist resort complex in Sithonia, Greece, designed in 1970 by The Architects Collaborative.

small, intimate cavelike space of the early Christians. The cathedral of the future may well be underground or in the most womblike internal place in the center of urban activity patterns. The smaller religious spaces may become an integral part of the street—an architectural interpretation of the store-window ghetto church. These places are more expressive of religious modern urban life than the ancient forms which fail to evoke the required emotion in modern man. An example of such a direct and straightforward modern solution is the Civic Center Synagogue by W. Breger in Manhattan, which provides a fluid, small and intimate space directly off the sidewalk—a religious oasis for the passerby.

Pages 281-283

Model of Sithonia tourist resort, Greece. The complex will include a golf course, a country club, convention hall, a casino, three chapels, a 2,000-seat amphitheatre, shopping center, and other ancillary tourist facilities.

The powerful and unusual form of the Beth Sholom Synagogue in Pennsylvania, designed by Frank Lloyd Wright and completed in 1959, generates a religious feeling in its monumental "memento mori" shape. The interior consists of a unified space, dramatically lit by day and night and imbued with a sense of fluidity.

The Unitarian Church in Wisconsin, Frank Lloyd Wright, architect, completed in 1947. The horizontal lines, characteristic of much of Wright's work, shoot up over the meeting place into a strong, diagonal, one-directional, folded-shape roof with a decisive and powerful determination.

The womblike spiritual space of the Ronchamp Chapel in France, designed by Le Corbusier, is the result of daring, brutalistic, and highly sculptured use of massive reinforced concrete forms. The interior of the chapel is lit through deep, small, and irregularly spaced recessed window openings which do not flood the sanctuary but admit light through clearly discernible sources, creating a feeling of a religious cave.

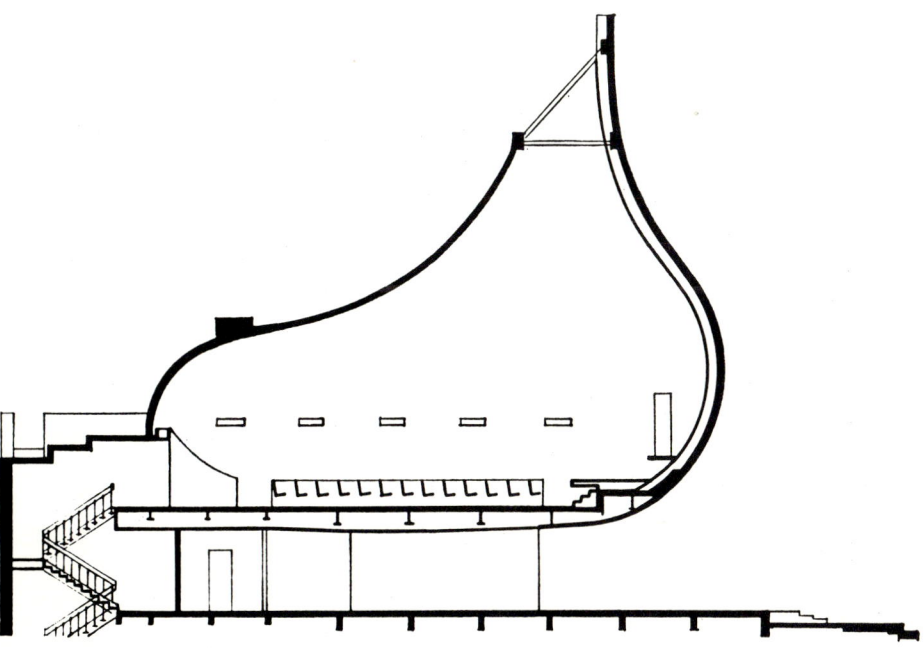

Cross section of the Civic Center Synagogue in New York City by William N. Breger, completed in 1967, is a small religious space carved out of an area formerly occupied by a New York brownstone apartment house.

The entire structure is only fifty feet wide, and its fluid facade expresses the purpose of the inner space but without disrupting the street as an urban unit.

282

The space of the sanctuary is located above the entrance court, defined by three concrete shells that are carried on the party walls of surrounding houses and lit by a space-frame skylight.

The charred cross of the bombed out Coventry Cathedral—a dramatic symbol of victory.

The new Coventry Cathedral in England designed by the well-known British architect Sir Basil Spence and consecrated in 1962. The war-destroyed old cathedral walls were retained as a war monument and the new structures well-integrated with the old in a direct and strong cultural and religious continuity.

The scale, texture, pattern, building materials and forms employed in the new structure have their roots deep in the spatial tradition of the old cathedral.

Chapter VII

The Evolving Microshelter

Although the connoisseur client who owns a house that has been designed for him by a master architect is becoming as rare as a person who owns a painting by Braque or Picasso, the study of these residential works of architecture gives an insight into the different philosophies and creative contribution of each artist-architect. Unfortunately, these custom-designed and custom-built residences cannot be experienced except by the few individuals who live in them. So far, no museums for these artifacts have been contemplated, and photographs of architecture are at best an unsatisfactory representation of the space contained. However, a discussion of these works of art is relevant to the subject of style in architecture.

Style is an abstraction. Among the leading twentieth-century architects there are almost as many styles as there are masters. Therefore, a style is only a useful means of classification of the general movements in twentieth-century architecture.

The master-architect-designed house is not the prisoner of its designer, since the space of the house is also an integral part of the overall environment and, after being lived in, contains not only the architect's ideas but especially the experiences of its inhabitants. House architecture is an extremely personal art in the creation of which both the client and the architect participate. The family that lives in such a house endows the space with its own influence and ideas.

The architecture of an individual house usually contains one dominant style, or two or more influences may be synthesized in a building, creating a new style. In modern house architecture one style may also be used by a variety of individual architects.

The foundation for twentieth-century architecture had been laid by the breaking of the Renaissance and Baroque sense of symmetry. During the nineteenth-century industrialization of the advanced countries, the whole social order changed, and architecture changed with it. As the large, educated middle class began to emerge, the form-givers were replaced by a renewed academic, theoretic approach to architecture; academicism and romanticism was the product, the reaction of sentiment against reason. Thus, Medieval, Roman, and Egyptian architectural elements became fashionable, finally evolving into the Victorian revival of past styles according to each man's fancy. Rationality became irrationality, and confidence became frustration.

Revivalism and romanticism in architecture did not mean a mere change of clothes; it meant an undiluted pursuit of historical forms and elements. By the mid-nineteenth century domestic architecture became completely academicized, that is, tight and rigid, easy to reproduce and to copy. Architects, instead of solving the new social problems, began to serve only those who could afford their services; and architecture, instead of being approached as a social art, became a highly personal affair. The concept that the design of the building should reflect the individuality and personality of the architect, the way a painting does a painter's, was easiest to apply in residential commissions for the very rich. This state of the art remained for almost one hundred years, and to shed its shackles twentieth-century architecture had to go through a great revolutionary movement.

In 1863, an English architect of French descent, A. W. Pugin, published his book in which he showed the artist for the first time since the Middle Ages, not as an isolated man but as a servant of society. Pugin's abhorrence of imitation in architecture and his calls for truth and reality had an important influence upon the later revolutionary movement.

John Ruskin and his advocate, William Morris, further advanced the cause against viewing architecture as a preconceived idea of what a building should look like and for working out its spatial composition according to its actual needs. The campaign of Morris' life was directed against the nineteenth-century lack of feeling for the essential unity of architecture and the world. He hated the architect's indifference to social needs and the separation of private space from public environment. Morris' theories, along with those of Ruskin and Pugin, formed the roots of the new idealism of twentieth-century architecture.

The remnants of the art-for-art's-sake theories, however, have remained to this day and are best exemplified in house architecture. While house architects were fighting the battle of styles, engineers were creating great new structures and spaces of a new era. By the beginning of the twentieth century the leading architects again assumed command and were among those who first understood the influence of mechanization, industrialization, and urbanization upon architecture. Among these architects were the members of the "international" school led by Le Corbusier in France and Walter Gropius in Germany.

In 1907, Peter Behrens was successful in founding the "Deutsche Werkbund," which gave impetus to the drive to get the architect in his rightful place in society and to bring art and industry into full collaboration. It was the first attempt towards the creation of a synoptic design team and eventually the systems approach to architecture and city planning. But it was not until after the First World War that this new architecture gained a real momentum.

Stein House, Les Terraces, Garches, near Paris, France, Le Corbusier and Pierre Jeanneret, 1927-28.

Savoye House, Poissey-sur-Seine, France, Le Corbusier and Pierre Jeanneret, 1929-30.

Walter Gropius represents this team approach to shaping architectural space. He was a member of the Werkbund, worked under Behrens, and his writing expressed his preoccupation with the application of modern technology towards solving modern problems of society. He was little interested, though, in individual house design throughout his long career.

Le Corbusier, a post-First World War celebrity, attempted to apply modern technology not only to macrostructures and city design, but also to the individual house which he believed could become a "house-machine" like the automobile. However, his houses, designed for the select connoisseur, are more interesting as works of art and not for their achievements in the application of prefabrication and mass production techniques.

Le Corbusier's houses possess a romantic, poetic spatial quality, although in his writings he is an advocate of the machine age. The Les Terraces House outside Paris at Garches, built in 1927, and the Villa Savoye at Poissey, built in 1930, are both masterful examples of creating moving, dynamic domestic spaces employing modern building materials.

Page 288

Romanticism found receptive soil in the United States in the nineteenth century. The American twentieth-century architects were hesitant, however, to use new materials in house architecture. Just as Le Corbusier did not believe in natural materials, since they could not be precise, clean, abstract and "colorless" as he wished, Frank Lloyd Wright loved them and his houses represent the indigenous organic school of architecture.

Wright despised the overcultivated man and his architecture. He saw academic sterility in such a man and in his space. While Le Corbusier spent great efforts in developing a mathematical formula for architectural proportions, to Wright, perceptual proportion in architecture was a result of philosophy rather than equations. Wright, in his domestic architecture, more than in the creation of any other space, expressed his philosophy that Nature ought to be the basic source of inspiration for architecture. The romantic love of nature, instead of the Renaissance drive to control it, was responsible for his great residential spaces.

Willets House, Highland Park, Illinois, Frank Lloyd Wright, 1902.

Robie House, Chicago, Illinois, Frank Lloyd Wright, 1908-09.

Barnsdall House, Hollywood, California, Frank Lloyd Wright, 1920.

Kaufmann House, Falling Water, Connellsville, Pennsylvania, Frank Lloyd Wright, 1936-37.

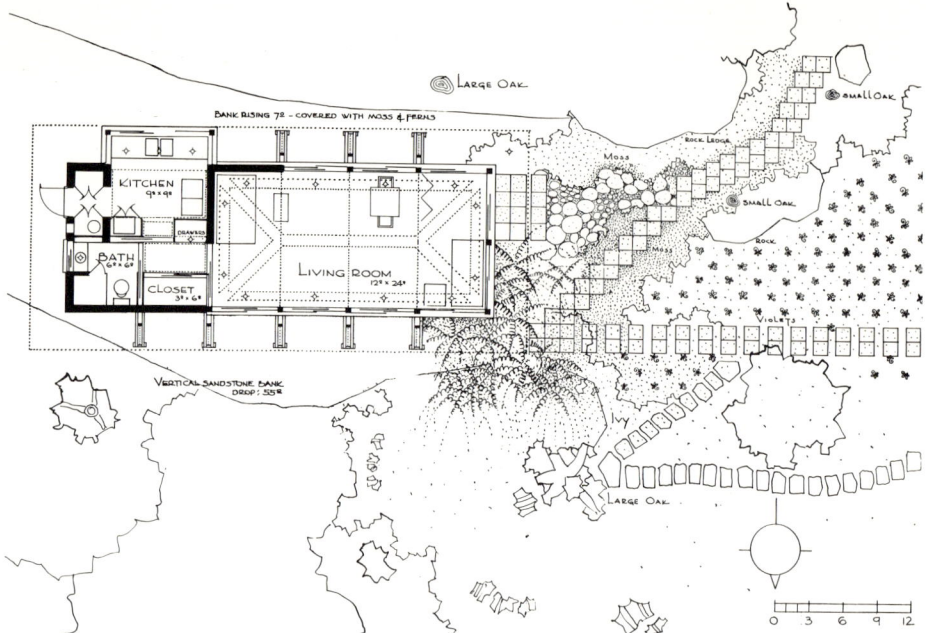

Plan of Fellowship Park House, Los Angeles, California, Harwell Hamilton Harris, 1936.

Interior of Fellowship Park House, Los Angeles, California, Harwell Hamilton Harris, 1936.

Ralph Johnson residence,
Los Angeles, California,
Harwell Hamilton Harris,
1948.

Bridgeman House, Stowe, Vermont, Daniel Urban Kiley and Julian Eugene Kulski, 1958.

Bridgeman House, Stowe, Vermont.

The Smith House,
Darien, Connecticut,
Richard Meier, 1968.

Plan of the Smith House,
Darien, Connecticut.

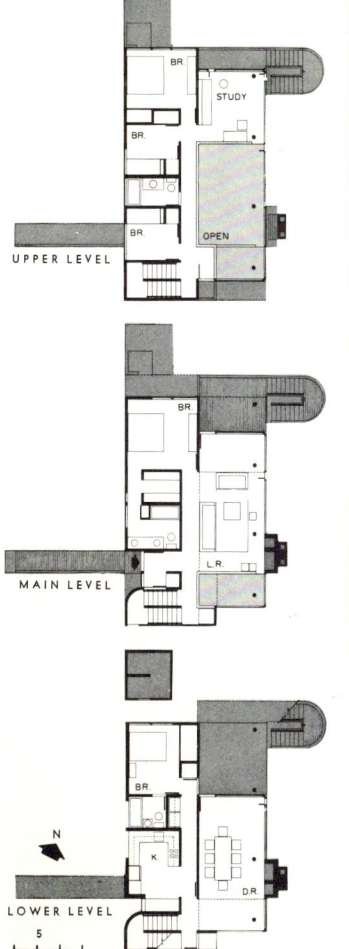

The Atrium House, Michigan, Gunnar Birkerts, 1967.

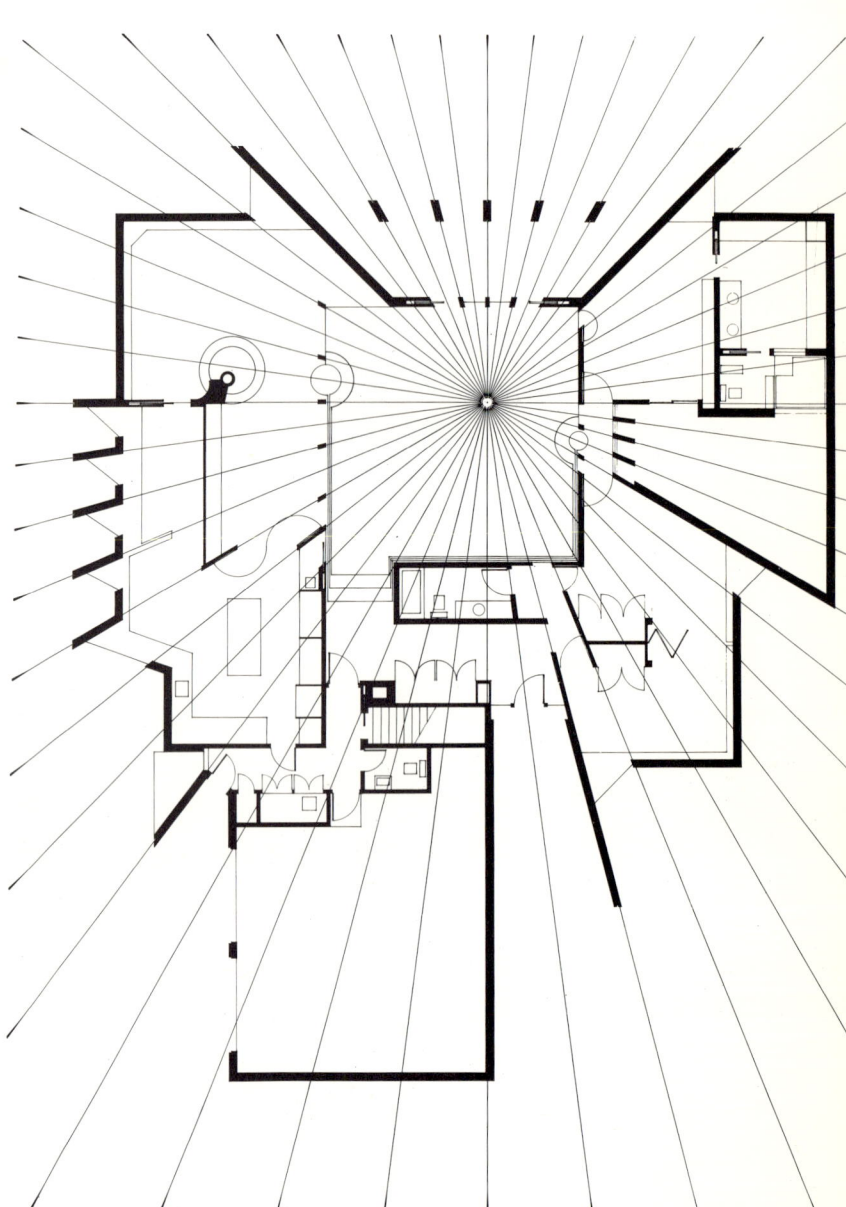

Plan of the Atrium House, Gunnar Birkerts.

296

Interior of the Atrium House, Gunnar Birkerts.

The Kreeger residence in Washington, D.C., is perhaps the best designed individual house of the 20th century—a contemporary version of the Renaissance Palazzo—housing the owner's exquisite collection of modern art. The design is based on the classic 22 foot square module which in the hands of Johnson turns into a space which is simple, dignified, and sophisticated.

Pages 299-301

The Ward Willits house in Highland Park, Illinois, is often considered the turning point in twentieth-century American residential architecture. The well-articulated elements of this house also indicate Wright's awareness of the changing nature of the American house, servants making way for household conveniences, life becoming less formal, and a new degree of flexibility and open planning becoming possible. Together with the Barnsdall House, the Robie House and the Kaufmann House, the Willits residence exemplified the total integration of the space of the family with the space of nature in a completely different medium, but equal poetically to the cubist architecture of Le Corbusier.

Pages 290, 291

Urbanization and increased leisure time, sports activity, skiing, boating, riding, have elevated the "summer home" of the early part of the twentieth century to the forefront of residential design. The Bridgeman House on the steep slopes of Stowe, Vermont, designed by the author, is an example of such a second home dedicated to communion with nature, to sports and to recreation.

Page 294

The Smith House by Richard Meier and the "Atrium House" by Gunnar Birkerts are perhaps the best examples of the master-architect-designed individual houses of the 1960s.

Pages 295-297

Japanese modular house construction had a tremendous influence upon the space of the modern house. The Fellowship Park House and the Johnson House at Los Angeles, California, by the American architect Harwell Hamilton Harris, are excellent examples of the application of the basketry of wood construction to creating spaces in a highly sophisticated understatement.

Pages 292, 293

In a world facing a threat of the extinction of architectural space and sociophysical chaos, the architect-environmentalist will no longer be able to confine his talents and efforts to the design of the individual house, using techniques which employ hand labor and hand-built materials. The future of the individual house as a work of art lies in the essence of the application of assembly-line type of production to shaping significant residential space.

David Lloyd Kreeger House in Washington, D.C., Philip Johnson, 1967.

Staircase, Kreeger House,
Washington, D.C.

The Great Hall, Kreeger
House, Washington, D.C.

PHOTO CREDITS

Frontispiece: Courtesy Litton Industries, Aero Service Division; pages 65-67, Courtesy Library of Congress; page 70, from *The Urban Pattern*, 2nd ed., by Arthur Gallion, (c) 1950, 1963 by Litton Educational Publishing Inc. by permission of Van Nostrand Reinhold Company; page 71, Courtesy The Museum of Modern Art, New York; page 73, Photo by Ollie Atkins; page 76 (top), Courtesy Whittlesey & Conklin; pages 76 (bottom) and 77-85, Photos by William A. Graham, Arlington, Va.; page 86, Photo by Julian E. Kulski; page 87, Courtesy Gulf Reston Inc.; page 88, Photo by Ezra Stoller Associates, Inc., Rye, N.Y., Courtesy James W. Rouse & Co., Inc.; pages 92-93, Photos by Winants Bros., Inc., Baltimore, Md.; page 94, Courtesy James W. Rouse & Co., Inc.; page 95, Photo by Max Araujo, Baltimore, Md.; page 97, Courtesy Library of Congress; pages 108-109, Courtesy Chandigarh Planning Office, Chandigarh, India; pages 111-112, Photos by Louis Checkman, Jersey City, N.J.; Courtesy Edward Durell Stone; pages 113 and 120-125, Courtesy Islamabad Planning Office, Islamabad, Pakistan; pages 130-131 and 134-135, Courtesy Information Office of the City of Brasilia, Brazil; page 138, Courtesy Library of Congress; page 140, Photo by A. K. Strobl, Courtesy Philadelphia City Planning Commission; page 141 (top), Courtesy Geddes, Brecher, Qualls & Cunningham; page 141 (bottom), Photo by Lawrence S. Williams, Inc., Courtesy Vincent Kling; page 144, Photo by Davis Studio, Washington, D.C.; pages 147-149, Courtesy Keyes, Lethbridge and Condon, Washington, D.C.; page 153, Courtesy Canadian Central Mortgage & Housing Corp.; pages 156-157, Photo by Allen, Washington, D.C., page 156 (bottom), Photo by J. Alexander, Wheaton, Md., all Courtesy Keyes, Lethbridge and Condon; pages 158-159, Courtesy Burger and Coplans; pages 160-161, Photos by David Hirsch, Brooklyn, N.Y., Courtesy The Architects Collaborative, Inc.; page 164, Courtesy Library of Congress; page 165 (bottom), Courtesy U.S. Department of Commerce, Bureau of Public Roads; pages 165 (top)-167, Courtesy Department of Public Works, Division of Highways, State of California; pages 170-171, Courtesy Burger and Coplans; pages 172-175, Courtesy Tube Transit, Inc.; pages 178-179, Courtesy The Port of New York Authority; pages 180-181, Photos by Charles P. Mills, Philadelphia, Pa., Courtesy Philadelphia City Planning Commission; page 183, Courtesy Chicago Area Transportation Study; page 185, Courtesy Roy P. Harrover & Associates, Memphis, Tenn.; page 187, Photos by Bill Engdahl, Hedrich-Blessing, Chicago, Ill.; pages 191-193, Courtesy Golemon, Rolfe, Pierce and Pierce; pages 194-195, Courtesy The Port of New York Authority; page 196, Photos by Liddle & Kohn, Miami, Fla., Courtesy John Andrews; pages 198-199, Courtesy The Museum of Modern Art, New York; pages 200-201, Courtesy Howard University, Washington, D.C.; page 203, Courtesy The Port of New York Authority; page 204, Courtesy New York City Planning Commission; pages 206-207 (top), Photos by Ezra Stoller Associates, Inc., Mamaroneck, N.Y., Courtesy Toronto City Planning Commission; page 207 (bottom), Courtesy New Zealand Embassy, Washington, D.C.; pages 208-209, Photos by Louis Reens, New York, Courtesy The Architects Collaborative, Inc.; pages 210-211, Photos by Ezra Stoller Associates, Inc., Rye, N.Y., Courtesy Edward Durell Stone; pages 212-213, Courtesy Gunnar Birkerts; page 214, Photo by Robert D. Harvey Studio, Boston, Mass., Courtesy The Architects Collaborative, Inc.; page 215, Courtesy The Architects Collaborative, Inc., Cambridge, Mass.; page 216, Photo by Louis Reens, New York, Courtesy The Architects Collaborative, Inc., pages 217-219, Photos by Ezra Stoller Associates Inc., Mamaroneck, N.Y., Courtesy The Architects Collaborative, Inc.; pages 222-223, Courtesy Eliot Noyes and Associates; top of pages 224-225, Courtesy Edward L. Barnes; bottom of pages 224-225, Photos by Orlando R. Cabanban, Oak Park, Ill., Courtesy Edward L. Barnes; page 226 (top), Courtesy Gunnar Birkerts; pages 226 (bottom)-229, Photos by Orlando R. Cabanban, Oak Park, Ill., Courtesy Gunnar Birkerts; page 231, Courtesy Hellmuth, Obata and Kassabaum; pages 234-235, Courtesy Philadelphia City Planning Commission; pages 233 and 236, Photo by Julian E. Kulski; page 237 (top), Photo by Robert D. Harvey Studio, Boston, Mass., Courtesy The Architects Collaborative, Inc.; page 237 (bottom), Photo Phokion Karas, Melrose, Mass., Courtesy The Architects Collaborative, Inc.; pages 238-239, Photos by George Cserna, New York, Courtesy John M. Johansen; page 242 (top), Photo by Morley Baer, Berkeley, Calif., page 242 (bottom), Photo by Karl H. Riek, San Francisco, Calif., both Courtesy Ernest J. Kump; page 243, Photo by Hatfield, Courtesy Ernest J. Kump; page 244 (top), Courtesy Ernest J. Kump; page 244 (bottom), Photo by Dudley, Hardin & Yang, Inc., Seattle, Wash.; pages 245-247, Courtesy Louis I. Kahn;

page 248, Courtesy Giancarlo De Carlo; page 249, Photo by Balthazar Korab, Birmingham, Mich., Courtesy Gunnar Birkerts; page 250 (top), Courtesy John Andrews; page 250 (bottom), Photo by John Reeves, Toronto, Canada, Courtesy John Andrews; pages 252-253, Photos by Orlando R. Cabanban, Oak Park, Ill., Courtesy Skidmore, Owings and Merrill; pages 254-255, Courtesy Skidmore, Owings & Merrill; page 256 (top), Photo by Harold Corsini, Pittsburgh, Pa., page 256 (bottom), Photo by Louis Checkman, Jersey City, N.J., both Courtesy Edward Durell Stone; page 257, Photo by Ezra Stoller Associates, Inc., Rye, N.Y., Courtesy Edward Durell Stone; page 258, Photo by Paolo Gasparini; page 262, Courtesy Edward Durell Stone; page 263, Photo by Louis Checkman, Jersey City, N.J., Courtesy Edward Durell Stone; page 264, Photo by M. K. Challenger, New South Wales, Wahroonga, Australia, Courtesy Australian Embassy, Washington, D.C.; page 266, Photo by Louis Checkman, Jersey City, N.J., Courtesy The Perkins and Will Partnership; page 267, Photo by Bob Serating, New York; page 268, Courtesy John F. Kennedy Center, Washington, D.C.; page 269, Photo by Ezra Stoller Associates, Inc., Mamaroneck, N.Y., Courtesy Edward Durell Stone; pages 270-271, Courtesy The Solomon R. Guggenheim Museum, New York; page 272 (top), Photo by H. de Burgh Galway and Hank Snock; page 272 (bottom), Courtesy Casson, Conder & Partners; pages 273-274, Courtesy Neill Smith and Associates; page 275, Courtesy R. Buckminster Fuller; page 276, Photos by Bill Engdahl, Hedrich-Blessing, Chicago, Ill., Courtesy Indianapolis Museum of Art; page 277 (top), Courtesy Norfolk City Planning Commission; pages 277 (bottom), Photo by Studio III, Norfolk, Va., Courtesy Norfolk City Planning Commission; pages 278-279, Photos by Robert D. Harvey Studio, Boston, Mass., Courtesy The Architects Collaborative, Inc.; page 280, Courtesy Howard University, Washington, D.C.; page 281 (top) Photo by Wayne Andrews; pages 281 (bottom)-283, Courtesy William N. Breger; pages 284-285, Photos by The British Travel Association, London, England; pages 288-291 (bottom), Courtesy The Museum of Modern Art, New York; page 291 (top) Courtesy Howard University, Washington, D.C.; page 292 (top) Courtesy Harwell Hamilton Harris; page 292 (bottom), Photo by Fred R. Dapprich, Los Angeles, Calif., Courtesy Harwell Hamilton Harris; page 293, Photo by Maynard L. Parker, Los Angeles, Calif., Courtesy Harwell Hamilton Harris; page 295, Courtesy Richard Meier; page 296 (top)-297, Photos by Bill Engdahl, Hedrich-Blessing, Chicago, Ill., Courtesy, Gunnar Birkerts; page 296 (bottom), Courtesy Gunnar Birkerts; page 299, Photos by Ezra Stoller Associates, Inc., Mamaroneck, N.Y.

COLOR TRANSPARENCY CREDITS

Pages 74-77, Julian E. Kulski; pages 90-91, Courtesy James W. Rouse & Co., Inc.; pages 99-123, page 126, Julian E. Kulski; pages 128-133, Courtesy Brazilian American Cultural Institute; pages 150-151, Julian E. Kulski; pages 176-177, Courtesy Washington Metropolitan Transit Authority; pages 188-189, Julian E. Kulski; page 261, (St. Louis) Courtesy St. Louis City Planning Commission; page 265, (Sydney) Courtesy Australian News and Information Bureau; page 294, Julian E. Kulski.

INDEX

academic commons—p. 221, 222, 240, 241
Academy of Environmental Sciences—p. 60, 61
Acorn housing project—p. 158, 159
Afghanistan—p. 110
African architecture—p. 258
agrarian urbanism—p. 69
Ahmedabad Business College—p. 240, 241, 244, 245, 246, 247
air passenger travel—p. 190
air pollution—p. 45
airport megastructures—p. 190
airports—p. 184, 186, 190
air-rights housing—p. 154, 155, 163, 170, 171
Albany, N.Y.—p. 249
American architecture—p. 21, 22, 40, 41, 51, 59, 60, 61
American Institute of Architects—p. 59, 60, 61, 214, 215
American Institute of Planners—p. 60
Andrews, John—p. 190, 196, 243, 250, 251
Appenine Hills—p. 241
architectometrics—p. 19
Architects Collaborative, The—p. 160, 208, 209, 214, 215, 216, 217, 218, 219, 237, 279
architecture and group psychology—p. 27, 28, 48, 49
architecture of movement—p. 18, 21, 22, 23, 24, 25, 26, 29, 30, 42, 162, 163, 172, 173, 182, 184, 186, 190
architectural space—p. 17, 18, 22, 23, 24, 28, 29, 30, 35, 36, 41, 51
Athens, Greece—p. 208, 209
Atlanta, Ga.—p. 43
"Atrium house"—p. 296, 297, 298
Atomic Research Institute, Islamabad—p. 110, 112, 114, 116, 117, 119
auditory system of perception—p. 35
Australia—p. 259
Aztec temples—p. 39
background architecture—p. 23, 24, 31, 32, 35, 36
balance of stimuli—p. 25, 26, 31, 32, 33, 34, 35, 36, 37
Baltimore, Md.—p. 89
Barnes, Edward Larrabee—p. 221, 224, 225
Barnsdall house—p. 291, 298
behavioral science and architecture—p. 17, 18, 19, 20, 21, 27, 28, 29, 30, 34, 35, 36
Behrens, Peter—p. 287

Bellevue Community College—p. 240
Berlin—p. 160, 161, 198, 199
Beth Sholom Synagogue—p. 262, 263, 280
Birkerts, Gunnar—p. 210, 212, 222, 226, 227, 228, 229, 241, 249, 295, 296, 297, 298
black inner city neighborhood—p. 58
black ghetto—p. 20
black removal—p. 58
black rural college—p. 241
black society—p. 20, 59
Boston—p. 43, 172, 175, 205, 207
Braque—p. 279
Brasilia—p. 98, 127, 128, 129, 130, 131, 132, 133, 134, 135, 136, 137, 139
Brazil—p. 98, 127
Breger, William—p. 279, 281, 282, 283
Bridgeman house—p. 294, 298
Brigden, S. W.—p. 120, 121
Broadacre city—p. 69, 70, 71
Buffalo, N.Y.—p. 197
Burger and Coplans—p. 155, 158, 159, 163, 170, 171
Calcutta—p. 110
Casson and Conder—p. 260, 272
Caudill, Rowlett, Scott—p. 84, 85, 230
central terminal spaces—p. 40, 42, 43
Chandigarh—p. 97, 98, 100, 101, 102, 103, 104, 105, 106, 107, 108, 109, 110, 205
Chicago—p. 43, 182, 183, 197
Chicago School of Architecture—p. 197
Christ-Janer, Victor—p. 233, 236
Cincinnati—p. 43
city design—p. 18, 19, 20, 22, 23, 24, 29, 30, 42, 43, 64, 68, 69, 72, 89, 96, 98, 101, 110, 127, 139, 140
Civic Center Synagogue—p. 279, 281, 282, 283
Clark University—p. 236, 238, 239
Cohen, Haft and Associates—p. 84, 85
college campus—p. 232, 240, 241, 243, 249
college enrollment—p. 240
Columbia, Md.—p. 69, 88, 89, 90, 91, 93, 94, 95
Columbia Plaza, Washington, D.C.—p. 142, 147
Columbus, Ind.—p. 221, 222, 223, 224, 225, 226, 227, 228, 229, 240
communion with space—p. 17, 21, 22, 23, 24, 25, 26, 27, 28, 29, 30

Congres Internationaux de l' Architecture Moderne
(CIAM)—p. 143
continuity of space—p. 22, 23, 24, 25, 26
contrast of spatial direction—p. 31, 32, 33, 34, 35, 36
conurbations—p. 43
Copenhagen—p. 182
Cornell University—p. 233
Costa, Lucio—p. 127, 130, 131
courthouse cluster—p. 143, 144
Coventry cathedral—p. 284, 285
Crane, David A.—p. 155
Cuba—p. 254
cultural continuity—p. 139
cultural ecology—p. 24, 41
custom-designed residence—p. 286, 287, 289, 298
Dalokay, Vedat—p. 113
Daytona, Fla.—p. 43
De Carlo, Giancarlo—p. 241, 248
density variation ratio—p. 31
Detroit—p. 43
diseconomies of urbanization—p. 48
Doxiadis, Constantinos—p. 110, 120, 121
Dulles International Terminal—p. 22, 186, 188, 189
dynamic asymmetry—p. 33
dynamic opposition of elements—p. 31, 32, 33
economic development and architecture—p. 17, 20,
 48, 49, 50, 52, 53, 54, 55, 56
economic values in architecture—p. 18, 19, 20, 21, 22
education and architecture—p. 56, 57
educational facilities—p. 220, 221, 222, 230, 232, 233,
 236, 240, 241, 243, 249, 254
educational noise center—p. 221
emotion-evoking variables—p. 31, 32, 33, 34, 35, 36,
 37, 38, 39
environmental architecture—p. 18, 19, 43, 44
environmental data processing centers—p. 53
Environmental Development Corporation—p. 53, 54,
 55, 56, 59
environmental development policy—p. 40, 49, 52, 53,
 54, 55
environmental design—p. 18, 19, 20, 25, 26
environmental design schools—p. 60
environmental megastructure—p. 25
environmental noise—p. 45
environmental policies—p. 40, 45, 46, 47, 48, 49, 50
environmental variables—p. 25, 35, 36, 37, 38, 39
Fellowship Park house—p. 292, 298
Finley, William—p. 89
Florence—p. 38
Fonseca, Gonzalo—p. 80, 81
Fort Lincoln, Washington, D.C.—p. 155, 156, 157
Foothill College—p. 240, 242, 243, 244
Franzen, Ulrich—p. 233
Fry, Maxwell—p. 98
Fuller, Buckminster—p. 260, 275
Garden city—p. 65, 66, 67, 72
Geddes, Brecher, Qualls, Cunningham—p. 141
Geddes, Patrick—p. 68
George Washington bridge—p. 176, 177
ghetto environment—p. 20
Golden Section—p. 34
Goleman, Rolfe, Pierce and Pierce—p. 190, 191, 192,
 193
Goodman, Charles—p. 74, 75, 78, 79, 83

government center—p. 205
Greek city space—p. 22
Greenbelt, Md.—p. 69
Greendale, Wis.—p. 69
Greenhills, Ohio—p. 69
Gropiusstadt—p. 160, 161
Gropius, Walter—p. 144, 160, 208, 209, 287, 289
Guggenheim Museum—p. 260, 270, 271
Habitat—p. 152, 153
Harris, Harwell Hamilton—p. 291, 292, 293, 298
Harrover, Roy—p. 184, 185, 187
Hashim, A. F. M.—p. 125
Havana School of Plastic Arts—p. 254, 258
Hellmuth, Obata and Kassabaum—p. 230, 231
hierarchy of sociophysical variables—p. 30
high-rise housing—p. 145, 152
historic continuity—p. 110, 139, 140
Hoppenfeld, Morton—p. 89
horizontal city—p. 64, 68, 69, 73, 89
housing—p. 17, 50, 55, 145, 147, 152, 153, 154, 155
housing megastructures—p. 154, 155
housing standards—p. 145
Houston—p. 43, 190, 191, 192, 193
Houston International Airport—p. 190, 191, 192, 193
Howard, Ebenezer—p. 64, 65, 66, 67, 72
imbalance of economies—p. 48, 49
India—p. 68, 98, 100, 101, 110, 210, 240, 244, 245,
 246, 247
Indianapolis Museum—p. 276
individual houses—p. 286, 287, 289, 298
individual space—p. 24, 27, 143, 145
integration of emotional stimuli—p. 36
international architect—p. 49, 287
International Bank for Reconstruction and
 Development—p. 230
Islamabad—p. 98, 110, 112, 113, 114, 115, 116, 117,
 119, 120, 121, 122, 123, 124, 125, 127
Islamabad, University of—p. 110
Italian renaissance—p. 38
Japanese house—p. 34, 298
Jeanneret, Pierre—p. 98
Jefferson, Thomas—p. 51
Jefferson Memorial Arch—p. 259, 261, 263
Johansen, John M.—p. 236, 238, 239
Johnson house—p. 293, 298
Johnson, Philip—p. 298, 299, 300, 301
Johnson Wax Company Building—p. 197, 200, 201
Kabul—p. 110
Kahn, Louis—p. 51, 232, 234, 235, 240, 241, 244, 245,
 246, 247
Kallmann, McKinnell and Knowles—p. 205, 207
Kaufmann house—p. 291, 298
Kennedy Center for the Performing Arts—p. 259,
 268, 269
Kennedy International Airport—p. 186
Keyes, Lethbridge and Condon—p. 145, 147, 155, 156,
 157
Kiley, Daniel Urban—p. 294
kinetic sequence—p. 25
Kling, Vincent G.—p. 140, 141
Krannert Pavilion—p. 276
Kreeger house—p. 298, 299, 300, 301
Kump, Masten and Hurd—p. 240, 242, 243, 244
Lahore Office Building—p. 126, 210

Lake Erie College—p. 233, 236
Larkin Company Building—p. 197
La Ville Contemporaine—p. 96
law of continuity—p. 32
law of proximity—p. 32
law of similarity—p. 32
Le Corbusier—p. 34, 37, 96, 97, 98, 100, 101, 102, 103, 104, 105, 106, 107, 144, 205, 262, 263, 281, 287, 288, 289
leisure space in architecture—p. 260
lender of last resort—p. 55
Les Terraces house—p. 289
Letchworth—p. 68
local color—p. 38
Logue, Edward—p. 155
Lincoln Center for the Performing Arts—p. 266, 267
London—p. 260, 272
low-interest loans—p. 56
Los Angeles—p. 43, 298
Louisville—p. 43
man and environment—p. 21, 24, 25, 26, 27, 28, 29, 30
Mann and Harrover—p. 184, 185, 187
mannerism—p. 36
Manhattan—p. 44, 172, 197, 202, 204, 279
Margalla mountains—p. 110
marine center—p. 260
Martins, M.—p. 133
mass education and architecture—p. 56, 220, 230, 232, 240
matrix of confusions—p. 32, 33
Mayan architecture—p. 38
Mayer, Albert—p. 98, 108
mechanical movement—p. 21, 22, 23, 24, 25, 26
medieval space—p. 23
Mediterranean—p. 143
mega-high school—p. 230, 231
Meier, Richard—p. 295, 298
memento mori in architecture—p. 240, 280
Memphis—p. 184, 185, 187
Metropolitan Cathedral—p. 128, 129
metropolitan sprawl—p. 44
Miami—p. 43, 190, 196
Miami Passenger Terminal—p. 190, 196
Mies van der Rohe—p. 197, 198, 199
Minneapolis—p. 210
Minneapolis Federal Reserve Bank—p. 210
modular housing cluster—p. 148
Mogul—p. 110, 210, 241
Montreal—p. 152, 260
Moretti, Luigi—p. 150, 151
Morris, William—p. 287
movement patterns—p. 24, 25, 26
movement scale—p. 24
movement systems—p. 25
multidimensional objects—p. 31, 32, 33
multivariable complexes—p. 44, 45
Narramore, Bain, Brady and Johnson—p. 240
National Bank of Reconstruction and Development—p. 59
National Geographic Society Headquarters—p. 210, 211, 260
national investment institution—p. 53, 54, 55, 56
Nervi, Pier Luigi—p. 172
Netsch, Walter—p. 250, 251, 252, 253, 254, 255

Newark Airport—p. 190, 194, 195
Newark, N.J.—p. 190, 194, 195
New Deal towns—p. 69
New Haven—p. 162
New Orleans—p. 43
new social demands—p. 20, 45, 46, 47, 48, 49, 50
New York—p. 43, 172, 175, 202, 204, 266, 267, 270, 271
New York State—p. 54
New York State University—p. 249, 256, 257
New Zealand Parliament Buildings—p. 207
Niemeyer, Oscar—p. 127, 128, 129, 131, 135, 136, 137
nineteenth century space—p. 20
no-interest credits—p. 56
noise pollution—p. 45
Northeast Megalopolis—p. 172, 174, 175
Notre Dame du Haut—p. 37
nonarchitectural space—p. 20
Nowicki, Matthew—p. 98, 108, 109
Noyes, Eliot—p. 221, 222, 223, 240
nucleated air megaterminal—p. 187
Oakland—p. 155, 159
office buildings—p. 197, 200, 202, 204, 205, 210
Pakistan—p. 68, 98, 110, 210
Palazzo Riccardi—p. 38
Paris—p. 289
Parker, Barry—p. 68
passenger port facility—p. 190
Penn, William—p. 51, 138, 139, 140
perception of architecture—p. 26, 162
perception of space—p. 24, 25, 29
perceptual orchestration—p. 36
perceptual proportion—p. 33, 34, 35, 36
perspective and psychoarchitecture—p. 28, 29, 30
Philadelphia—p. 138, 139, 140, 141, 142, 173
Picasso, Pablo—p. 279
Pinney and Ong—p. 155
Pittsburgh—p. 43, 230
pollution and architecture—p. 44, 45, 46, 47
Ponti, Gio—p. 110, 118, 122, 124
Portland—p. 43
Porro, Ricardo—p. 254, 258
post-moon movement—p. 24, 25, 26, 27, 28
postwar architecture—p. 51
Potwar Plateau—p. 110
prefabricated buildings—p. 57, 152, 153
pre-moon movement—p. 22, 23, 24
Professional Development Program—p. 59
psychoarchitecture—p. 26
psychology of architecture—p. 19
psychophysics—p. 31
Puerto Rico—p. 154
Pugin, A. W.—p. 287
Punjab—p. 100, 110
racial and economic inequities—p. 50
racial minorities—p. 50
Racine, Wis.—p. 197, 200, 201
Radburn, N.J.—p. 68
radial corridor—p. 44
Raleigh, N.C.—p. 43
recreational facilities—p. 259, 260
Rawalpindi—p. 110
religious facilities—p. 262, 263, 279
religious school buildings—p. 241

religious space—p. 262, 263, 279
renaissance perspective—p. 29
renaissance space—p. 23
residential overcrowding—p. 145
Reston, Va.—p. 69, 72, 73, 74, 75, 76, 77, 78, 79, 80, 81, 82, 83, 84, 85, 86, 87
Revell, Viljo—p. 205, 206
revivalism and romanticism—p. 287
rhythm in architecture—p. 36
Richards Medical Laboratories—p. 232, 234, 235
Richardson, Severns, Scheeler—p. 276
Ried, Rockewell, Barnwell and Tarics—p. 232
Robie house—p. 290, 298
Ronchamp Chapel—p. 262, 263, 281
Rouse, James—p. 89
Rudolph, Paul—p. 51, 162, 168, 169
Ruskin, John—p. 287
Saarinen, Eero—p. 184, 186, 188, 189, 232, 233, 259, 261, 263
Safdie, Moshe—p. 152
San Francisco—p. 43, 163, 170, 171, 232
satellite cities—p. 22, 44, 64, 66
Sauer, Louis—p. 85
Scarborough College—p. 243, 250, 251
science of architecture—p. 19
science of environics—p. 19
scientific perspective—p. 29, 30
Scull, Nicholas—p. 138
sculpting of space—p. 27, 29, 31, 37, 49
Seattle—p. 43
Shahrazad hotel—p. 118, 124
Shiwalaks—p. 98
Simon, Robert—p. 72
Sithonia, Greece—p. 278
Skidmore, Owings and Merrill—p. 243, 252, 253, 254, 255
Smith, Chloethiel Woodard—p. 82, 83
Smith house—p. 295, 298
Smith, Neill—p. 260, 273, 274
Smithsonian Museum—p. 260
social investments—p. 57
social psychology—p. 19
socioenvironmental diseconomies—p. 48
sociophysical design—p. 19
space and movement—p. 21, 22
space exploration—p. 24, 25, 26, 28, 29
spatial disorientation—p. 25
spatial experience—p. 18, 20, 21, 22
spatial movement systems—p. 22, 23, 24, 25, 26
Spence, Sir Basil—p. 207, 284, 285
sports facilities—p. 259, 260
Stein, Clarence—p. 68
St. Louis—p. 259, 261, 262, 263
Stone, Edward Durell—p. 112, 114, 116, 117, 119, 126, 210, 211, 249, 256, 257, 259, 260, 262, 268, 269
Stonehenge—p. 35
structure of city architecture—p. 42, 43, 44
structure of psychoenvironment—p. 28
suburban subdivision—p. 142, 143,
Sydney, Australia—p. 213, 259, 264, 265
Sydney Opera House—p. 259, 264, 265
symmetrical balance—p. 33
synthetic materials—p. 57
synoptic design team—p. 287

synoptic environment—p. 20
Task Force on Social Responsibility—p. 59, 61
technical assistance—p. 55
teletransportation systems—p. 172
textural variation—p. 38
Thai architecture—p. 38
time-space perception—p. 25
transportation megastructure—p. 96
Toronto—p. 205, 206
Toronto City Hall—p. 205
Tougaloo College—p. 241, 249
Tube Transit, Inc.—p. 174, 175
uneconomical uncertainties—p. 34
university building—p. 232, 233, 234, 236
university campus—p. 243, 249
University of California—p. 232
University of Illinois Chicago Circle Campus—p. 243, 249, 252, 253, 254, 255
University of Pennsylvania—p. 232
University of Tunis—p. 237
university library—p. 233, 234
Unitarian Church—p. 262, 263, 280
United States—p. 22, 40, 41, 43, 45, 46, 47, 48, 51, 52, 53, 54, 59, 140, 142, 190, 289
U.S. Department of Commerce—p. 56
U.S. Department of Health, Education and Welfare—p. 56, 240
U.S. Housing and Home Finance Agency—p. 53
U.S. Department of Housing and Urban Development—p. 53, 56
U.S. Department of Interior—p. 56
U.S. Public Health Service—p. 45
U.S. Department of Transportation—p. 56
Unwin, Raymond—p. 68
urban activity systems—p. 57
urban design—p. 19, 20, 40, 42, 43, 44, 45, 46, 47, 64, 68, 69, 72, 89, 96, 98, 101, 110, 127, 139, 140
Urban Design Center—p. 61
urban museum—p. 260
Urbino, Italy—p. 241, 248
Utzon, Jon—p. 259, 264, 265
value contrasts in architecture—p. 37
Verrazano-Narrows bridge—p. 165
vertical city—p. 96
Victorian revival—p. 286
Villa Savoye—p. 289
Ward Willits house—p. 290, 298
Wampler, Jan—p. 154
Washington, D.C.—p. 22, 43, 44, 72, 89, 144, 145, 147, 148, 149, 150, 151, 155, 156, 157, 166, 172, 175, 180, 181, 186, 210, 211, 259, 260, 298, 299, 300, 301
water pollution—p. 47
Watergate, Washington, D.C.—p. 147, 148, 149
Weese, Harry—p. 180, 181
Whittlesey and Conklin—p. 73
Wellington, N.Z.—p. 207
Wright, Frank Lloyd—p. 45, 51, 69, 70, 71, 197, 200, 201, 260, 262, 263, 270, 271, 280, 289, 290, 291, 298
Wright, Henry—p. 68
Wright, Porteous and Lowe—p. 276
World Health Organization—p. 45
World Trade Center—p. 202, 203
Yamasaki, Minoru—p. 202
Yale University—p. 232, 233